SWEET T[illegible]

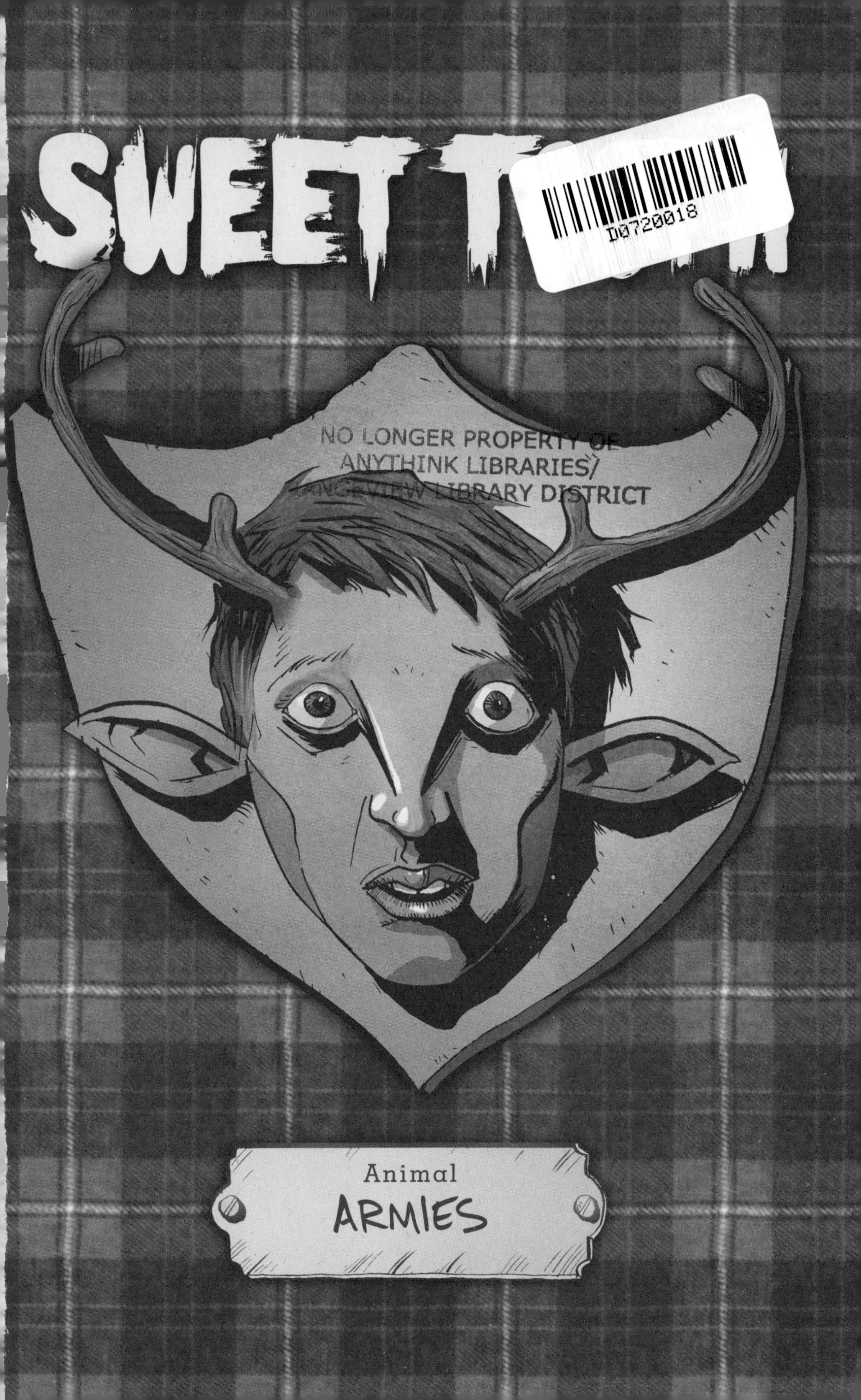

Animal
ARMIES

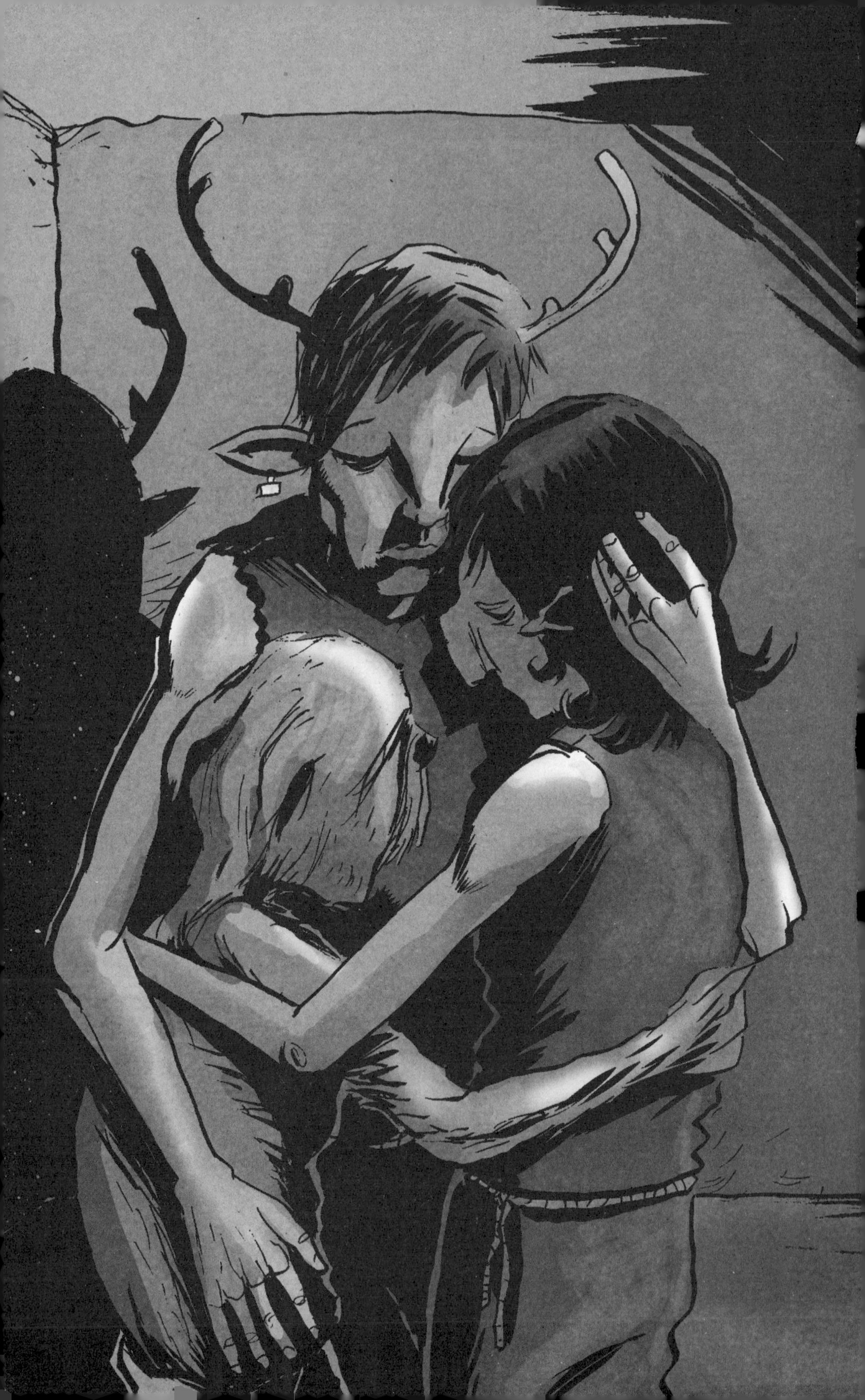

SWEET TOOTH

ANIMAL ARMIES

JEFF LEMIRE
story & art

JOSE VILLARRUBIA
colors

PAT BROSSEAU
letters

Robbie Biederman
publication design

SWEET TOOTH
created by Jeff Lemire

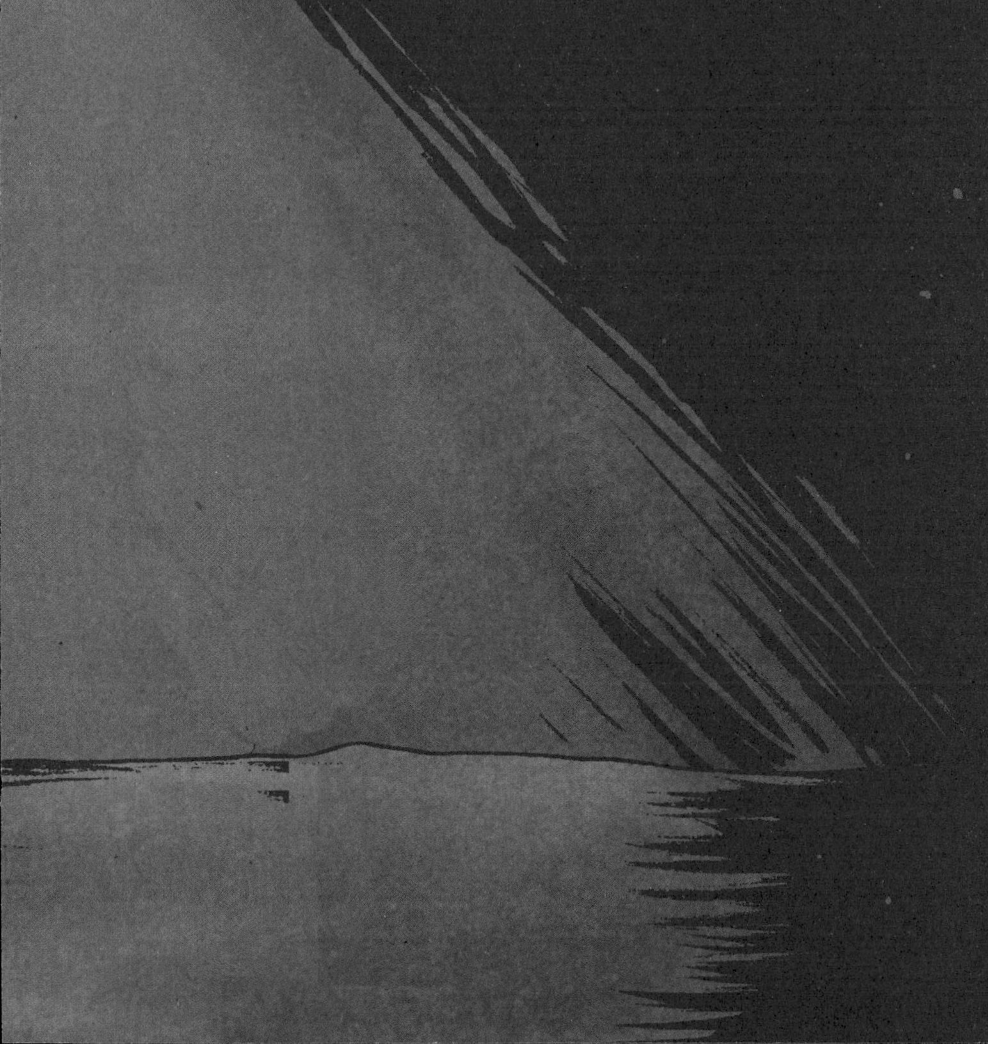

PORNSAK PICHETSHOTE Editor-Original series IAN SATTLER Director Editorial, Special Projects and Archival Editions
SCOTT NYBAKKEN Editor ROBBIN BROSTERMAN Design Director – Books

KAREN BERGER Senior VP – Executive Editor, Vertigo BOB HARRAS VP – Editor in Chief

DIANE NELSON President DAN DIDIO and JIM LEE Co-Publishers GEOFF JOHNS Chief Creative Officer
JOHN ROOD Executive VP – Sales, Marketing and Business Development AMY GENKINS Senior VP – Business and Legal Affairs NAIRI GARDINER Senior VP – Finance
JEFF BOISON VP – Publishing Operations MARK CHIARELLO VP – Art Direction and Design JOHN CUNNINGHAM VP – Marketing
TERRI CUNNINGHAM VP – Talent Relations and Services ALISON GILL Senior VP – Manufacturing and Operations DAVID HYDE Senior VP – Publicity
HANK KANALZ Senior VP – Digital JAY KOGAN VP – Business and Legal Affairs, Publishing JACK MAHAN VP – Business Affairs, Talent
NICK NAPOLITANO VP – Manufacturing Administration RON PERAZZA VP – Online COURTNEY SIMMONS Senior VP – Publicity BOB WAYNE Senior VP – Sales

DC Comics, 1700 Broadway, New York, NY 10019
A Warner Bros. Entertainment Company
Printed in the USA. First Printing.
ISBN: 978-1-4012-3170-5

SUSTAINABLE FORESTRY INITIATIVE
Certified Fiber Sourcing
www.sfiprogram.org

Fiber used in this product line meets the sourcing requirements of the SFI program.
www.sfiprogram.org SGS-SFICOC-0130

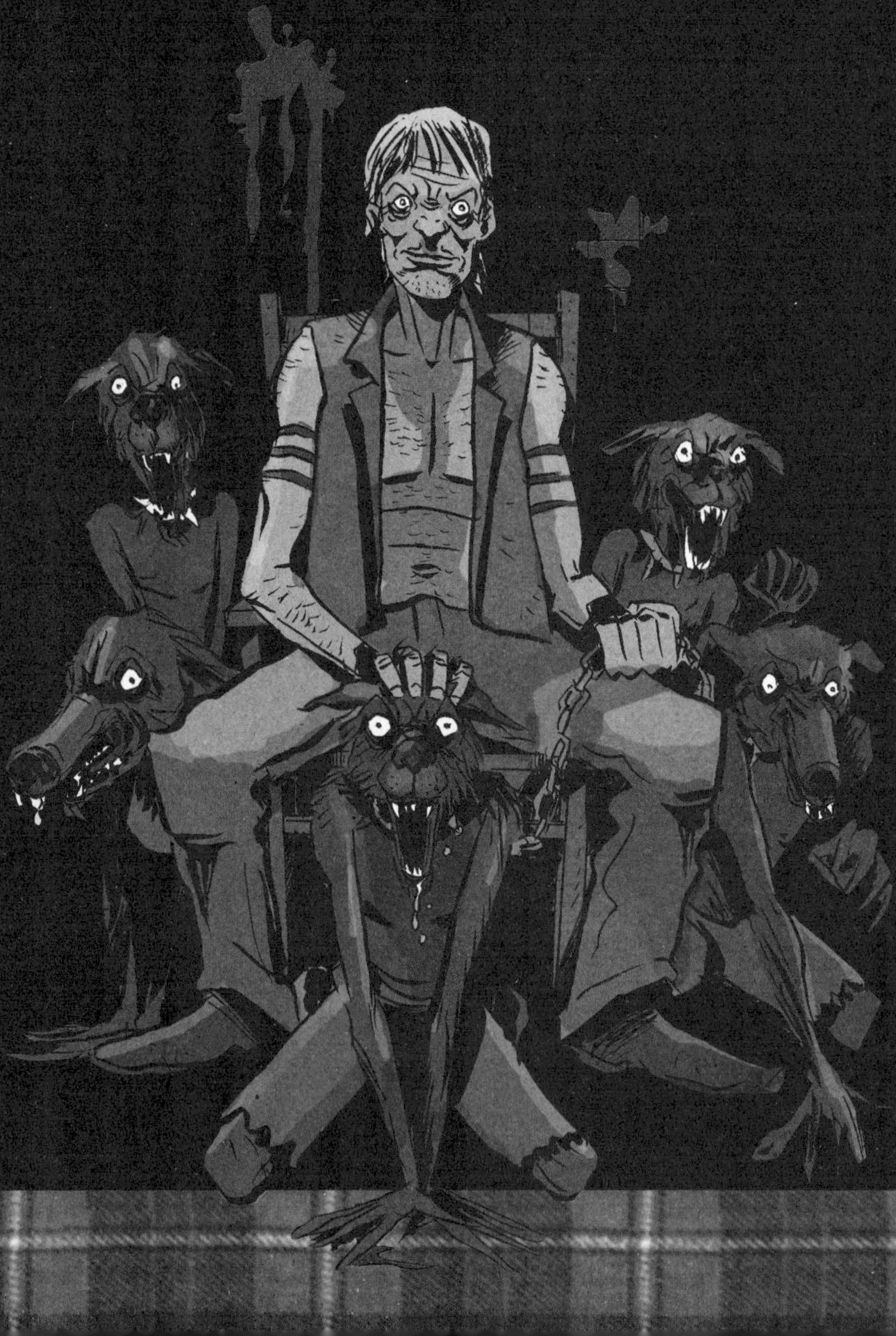

PREVIOUSLY

A decade ago a horrible disease raged across the world killing billions. Adding to the mystery surrounding the origins of the plague are a new breed of human/animal hybrid children... the only children born since the plague.

GUS is one such hybrid. A young boy with a sweet soul, a sweeter tooth — and the features of a deer. After his father died and he finally left the seclusion of his forest home, Gus hooked up with a hulking and violent drifter named JEPPERD. Jepperd promised to take him to a safe haven for hybrid children called "The Preserve," but at the last minute he betrayed Gus, selling him to the vicious Militia in exchange for a mysterious duffle bag, which later turned out to contain the remains of his dead wife LOUISE.

In captivity Gus met other hybrid children, including the sweet pig-girl named Wendy and the lovable groundhog boy named Bobby. Even in the face of horrible treatment at the hands of the Militia and their leaders, a brutal man named ABBOT and a misguided doctor named SINGH, Gus found solace with these other children.

Meanwhile we learned the truth about Jepperd's past. He and his wife became pregnant with a hybrid child of their own, but Abbot and the Militia tricked them and imprisoned them. Jepperd escaped from the Militia jail with the help of a timid guard named JOHNNY, only to discover both Louise and the baby died in childbirth. The militia set Jepperd free, promising only to give him Louise's remains if he brought them more hybrids to experiment on in hopes of finding a cure for the plague.

After burying his wife on their farm, Jepperd set out across the country, plagued by the guilt of what he had done to Gus. He was brutally beaten by a group of scavengers and found himself returning to Rockbridge, Nebraska, where Lucy, a hard woman whom Jepperd previously saved from a prostitution ring, and her teenaged companion Becky nursed him back to health.

As Singh and Abbot become more and more convinced that Gus's past hold the secrets of the plague, Jepperd, Lucy and Becky head out, determined to rescue the boy...

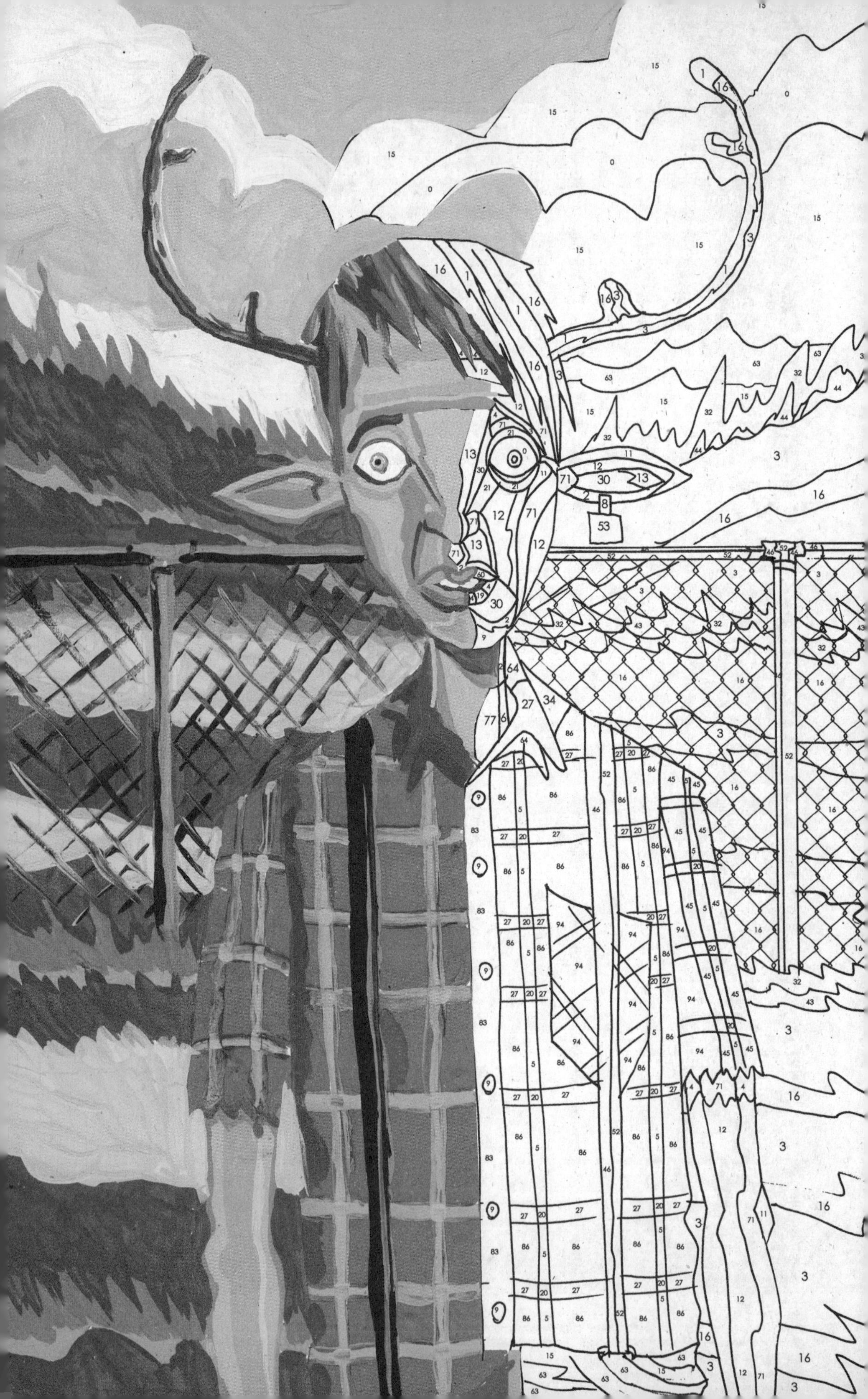

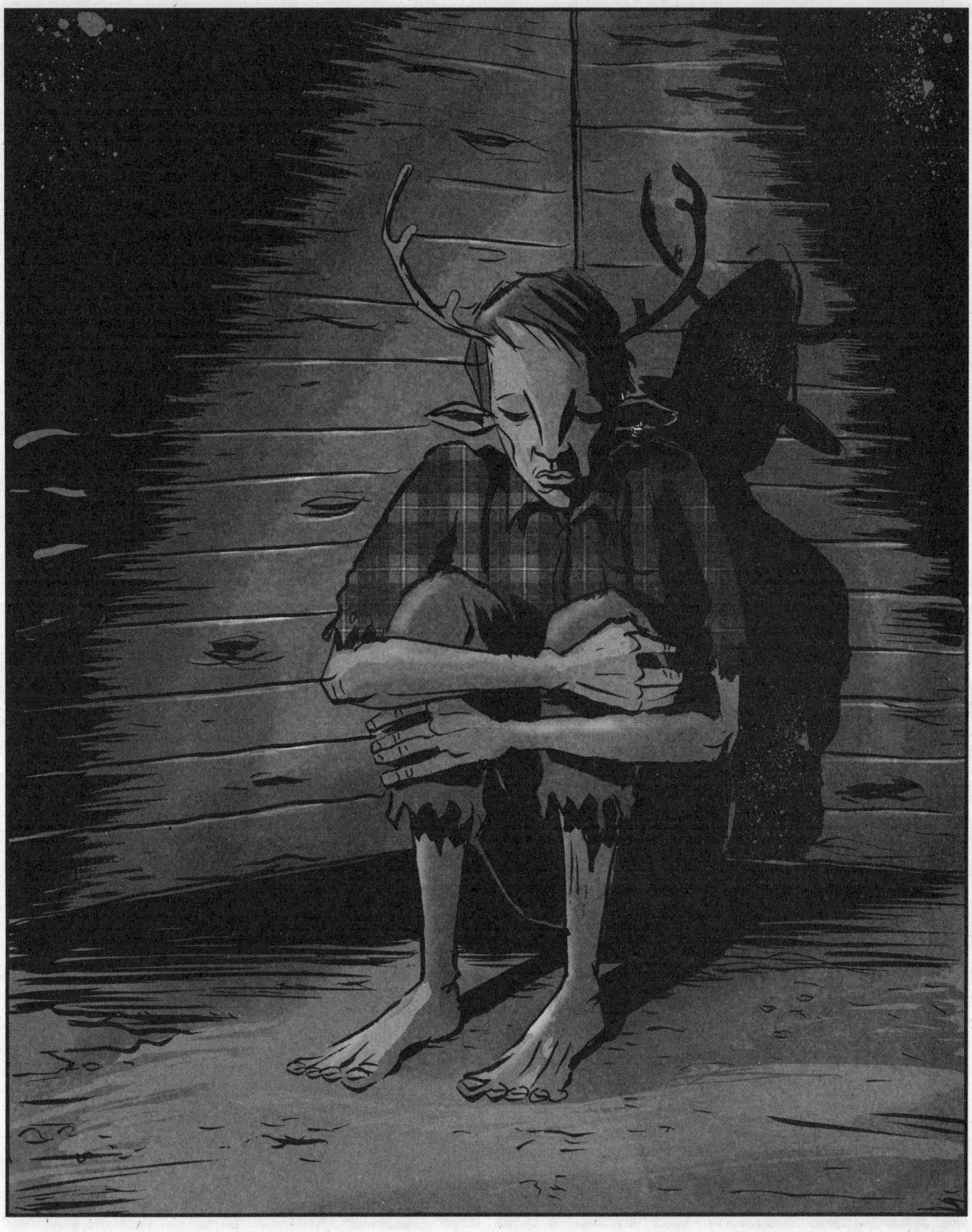

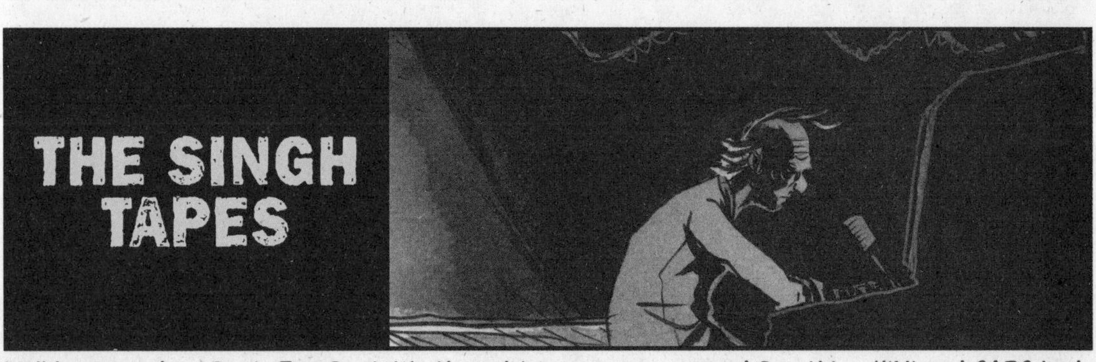
THE SINGH TAPES

It all happened so fast. *Too* fast. We thought we were prepared for this. HINI and SARS had hit only years before. We had fair warning. We had time to prepare. But it didn't matter. *None* of it mattered. Any safeguards and provisions we had in place were instantly overwhelmed. Millions died in mere weeks.

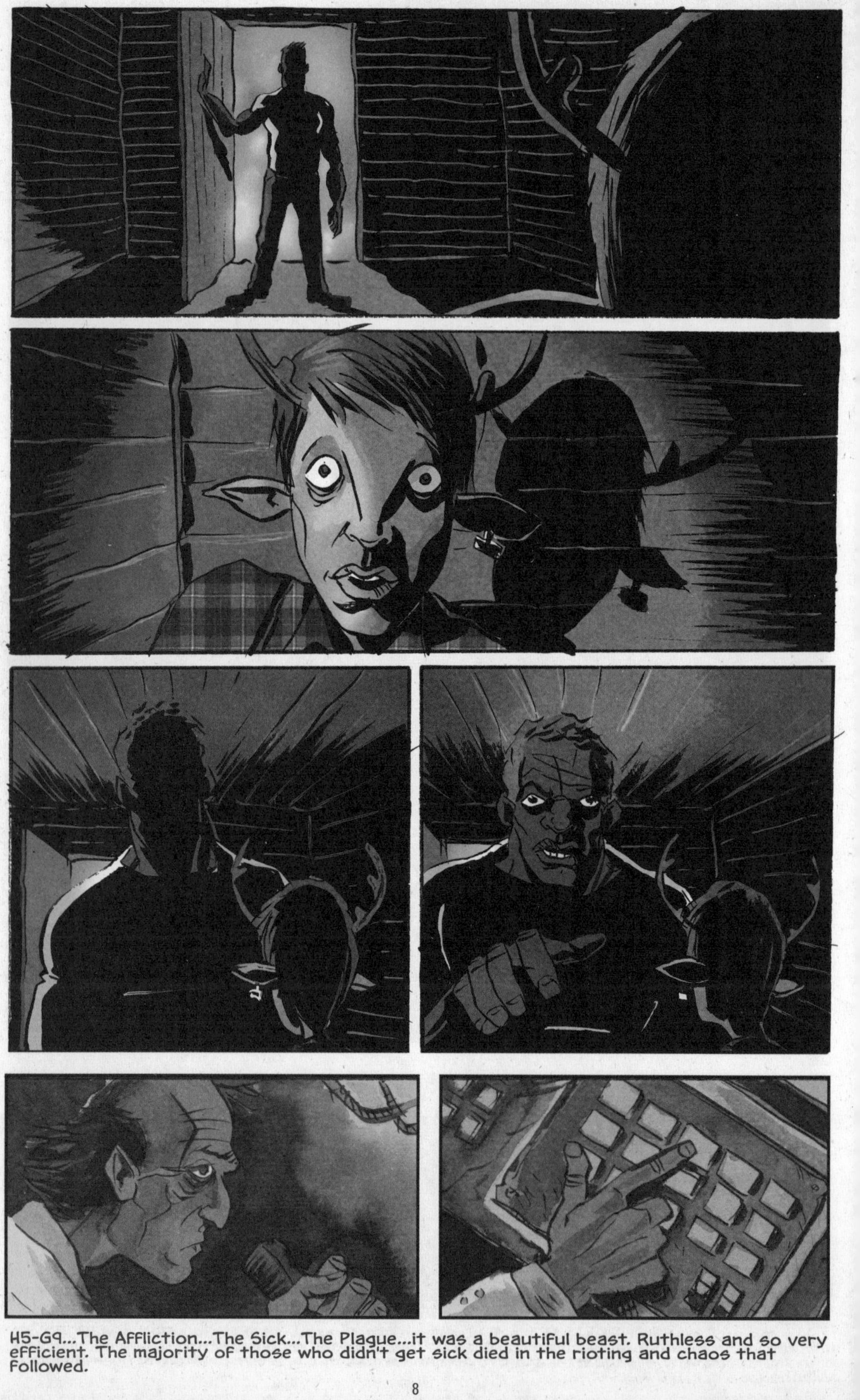

H5-G9...The Affliction...The Sick...The Plague...it was a beautiful beast. Ruthless and so very efficient. The majority of those who didn't get sick died in the rioting and chaos that followed.

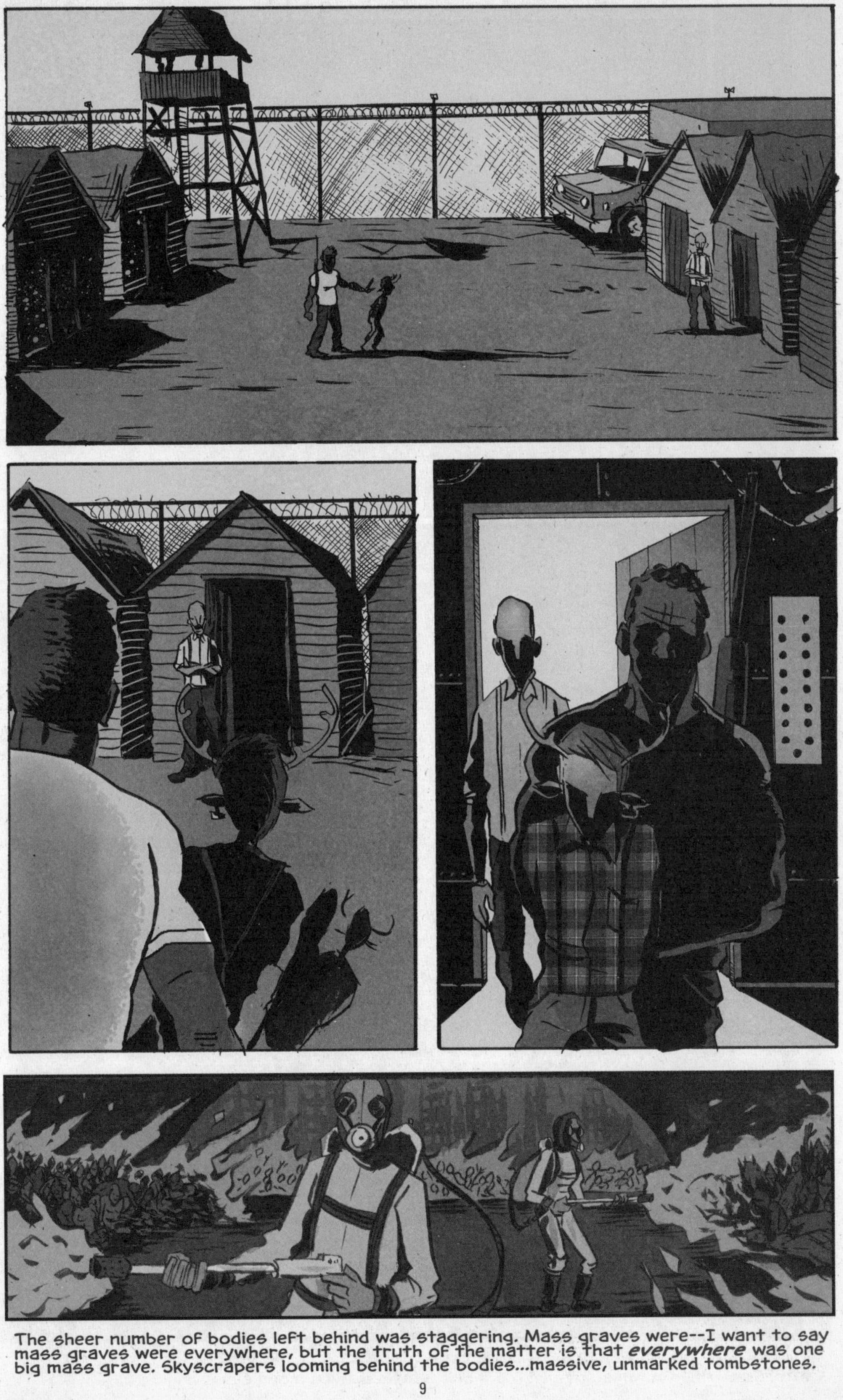

The sheer number of bodies left behind was staggering. Mass graves were--I want to say mass graves were everywhere, but the truth of the matter is that *everywhere* was one big mass grave. Skyscrapers looming behind the bodies...massive, unmarked tombstones.

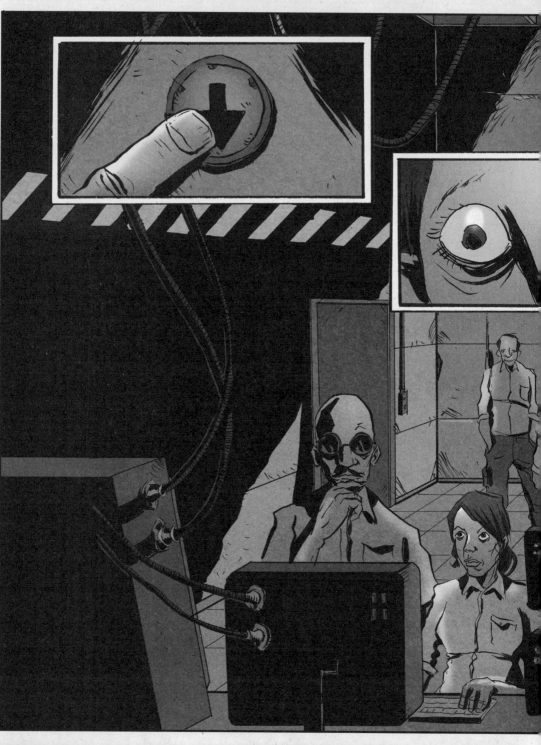

Everything collapsed. Global communication systems...the Internet...all of it obsolete within months. We were cut off from one another...even more alone and terrified.

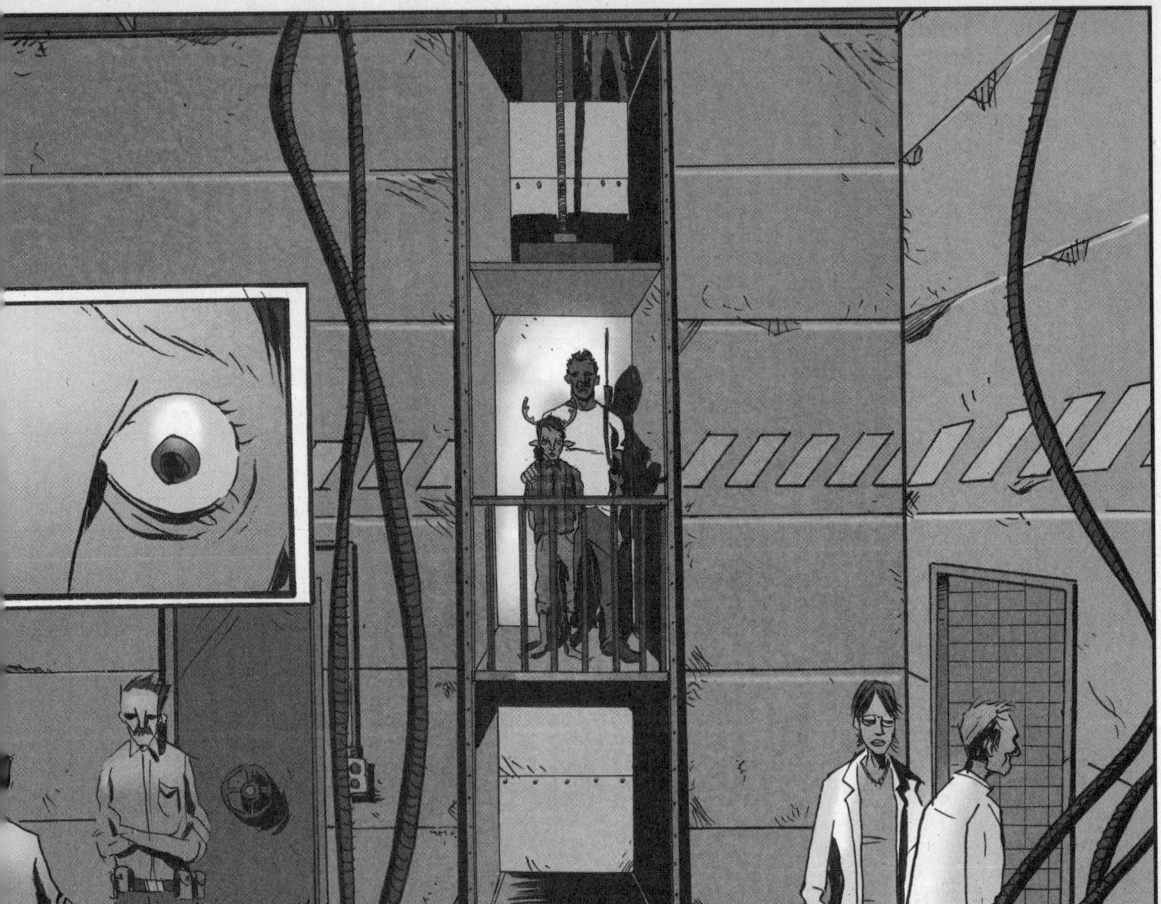

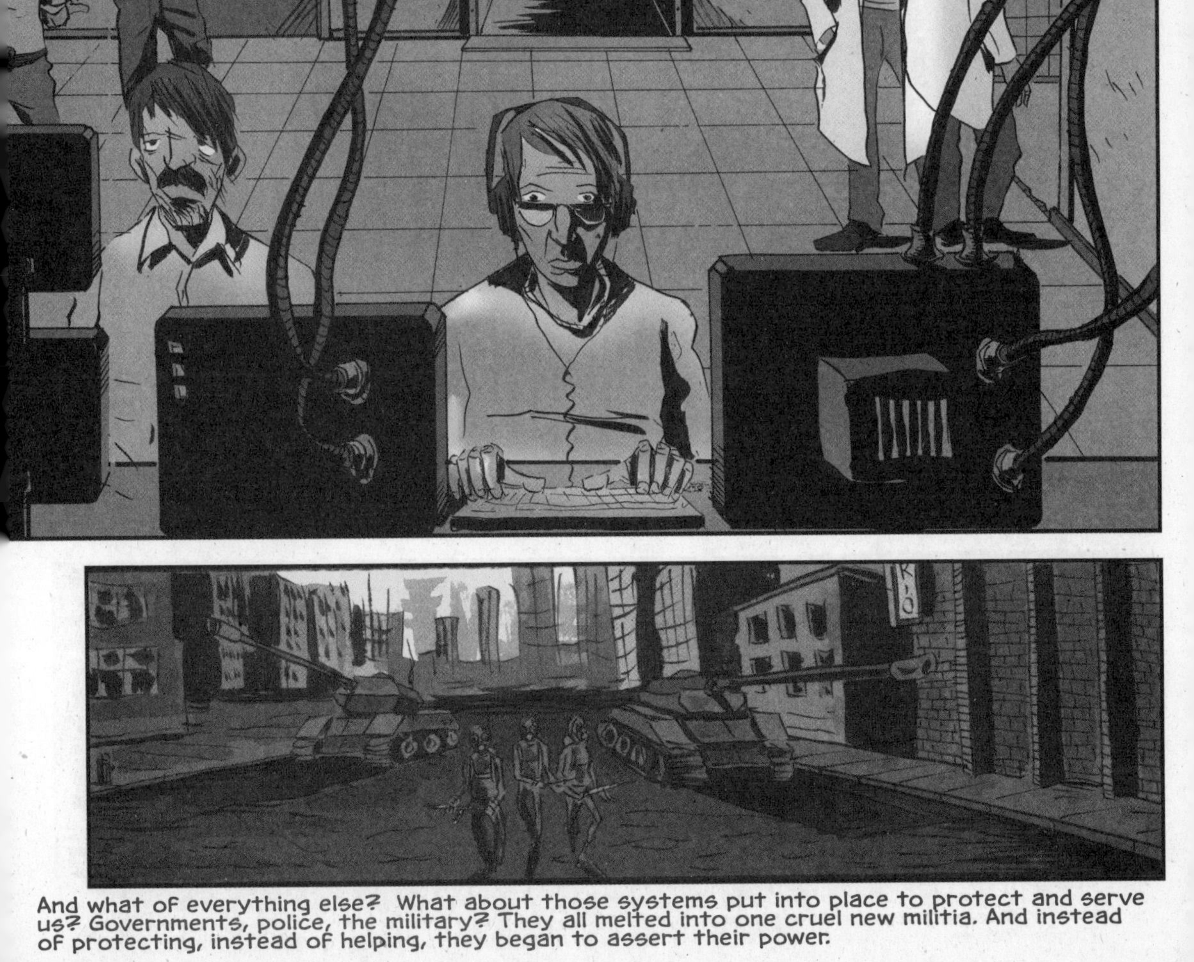

And what of everything else? What about those systems put into place to protect and serve us? Governments, police, the military? They all melted into one cruel new militia. And instead of protecting, instead of helping, they began to assert their power.

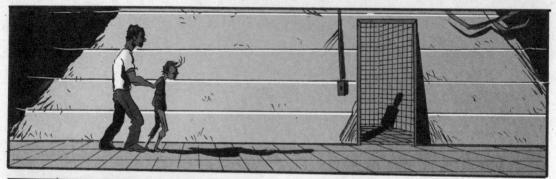

They swept through the cities, hoarding anything they saw as a commodity. Gasoline, medicine, weapons, food.

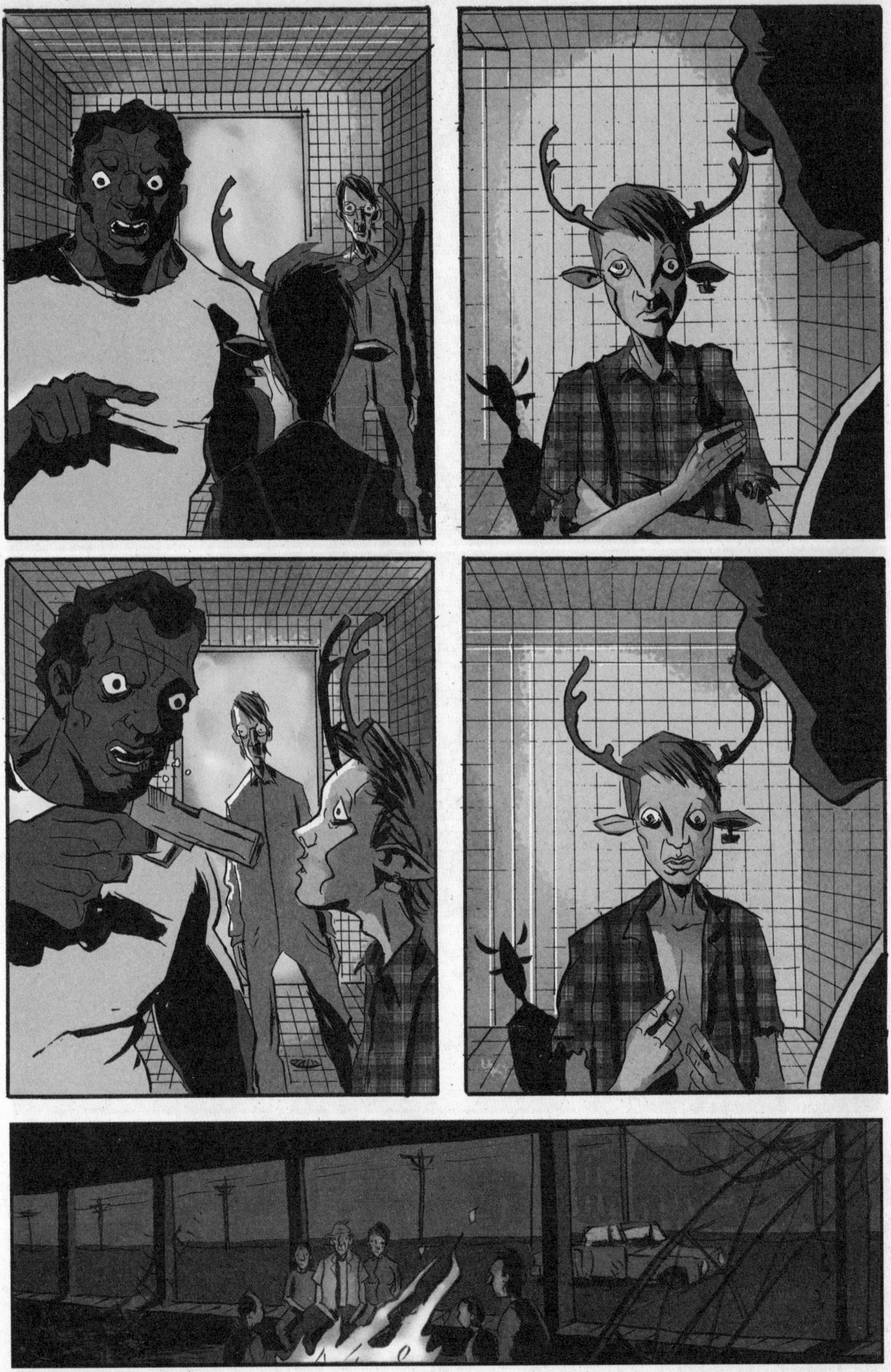

They left nothing for the rest of us. We scavenged for what we could. Starvation and exposure were the new threat. If we didn't have something they needed...something they could use, we were invisible to them.

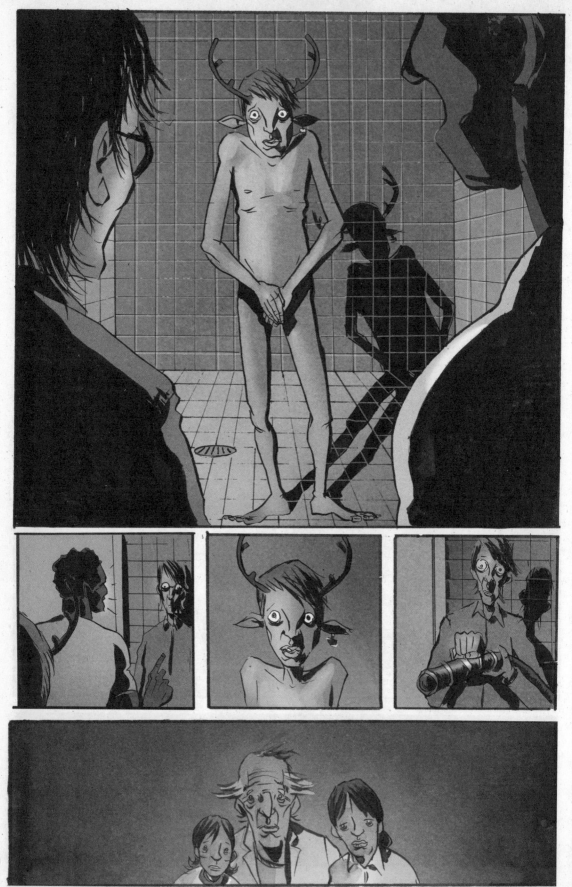

And lurking behind it all...coiled and ready in the shadows, H5-G9 waited. After its first deadly strike, it learned to be patient. Learned to wait before it pounced. We initial survivors presumed we were immune. We presumed we were safe from The Sick. We were wrong.

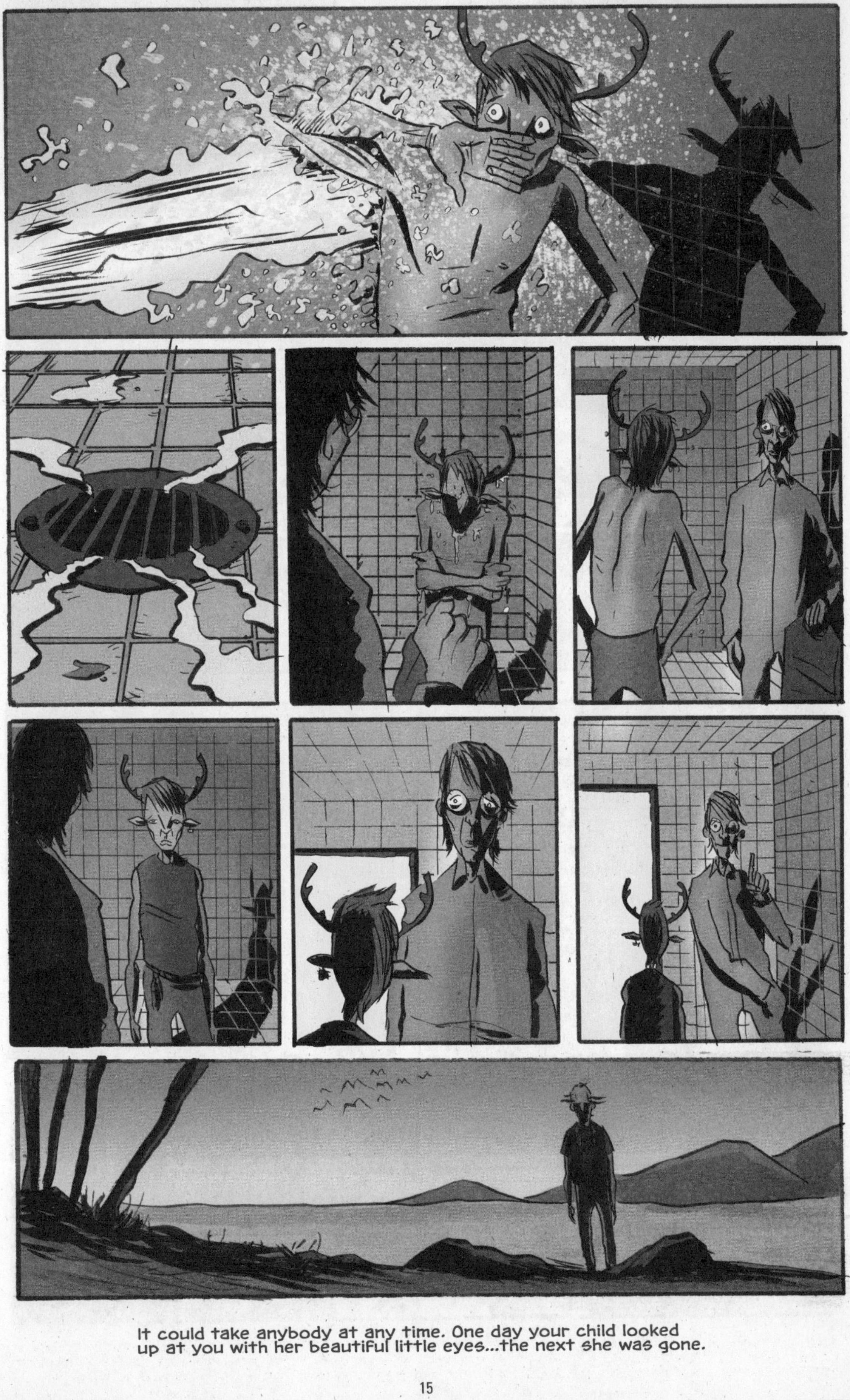

It could take anybody at any time. One day your child looked up at you with her beautiful little eyes...the next she was gone.

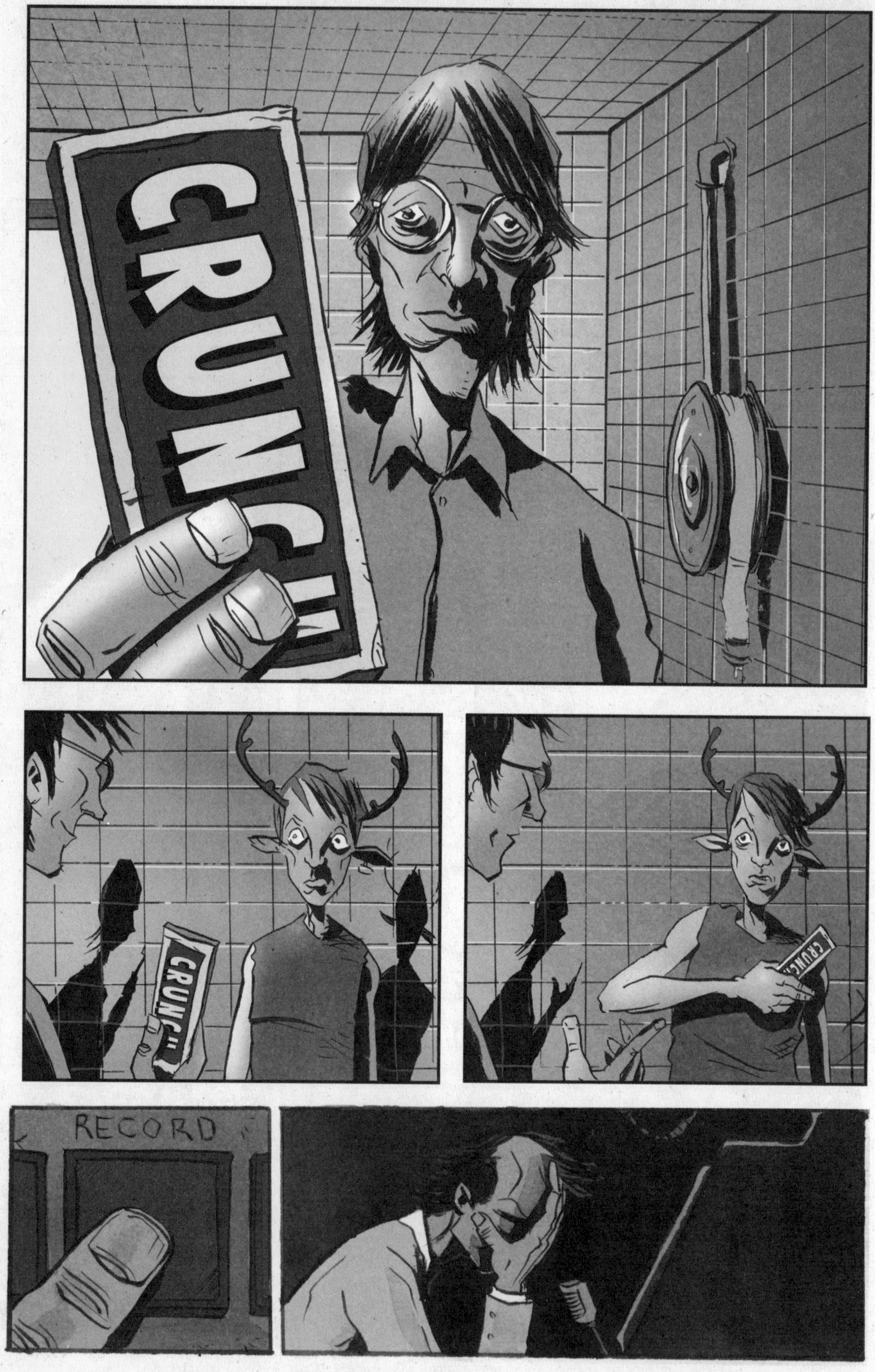
CRUNCH
CRUNCH
CRUNCH
RECORD

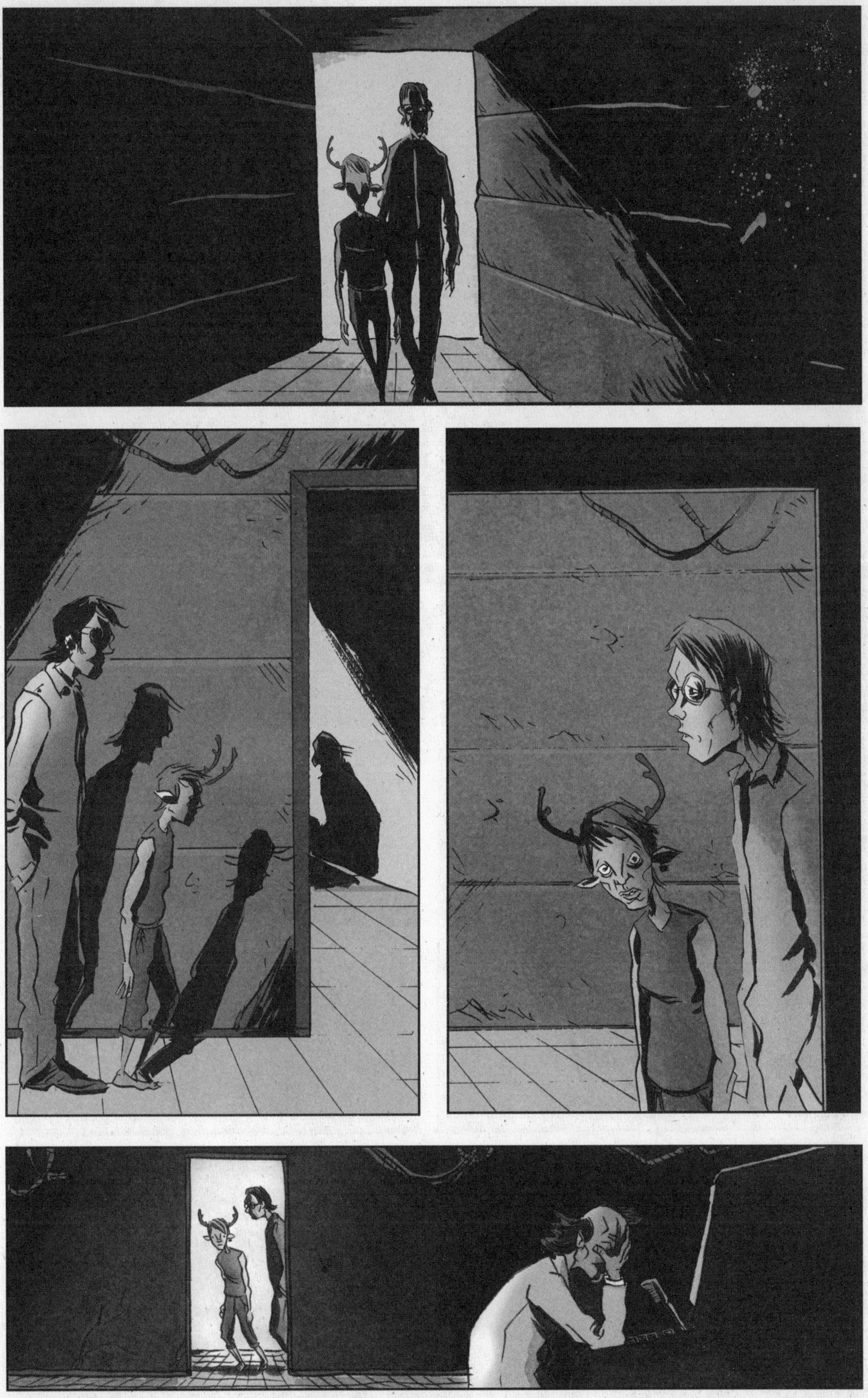

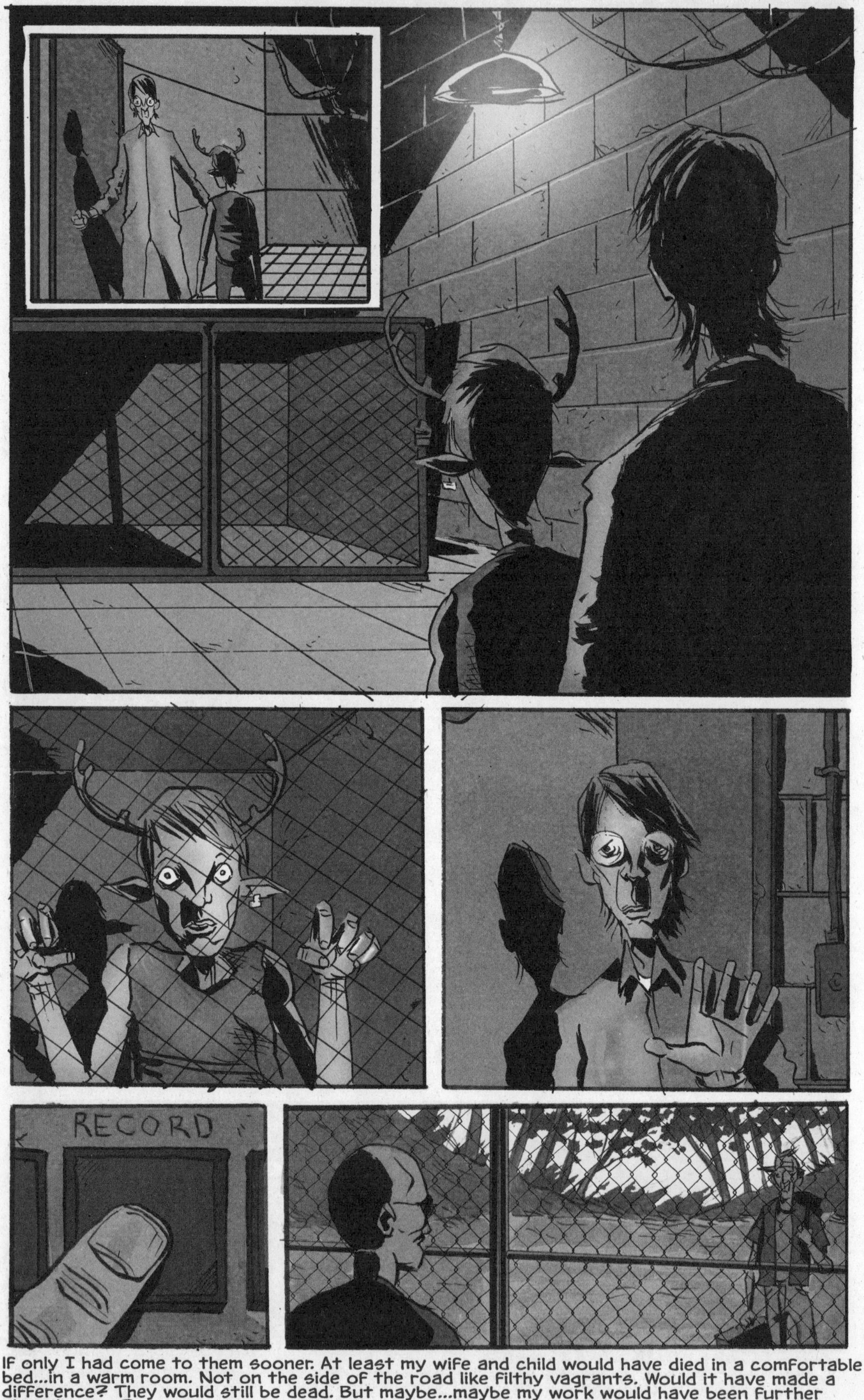
RECORD

IF only I had come to them sooner. At least my wife and child would have died in a comfortable bed...in a warm room. Not on the side of the road like filthy vagrants. Would it have made a difference? They would still be dead. But maybe...maybe my work would have been further along by now?

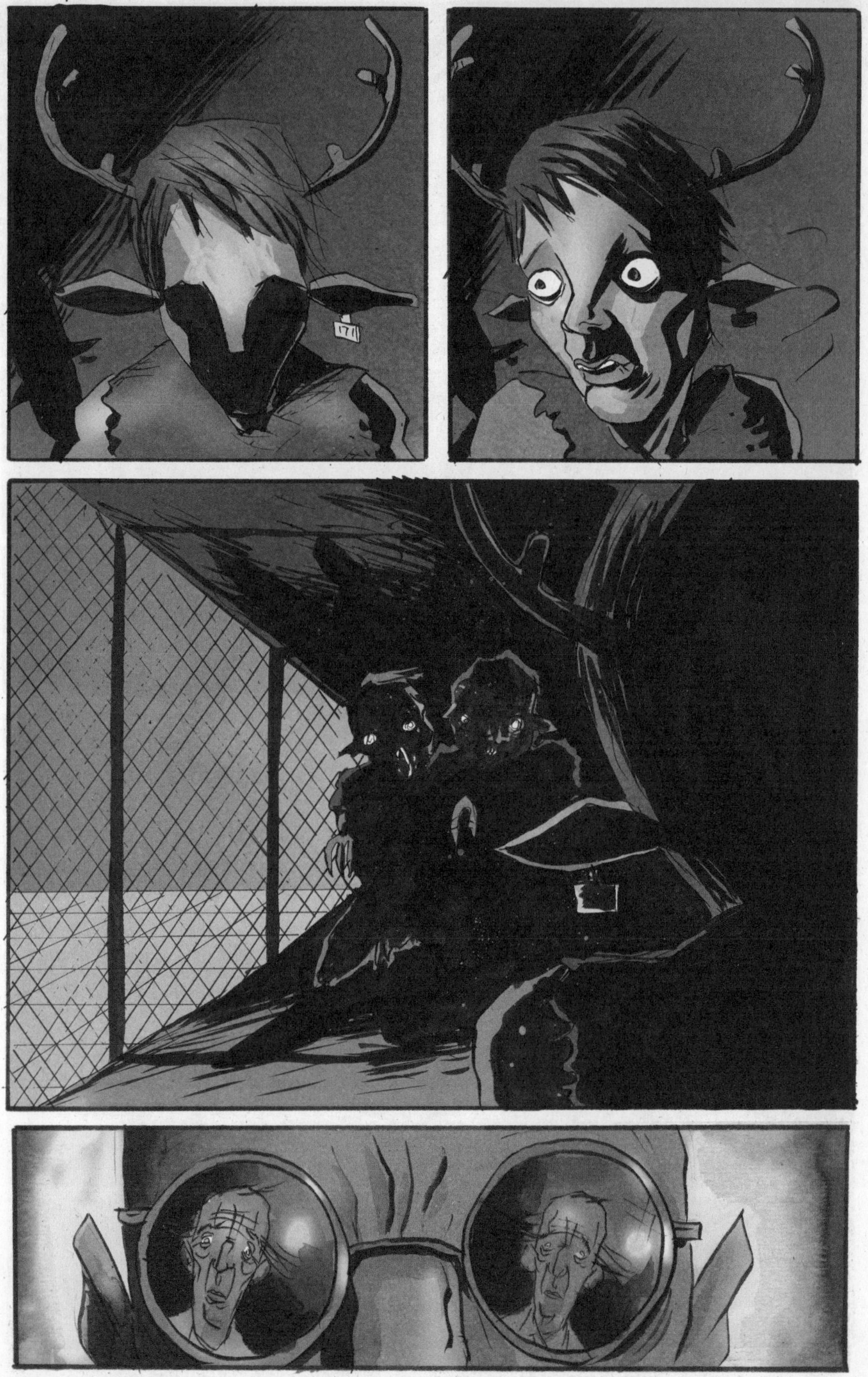
171

I Knew they needed men like me...educated men. Men of science. It's all so...so ironic. When I came to this country I was told I didn't have the proper qualifications to practice medicine, despite having been trained and certified in the finest schools in India.

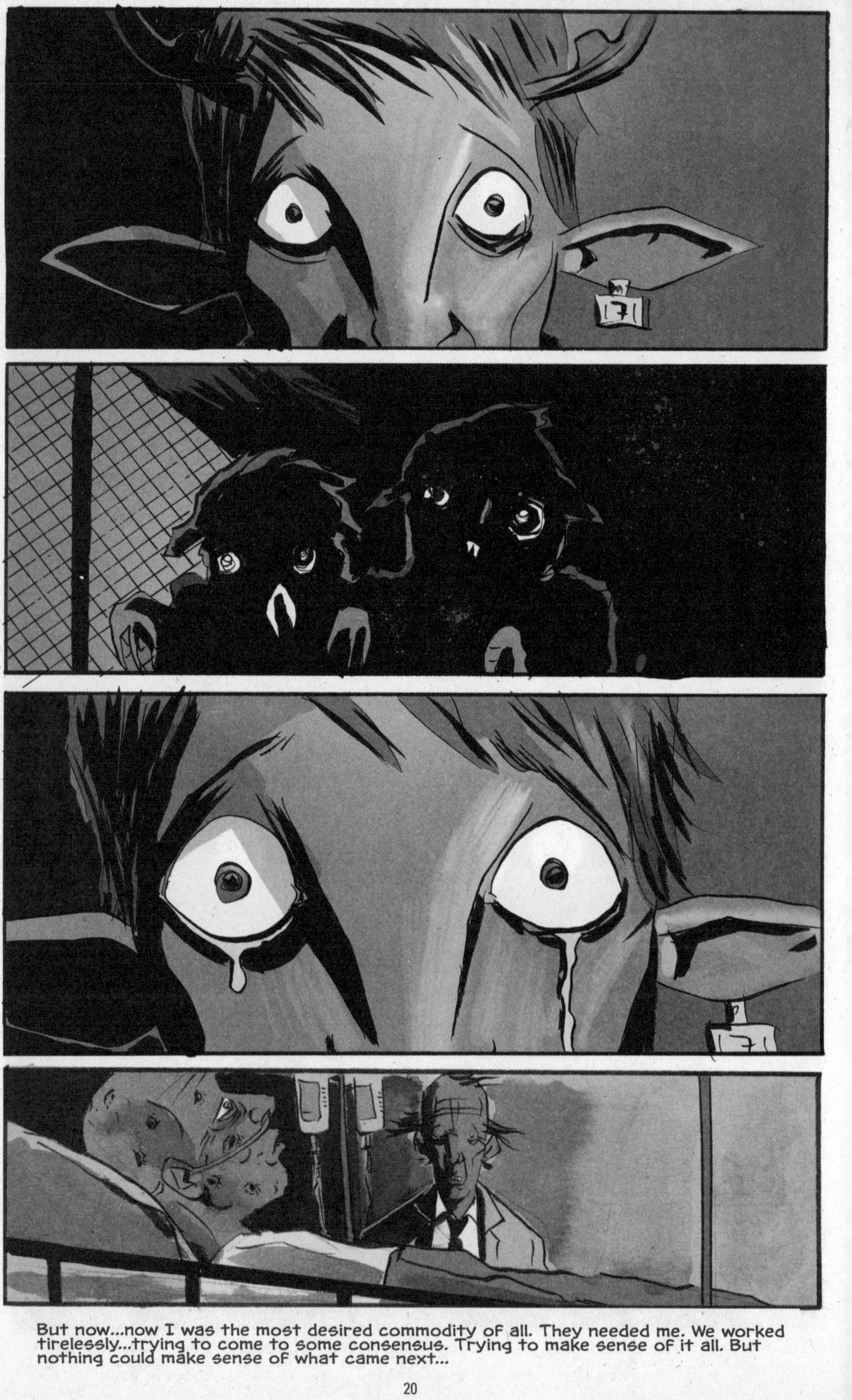

But now...now I was the most desired commodity of all. They needed me. We worked tirelessly...trying to come to some consensus. Trying to make sense of it all. But nothing could make sense of what came next...

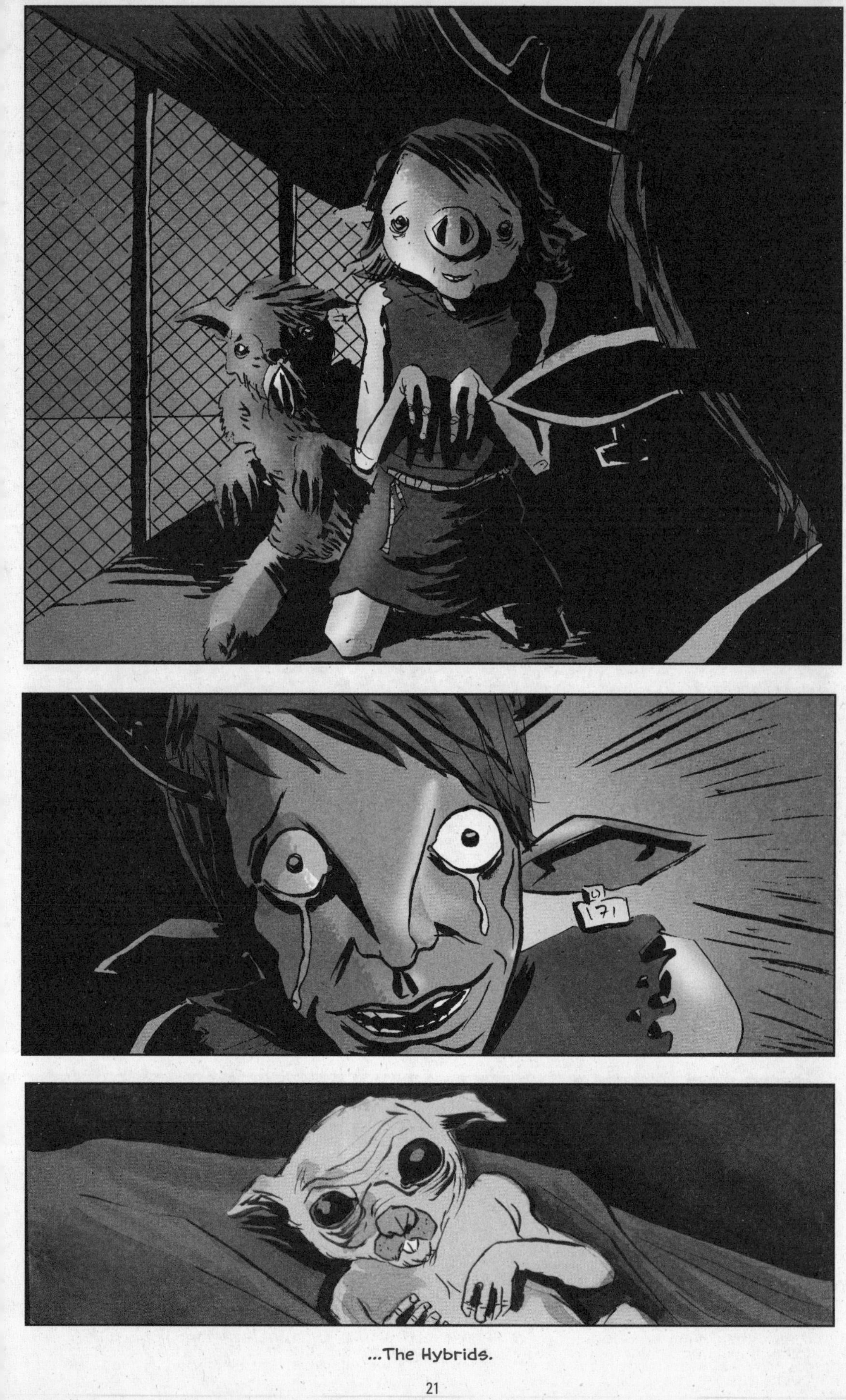
171

...The Hybrids.

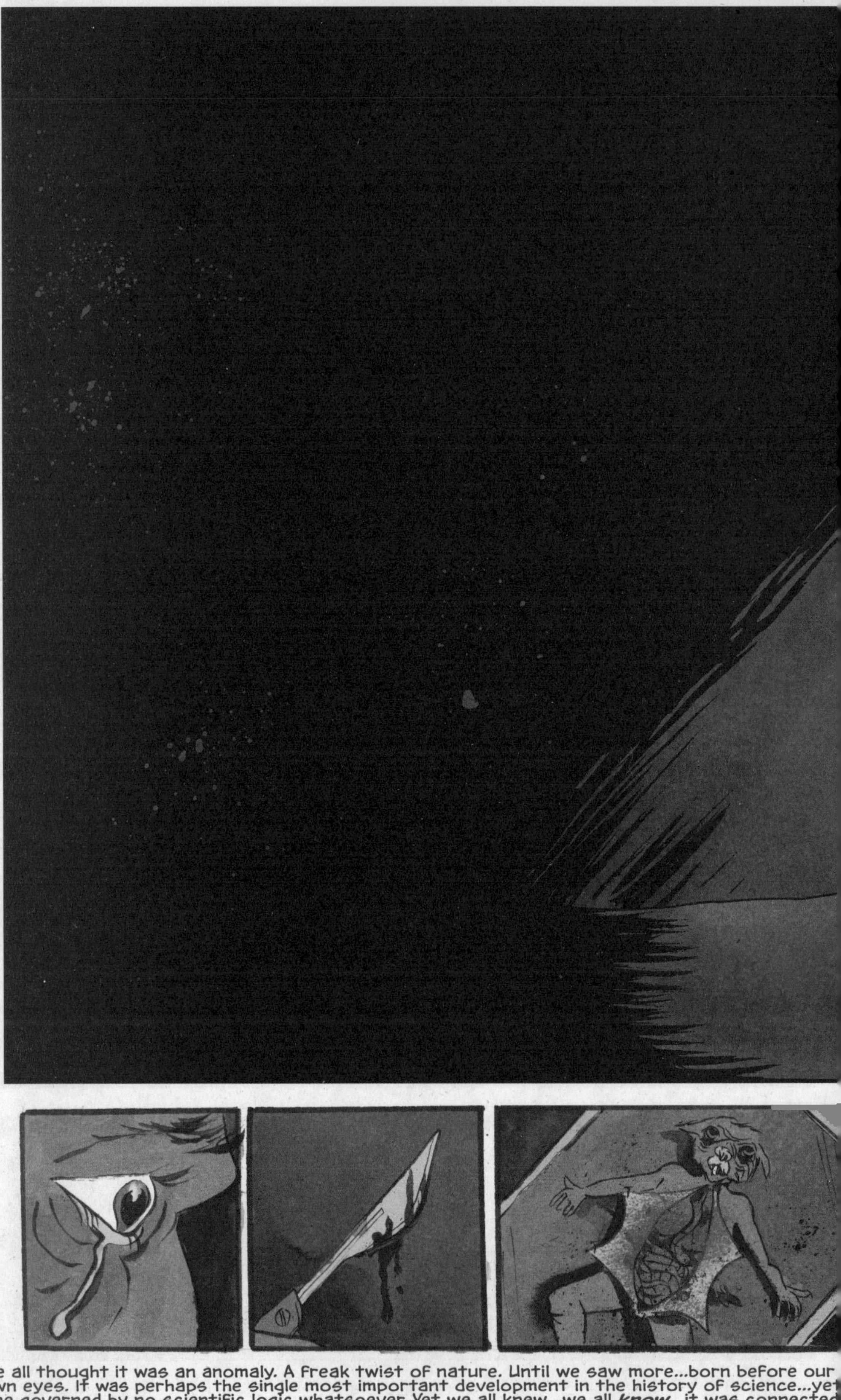

We all thought it was an anomaly. A freak twist of nature. Until we saw more...born before our own eyes. It was perhaps the single most important development in the history of science...yet one governed by no scientific logic whatsoever. Yet we all knew...we all ***know...*** it was connected. They were the key to it all.

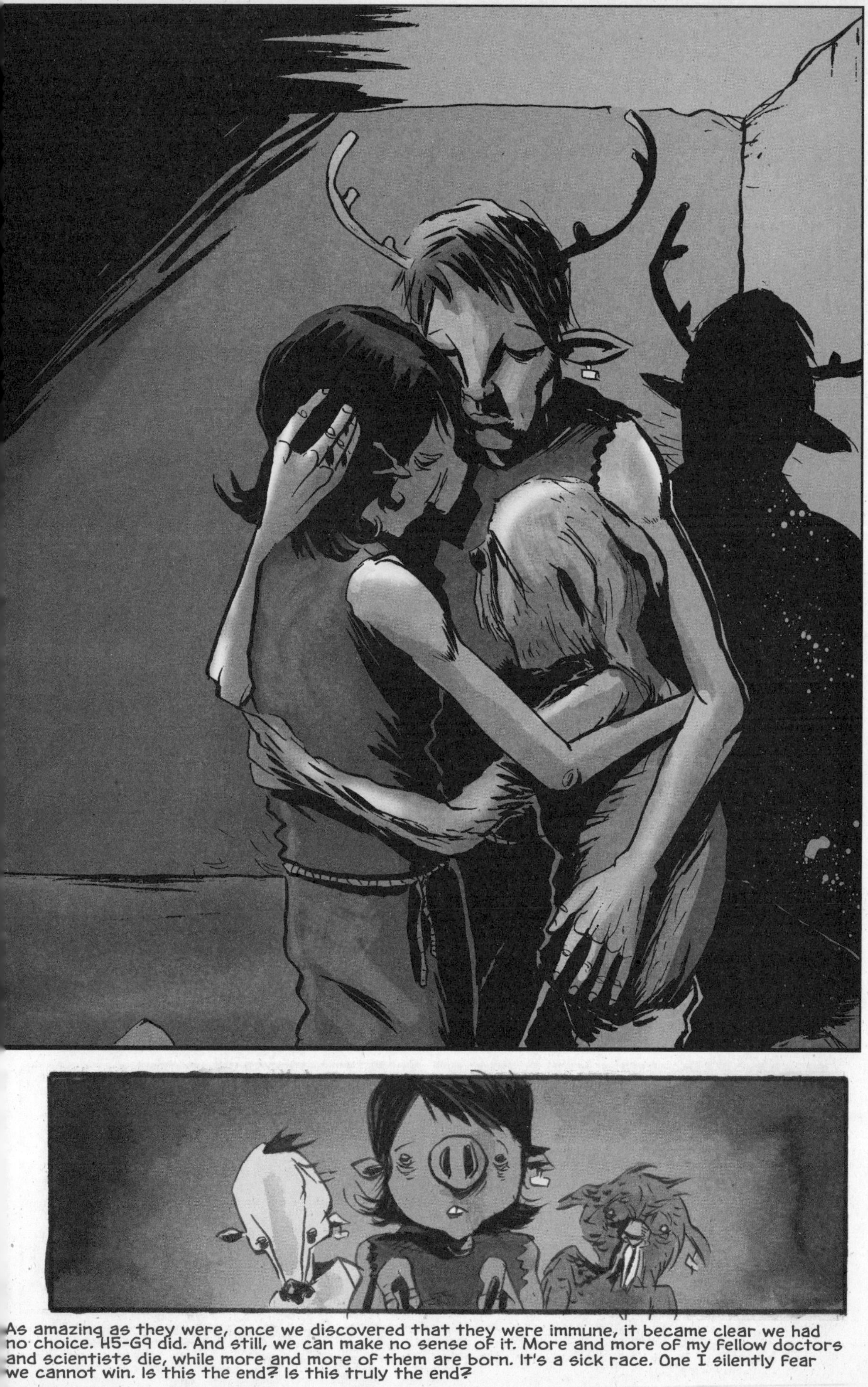

As amazing as they were, once we discovered that they were immune, it became clear we had no choice. H5-G9 did. And still, we can make no sense of it. More and more of my fellow doctors and scientists die, while more and more of them are born. It's a sick race. One I silently fear we cannot win. Is this the end? Is this truly the end?

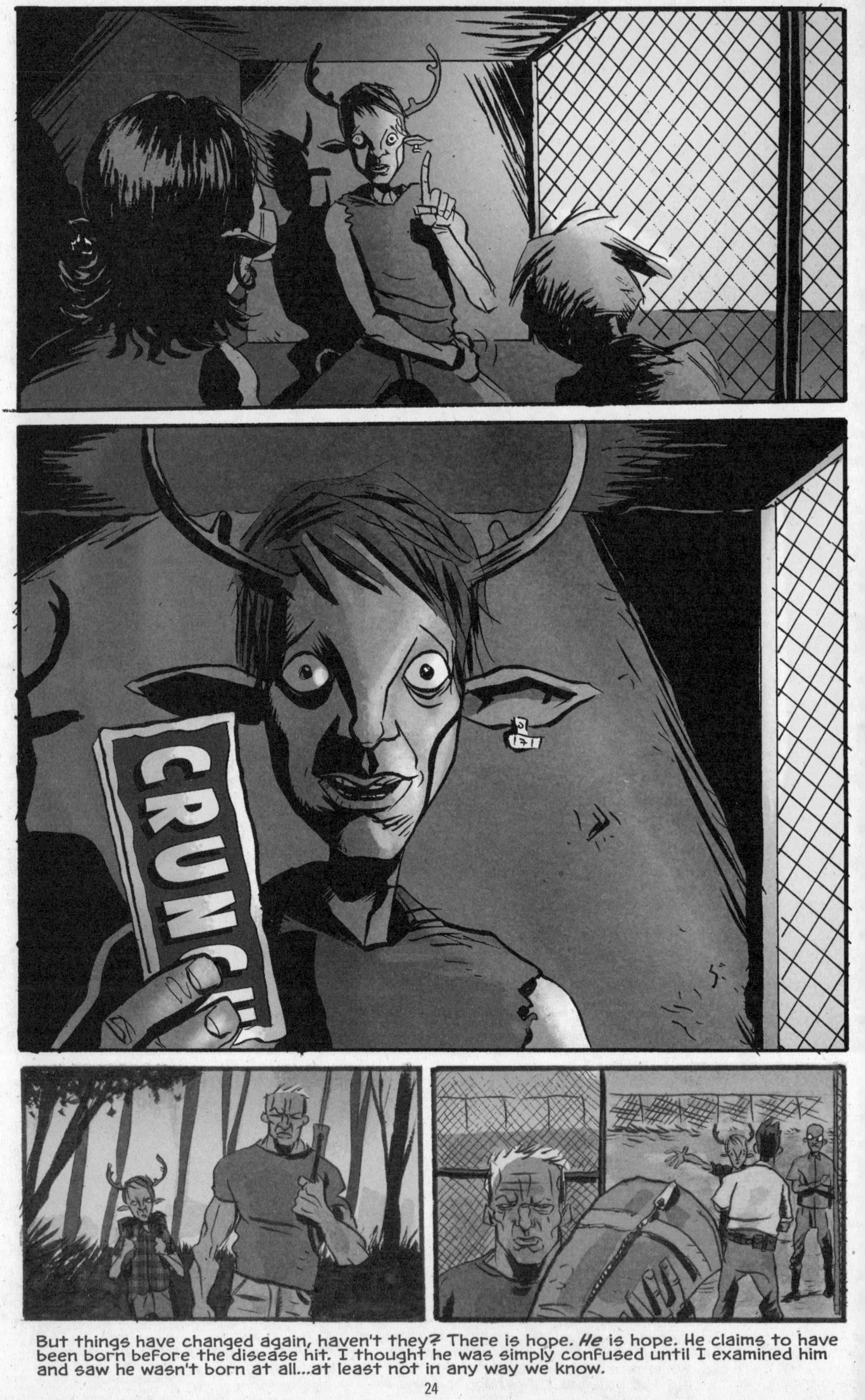
CRUNC

But things have changed again, haven't they? There is hope. *He* is hope. He claims to have been born before the disease hit. I thought he was simply confused until I examined him and saw he wasn't born at all...at least not in any way we know.

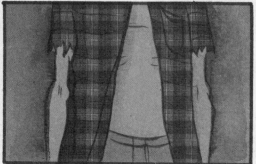

So where did he come from? How did he get here? And if he did come first...if what he says is true...It raises a very disturbing thought...

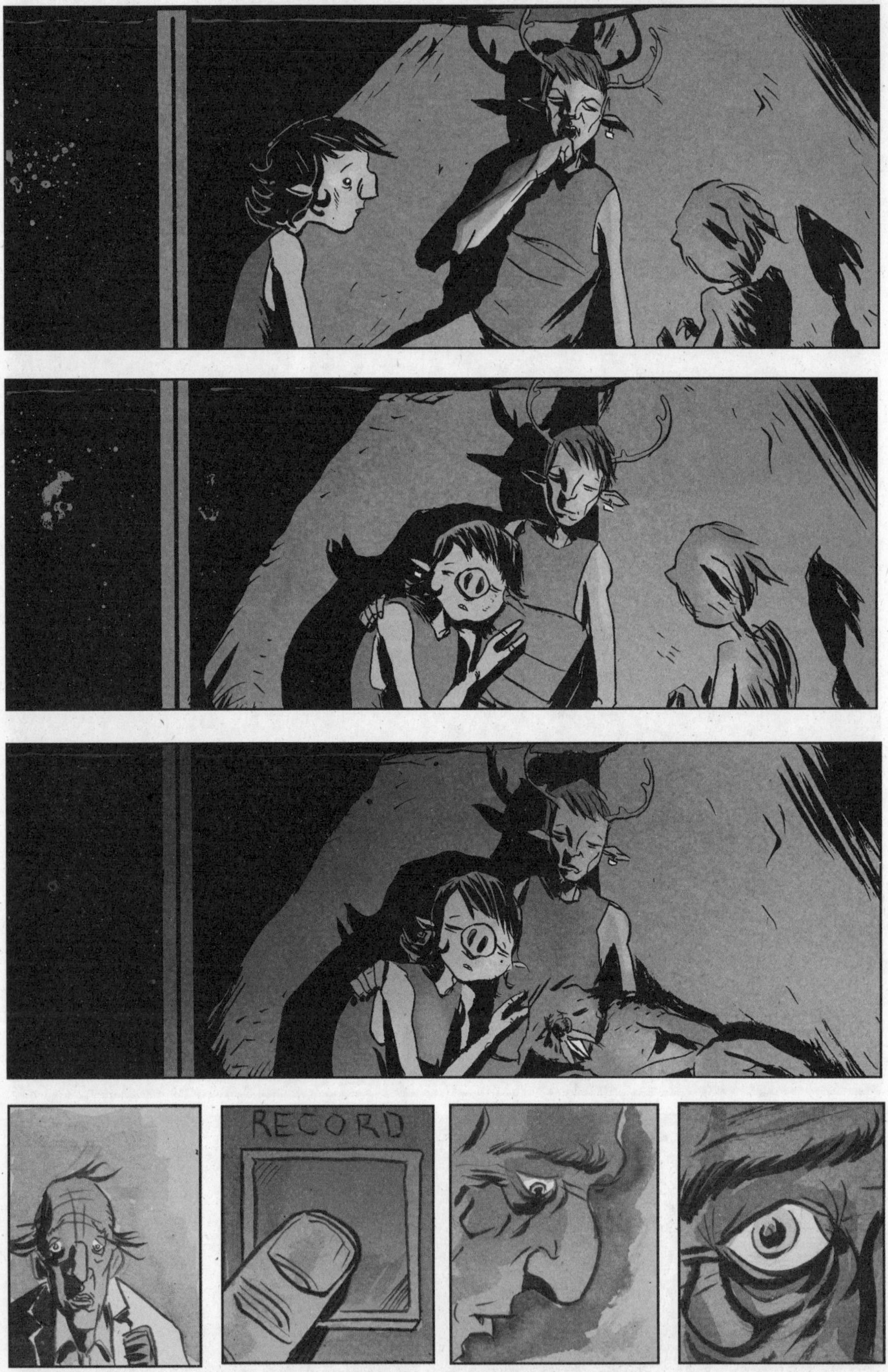
RECORD

What if they aren't the solution at all, but the problem? What if they caused it?

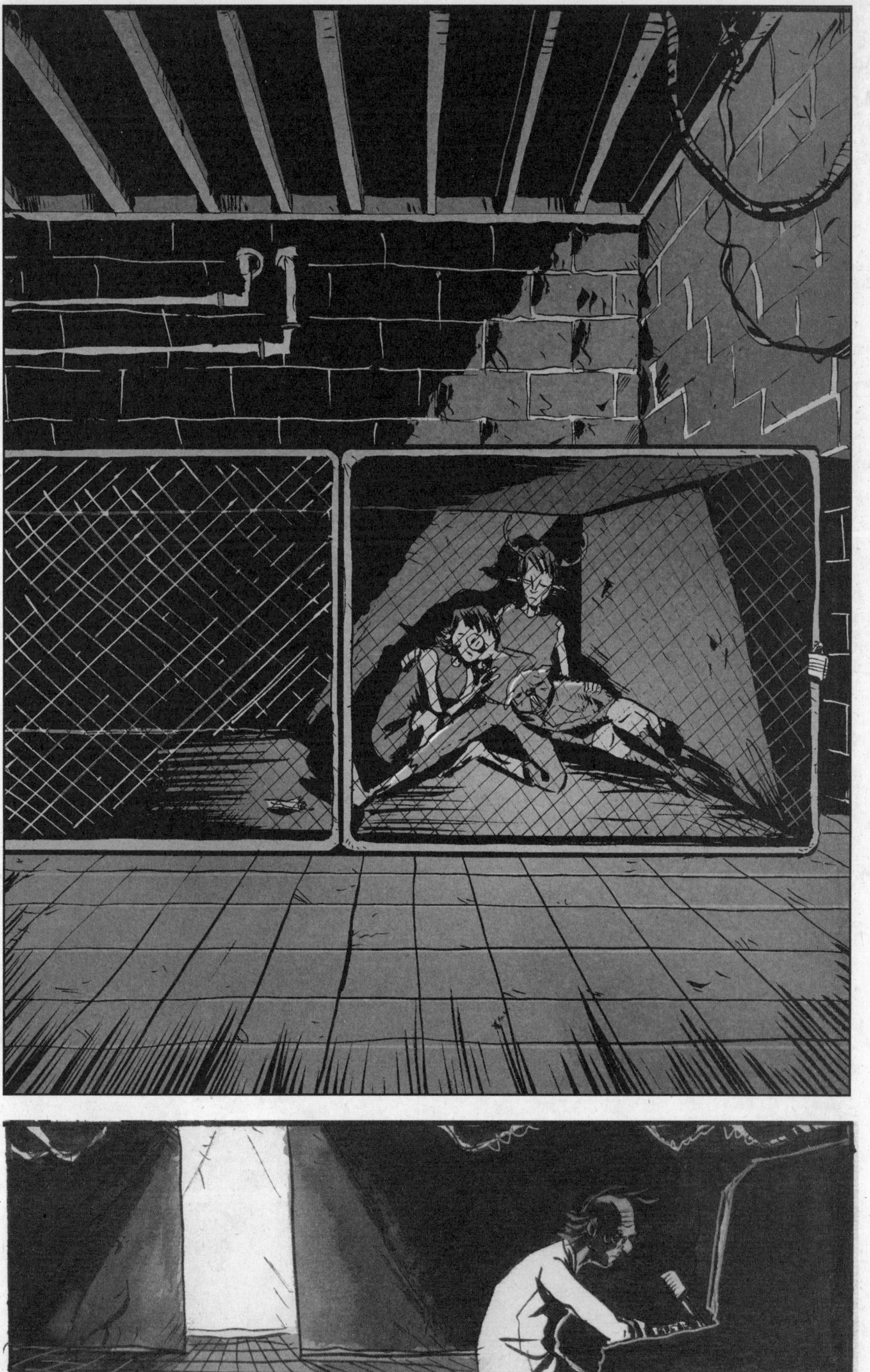
FOR WOLFMAN + PEREZ!

What if *he* caused it?

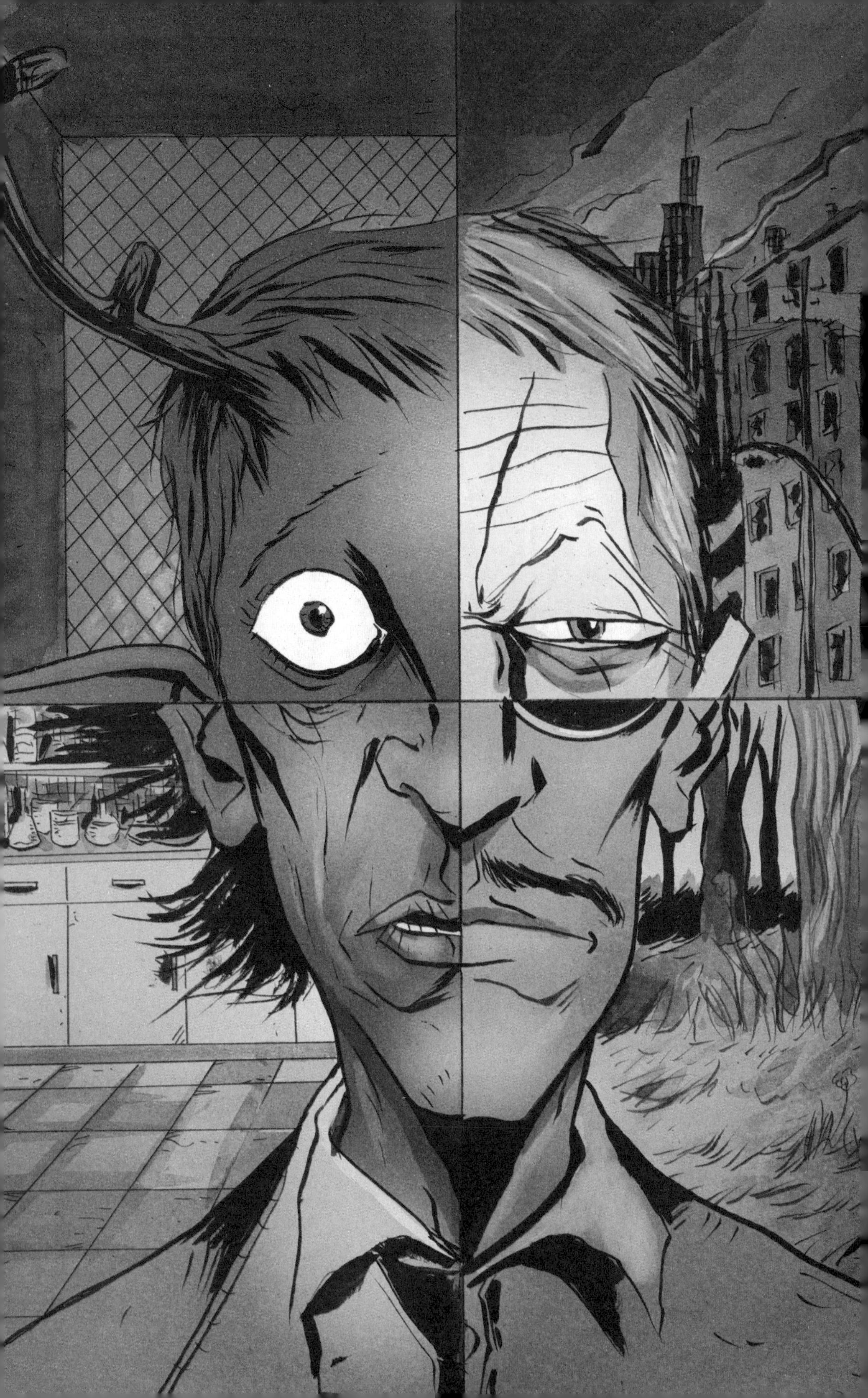

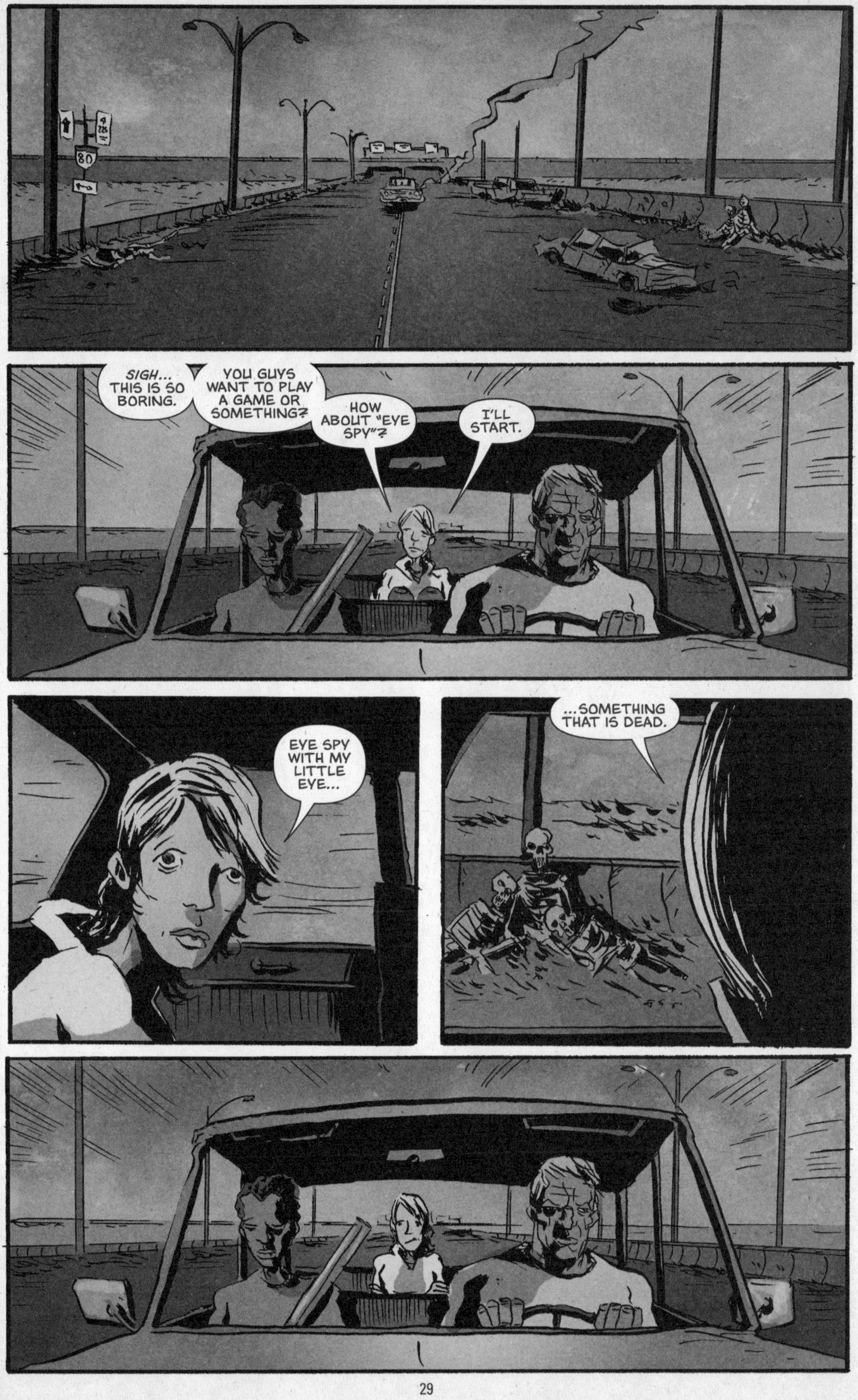

SIGH... THIS IS SO BORING.
YOU GUYS WANT TO PLAY A GAME OR SOMETHING?
HOW ABOUT "EYE SPY"?
I'LL START.
EYE SPY WITH MY LITTLE EYE...
...SOMETHING THAT IS DEAD.
80

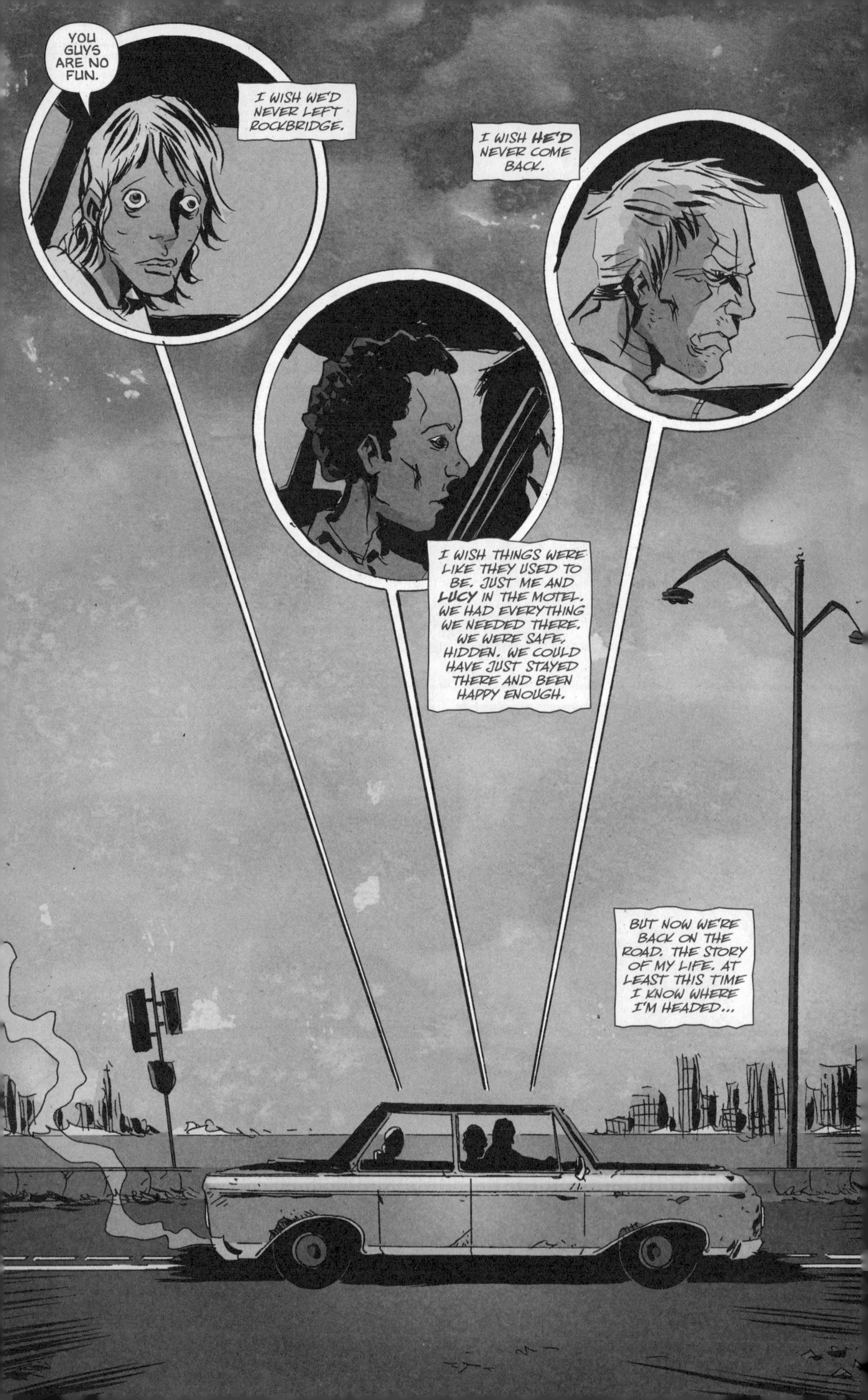
YOU GUYS ARE NO FUN.
I WISH WE'D NEVER LEFT ROCKBRIDGE.
I WISH HE'D NEVER COME BACK.
I WISH THINGS WERE LIKE THEY USED TO BE. JUST ME AND LUCY IN THE MOTEL. WE HAD EVERYTHING WE NEEDED THERE. WE WERE SAFE, HIDDEN. WE COULD HAVE JUST STAYED THERE AND BEEN HAPPY ENOUGH.
BUT NOW WE'RE BACK ON THE ROAD. THE STORY OF MY LIFE. AT LEAST THIS TIME I KNOW WHERE I'M HEADED...

...'COURSE THAT'S THE SCARIEST PART OF ALL.
13-3
ANIMAL ARMIES
PART ONE

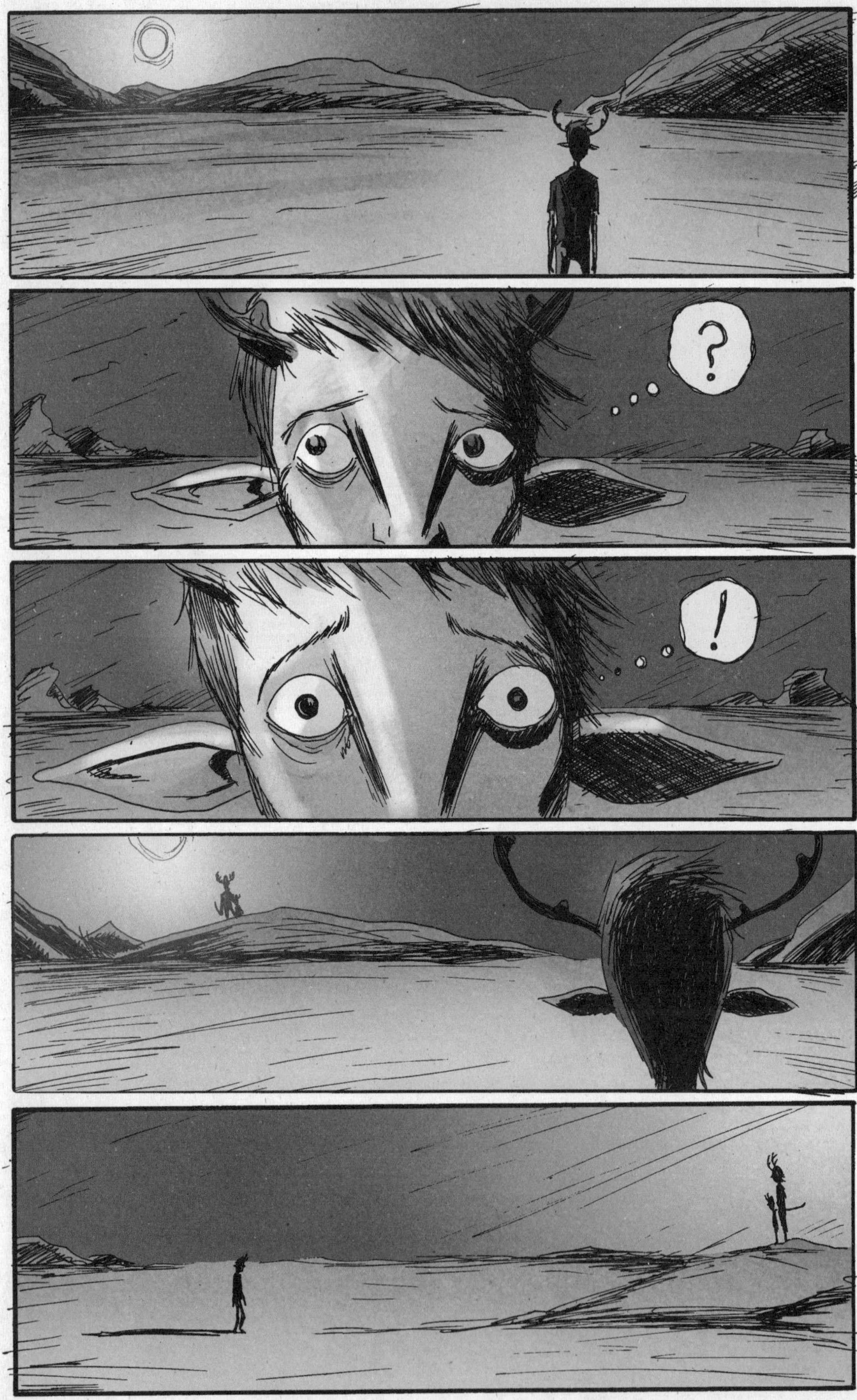
?
!

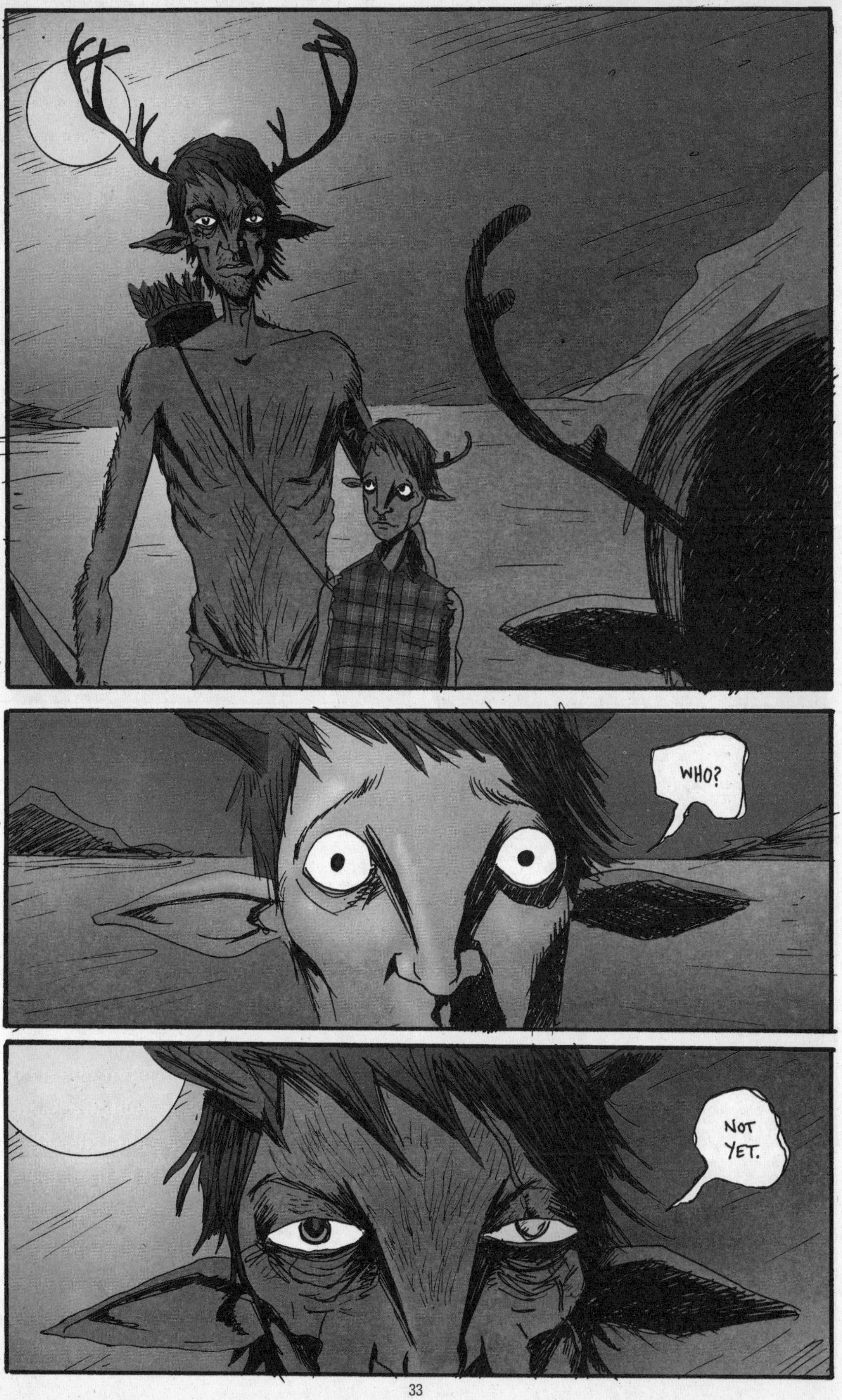
WHO?
NOT YET.

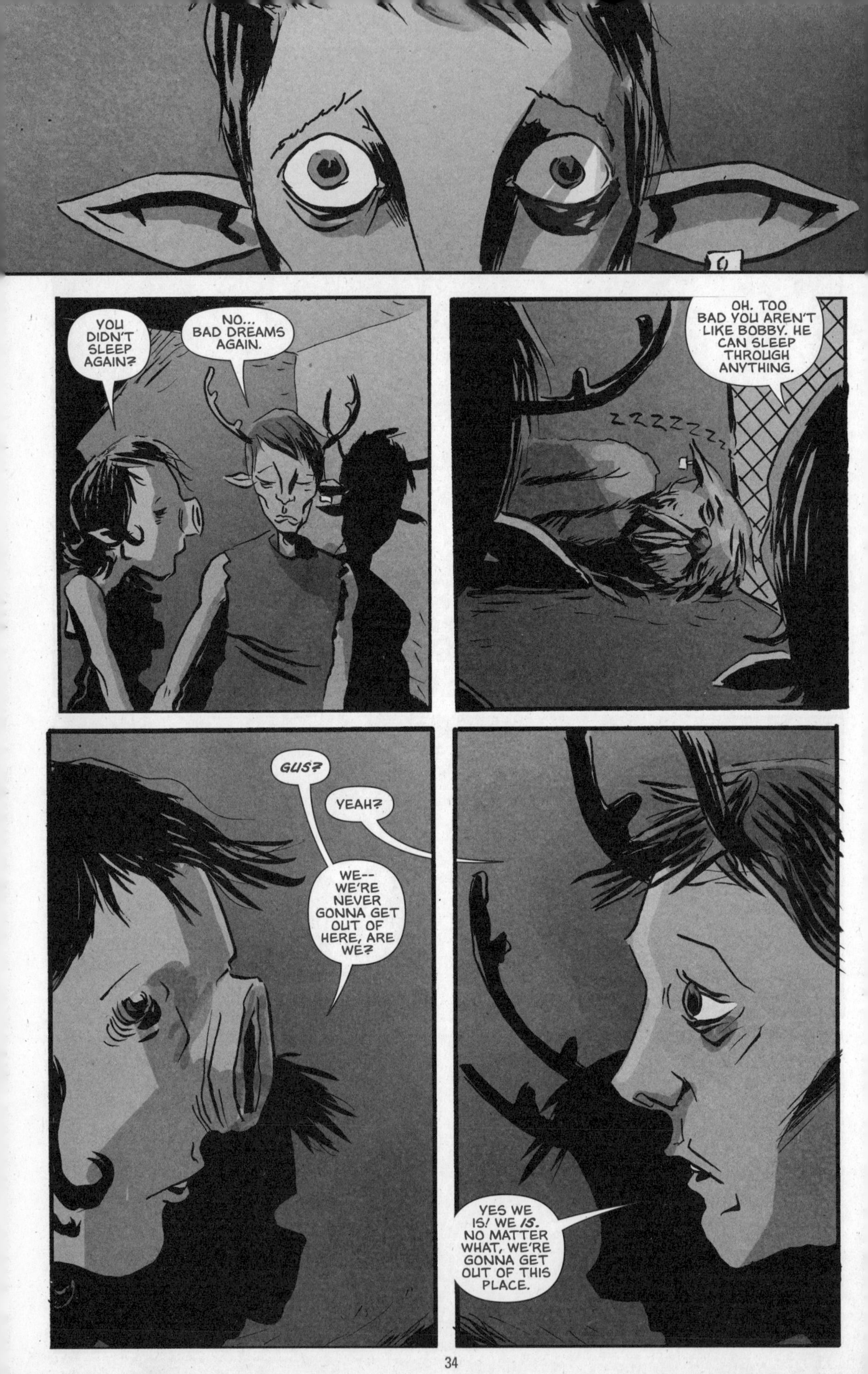
YOU DIDN'T SLEEP AGAIN?
NO... BAD DREAMS AGAIN.
OH. TOO BAD YOU AREN'T LIKE BOBBY. HE CAN SLEEP THROUGH ANYTHING.
ZZZZZZZZ
GUS?
YEAH?
WE-- WE'RE NEVER GONNA GET OUT OF HERE, ARE WE?
YES WE IS! WE *IS*. NO MATTER WHAT, WE'RE GONNA GET OUT OF THIS PLACE.

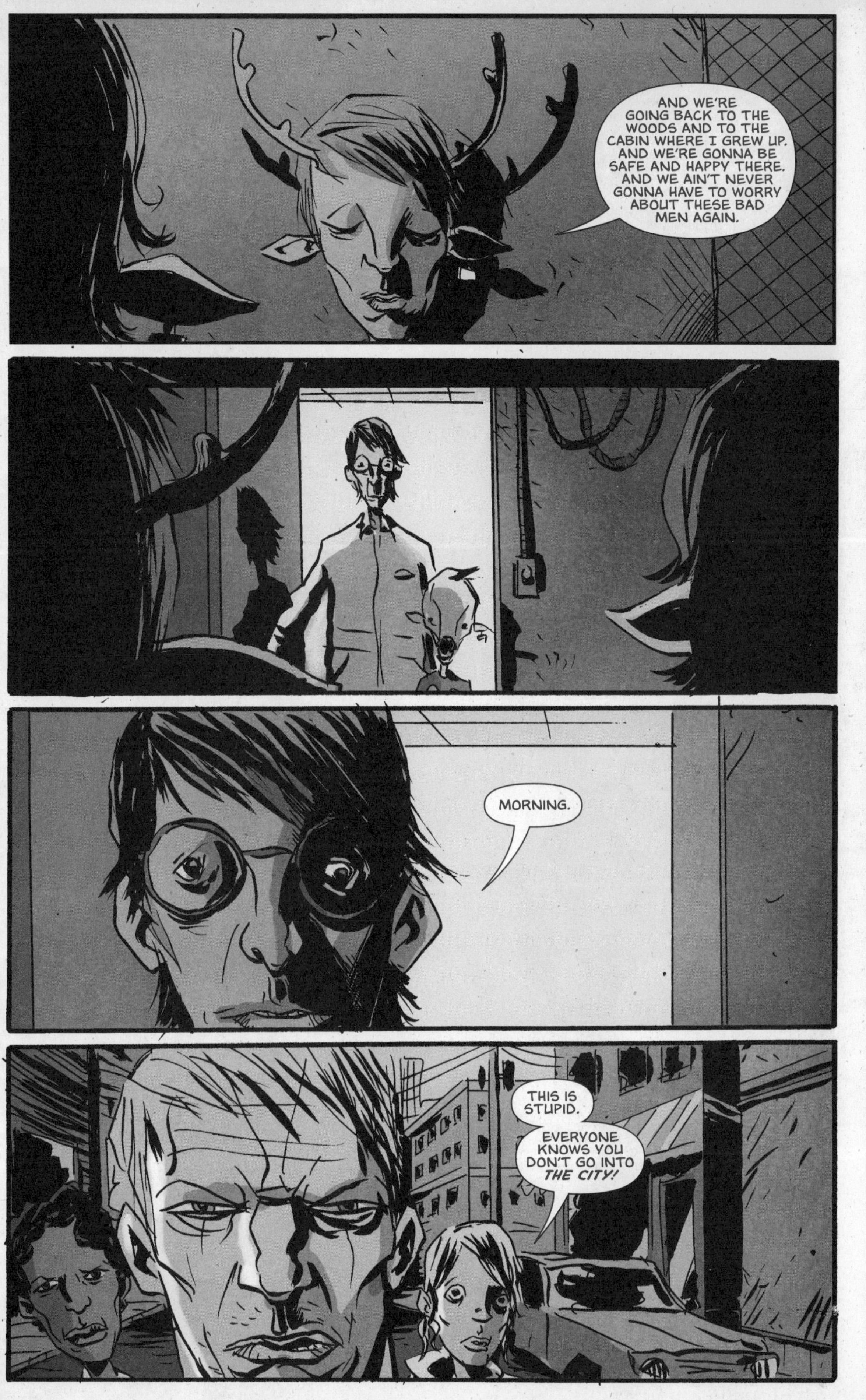
AND WE'RE GOING BACK TO THE WOODS AND TO THE CABIN WHERE I GREW UP. AND WE'RE GONNA BE SAFE AND HAPPY THERE. AND WE AIN'T NEVER GONNA HAVE TO WORRY ABOUT THESE BAD MEN AGAIN.
MORNING.
THIS IS STUPID.
EVERYONE KNOWS YOU DON'T GO INTO *THE CITY!*

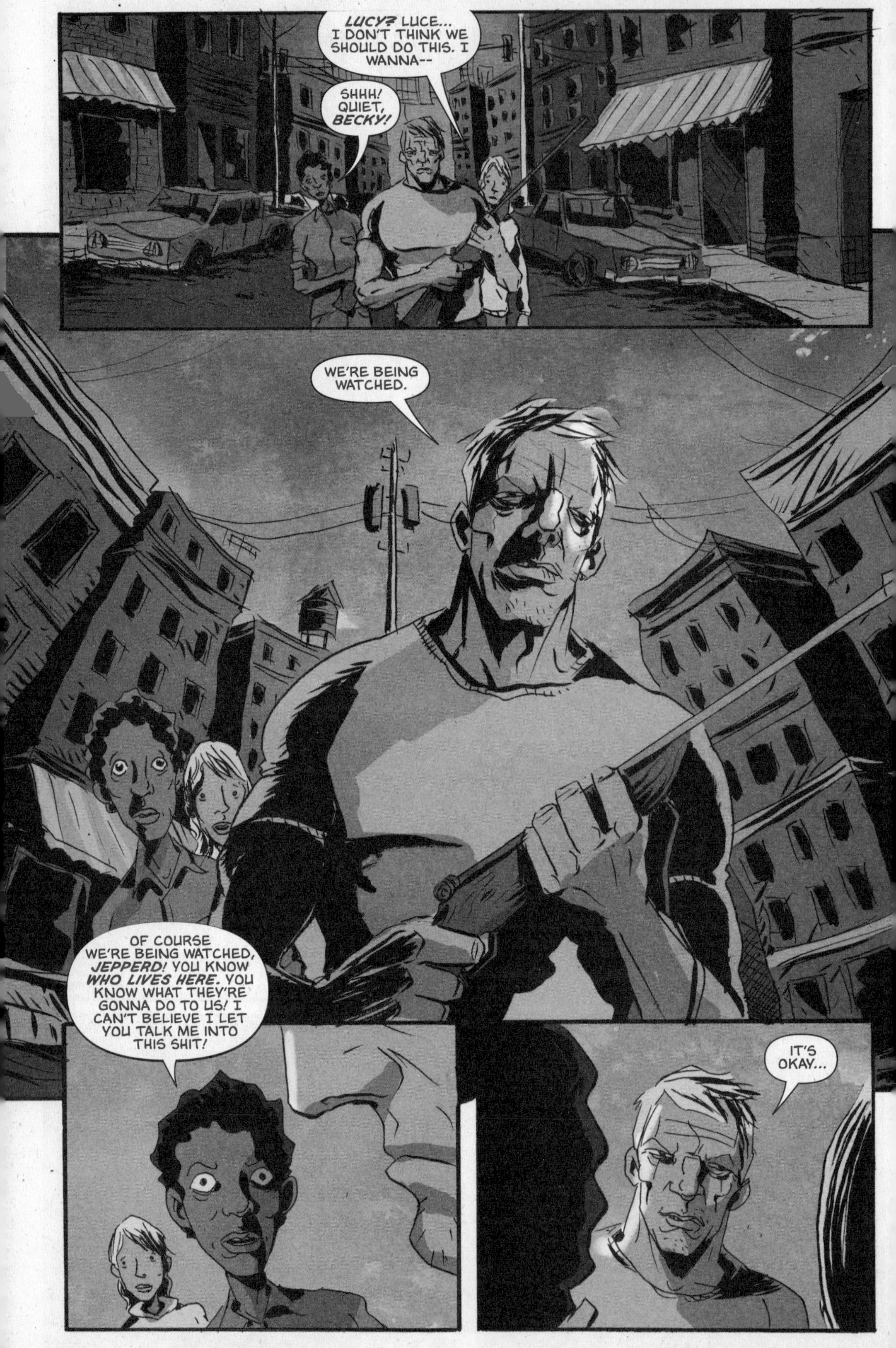
LUCY? LUCE... I DON'T THINK WE SHOULD DO THIS. I WANNA--
SHHH! QUIET, BECKY!
WE'RE BEING WATCHED.
OF COURSE WE'RE BEING WATCHED, JEPPERD! YOU KNOW WHO LIVES HERE. YOU KNOW WHAT THEY'RE GONNA DO TO US! I CAN'T BELIEVE I LET YOU TALK ME INTO THIS SHIT!
IT'S OKAY...

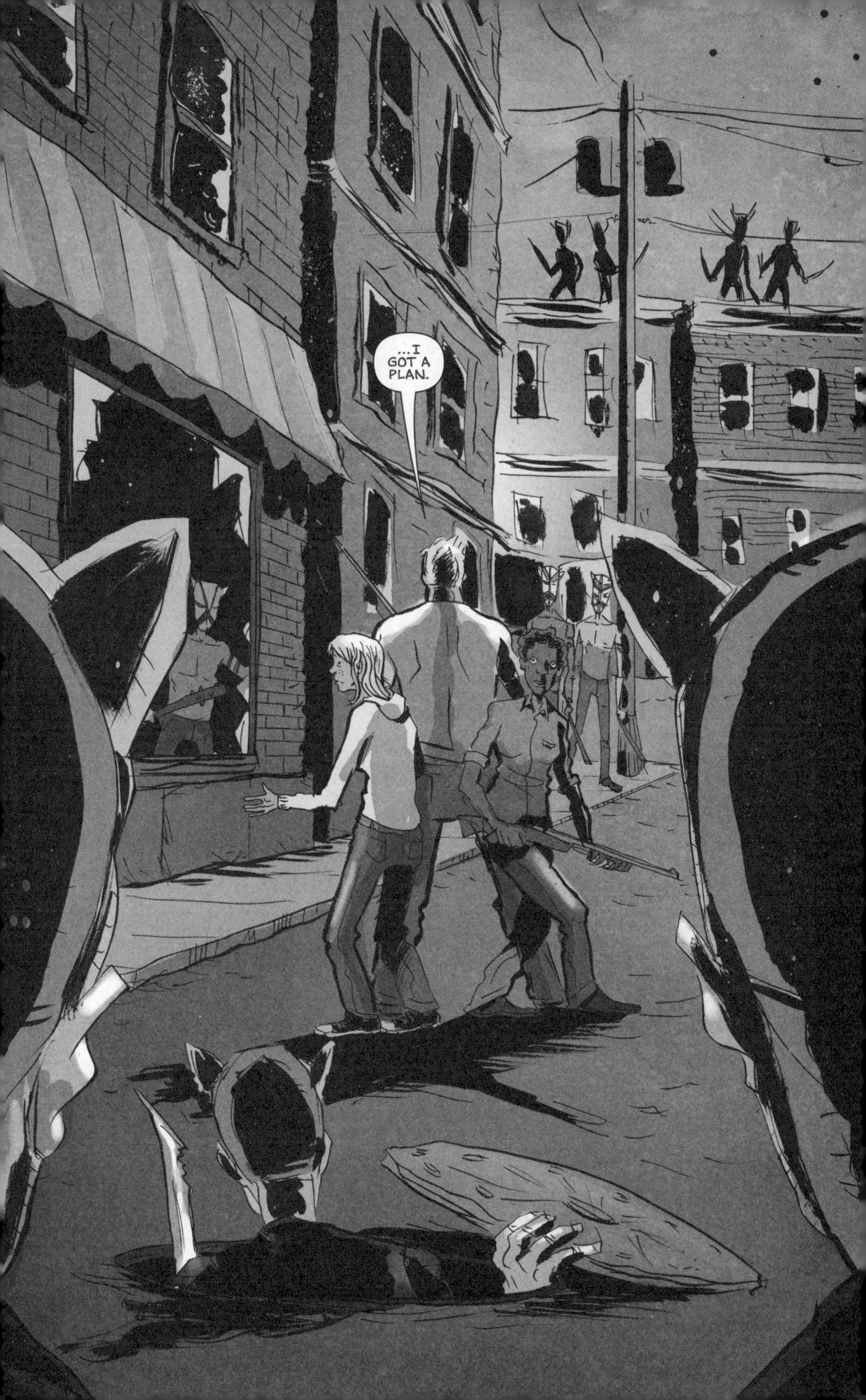
...I GOT A PLAN.

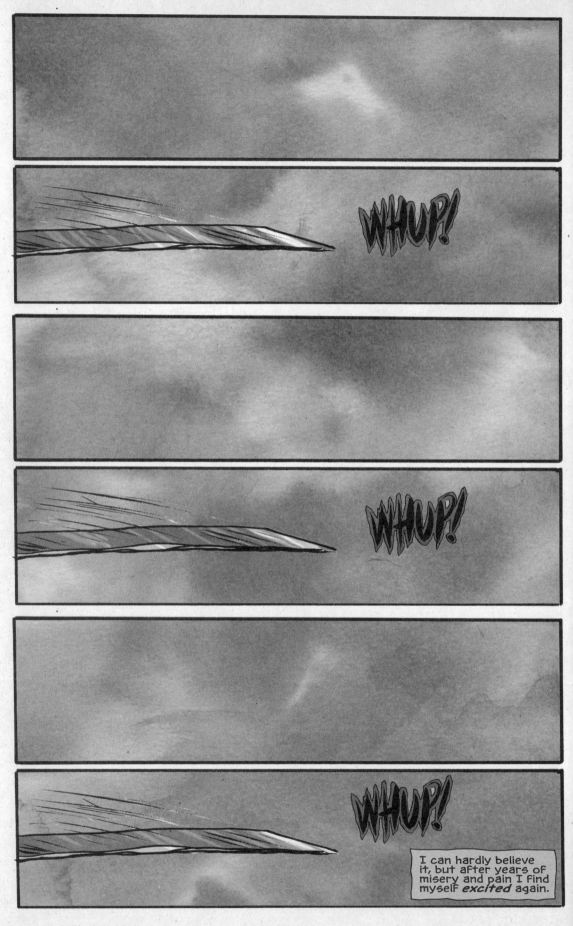

WHUP!

WHUP!

WHUP!

I can hardly believe it, but after years of misery and pain I find myself *excited* again.

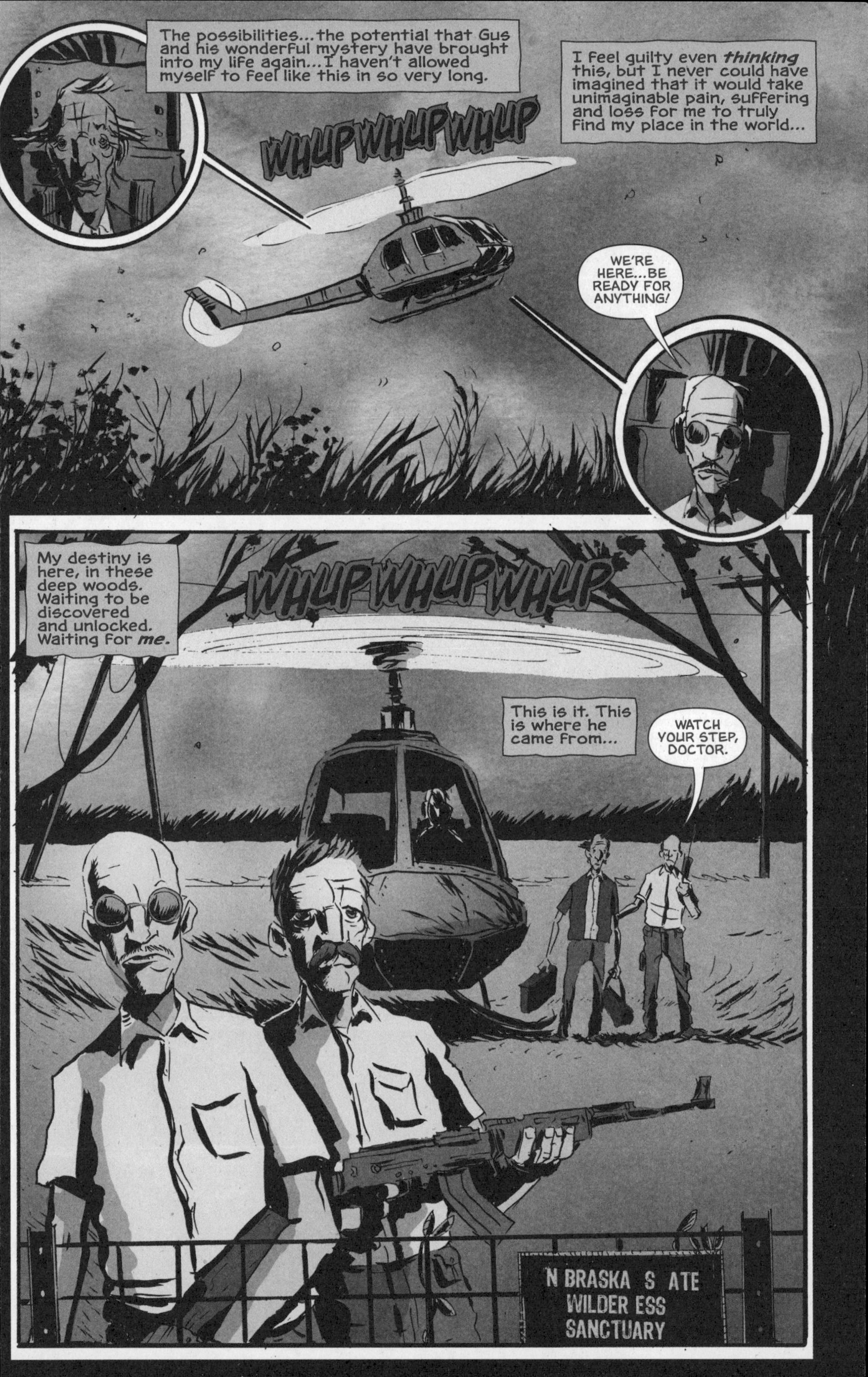

The possibilities...the potential that Gus and his wonderful mystery have brought into my life again...I haven't allowed myself to feel like this in so very long.
I feel guilty even *thinking* this, but I never could have imagined that it would take unimaginable pain, suffering and loss for me to truly find my place in the world...
WHUPWHUPWHUP
WE'RE HERE...BE READY FOR ANYTHING!
My destiny is here, in these deep woods. Waiting to be discovered and unlocked. Waiting for *me*.
WHUPWHUPWHUP
This is it. This is where he came from...
WATCH YOUR STEP, DOCTOR.
N BRASKA S ATE
WILDER ESS
SANCTUARY

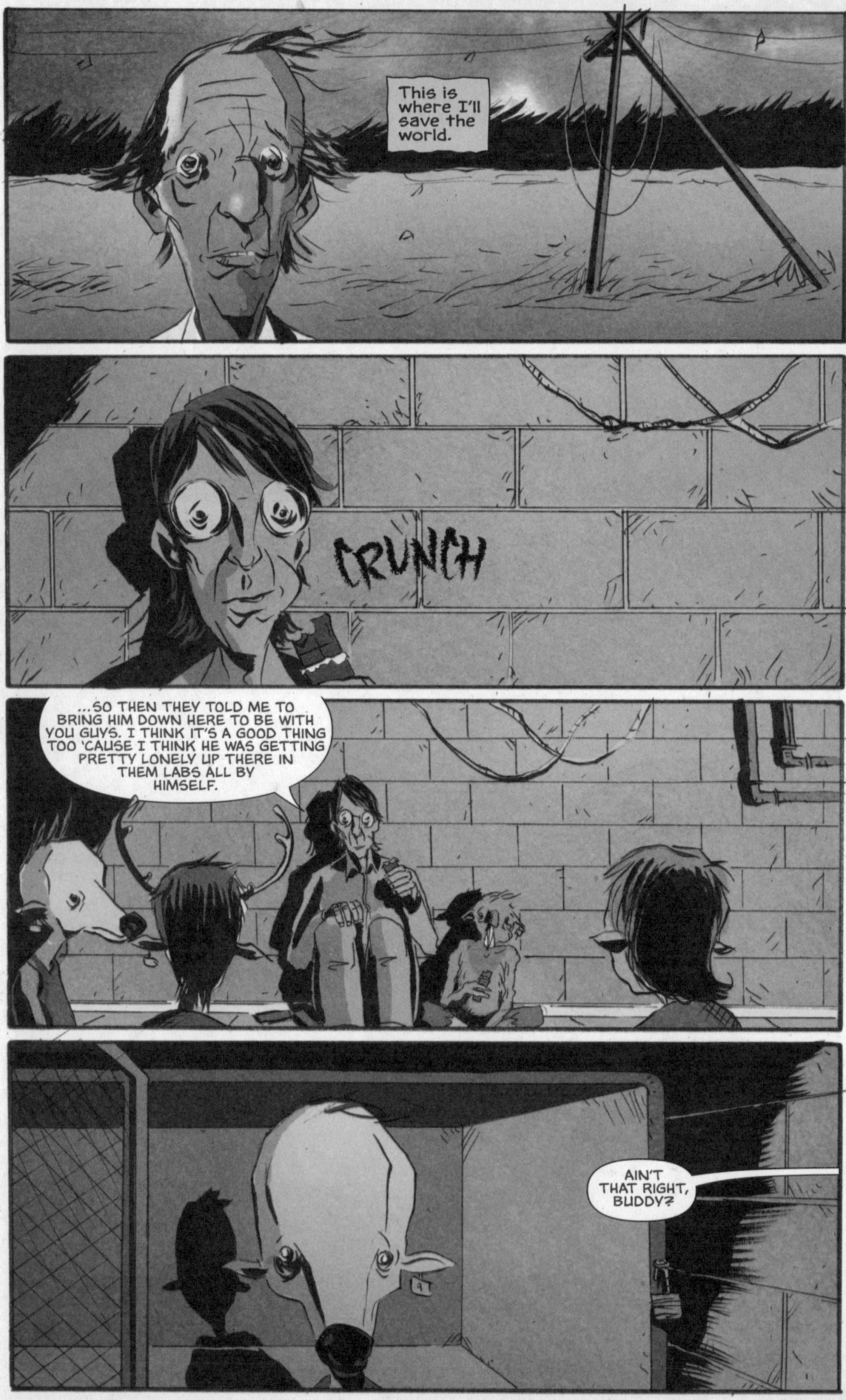
This is where I'll save the world.
CRUNCH
...SO THEN THEY TOLD ME TO BRING HIM DOWN HERE TO BE WITH YOU GUYS. I THINK IT'S A GOOD THING TOO 'CAUSE I THINK HE WAS GETTING PRETTY LONELY UP THERE IN THEM LABS ALL BY HIMSELF.
AIN'T THAT RIGHT, BUDDY?

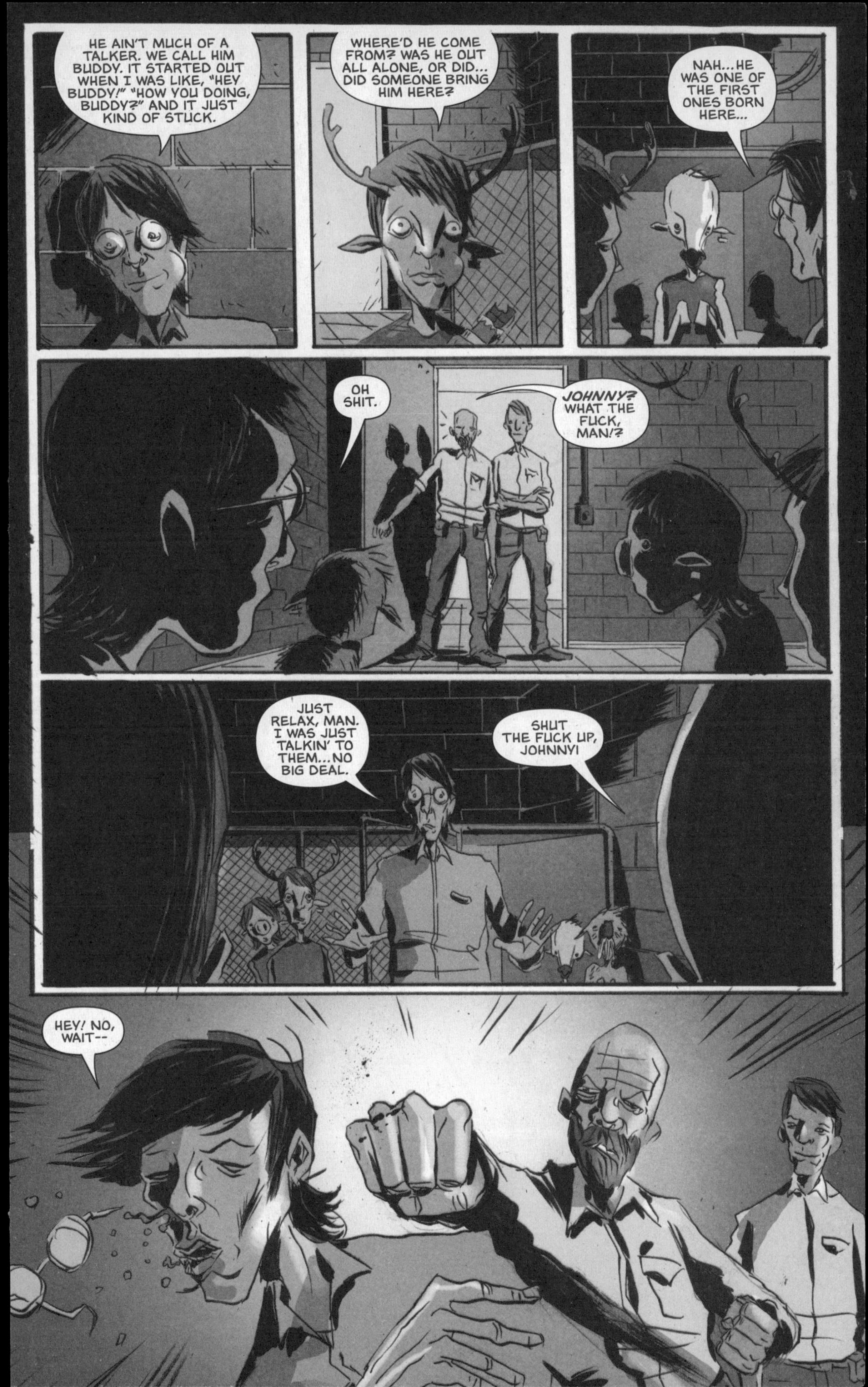
HE AIN'T MUCH OF A TALKER. WE CALL HIM BUDDY. IT STARTED OUT WHEN I WAS LIKE, "HEY BUDDY!" "HOW YOU DOING, BUDDY?" AND IT JUST KIND OF STUCK.
WHERE'D HE COME FROM? WAS HE OUT ALL ALONE, OR DID... DID SOMEONE BRING HIM HERE?
NAH... HE WAS ONE OF THE FIRST ONES BORN HERE...
OH SHIT.
JOHNNY? WHAT THE FUCK, MAN!?
JUST RELAX, MAN. I WAS JUST TALKIN' TO THEM... NO BIG DEAL.
SHUT THE FUCK UP, JOHNNY!
HEY! NO, WAIT--

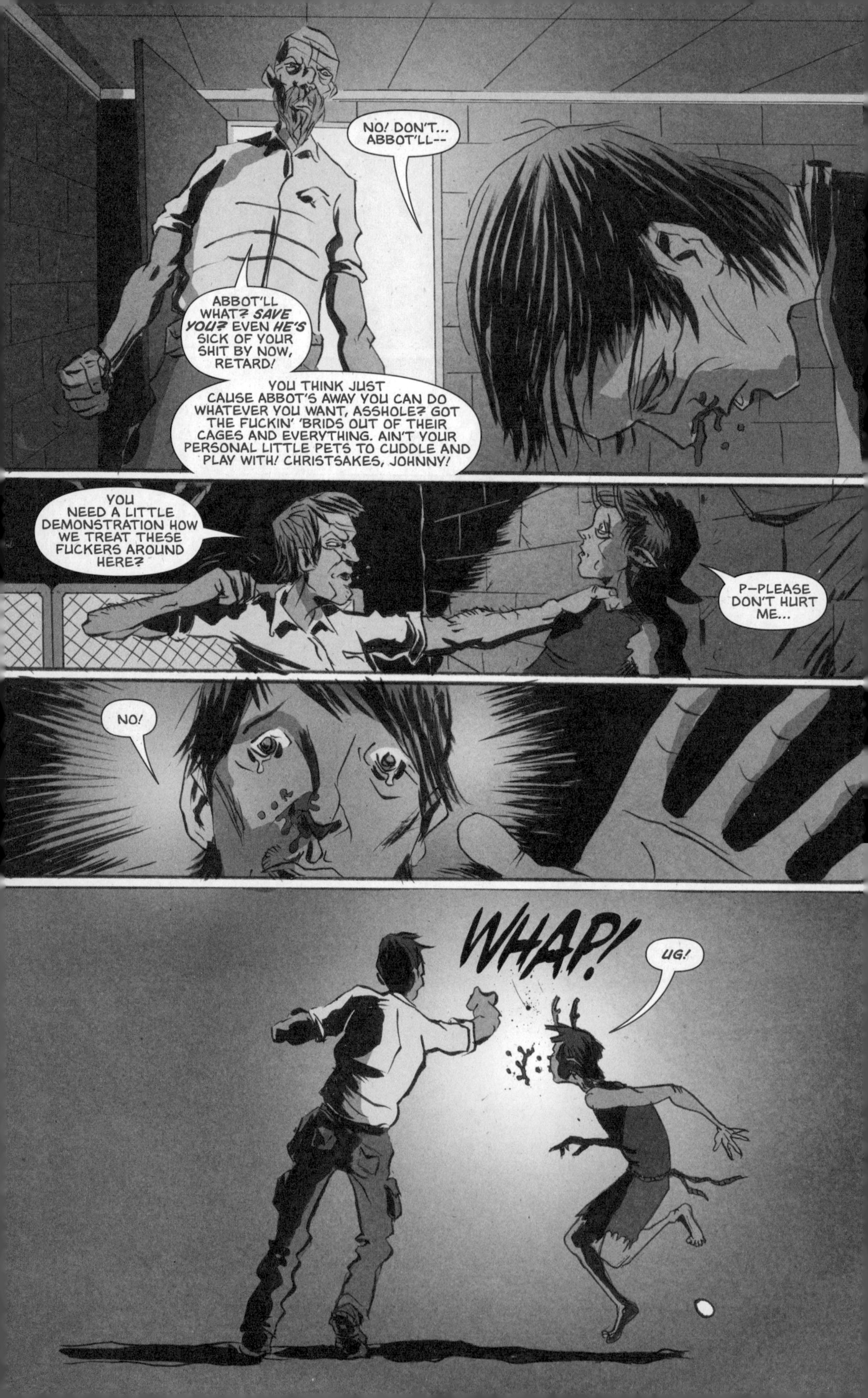
NO! DON'T... ABBOT'LL--
ABBOT'LL WHAT? SAVE YOU? EVEN HE'S SICK OF YOUR SHIT BY NOW, RETARD!
YOU THINK JUST CAUSE ABBOT'S AWAY YOU CAN DO WHATEVER YOU WANT, ASSHOLE? GOT THE FUCKIN' 'BRIDS OUT OF THEIR CAGES AND EVERYTHING. AIN'T YOUR PERSONAL LITTLE PETS TO CUDDLE AND PLAY WITH! CHRISTSAKES, JOHNNY!
YOU NEED A LITTLE DEMONSTRATION HOW WE TREAT THESE FUCKERS AROUND HERE?
P-PLEASE DON'T HURT ME...
NO!
WHAP!
UG!

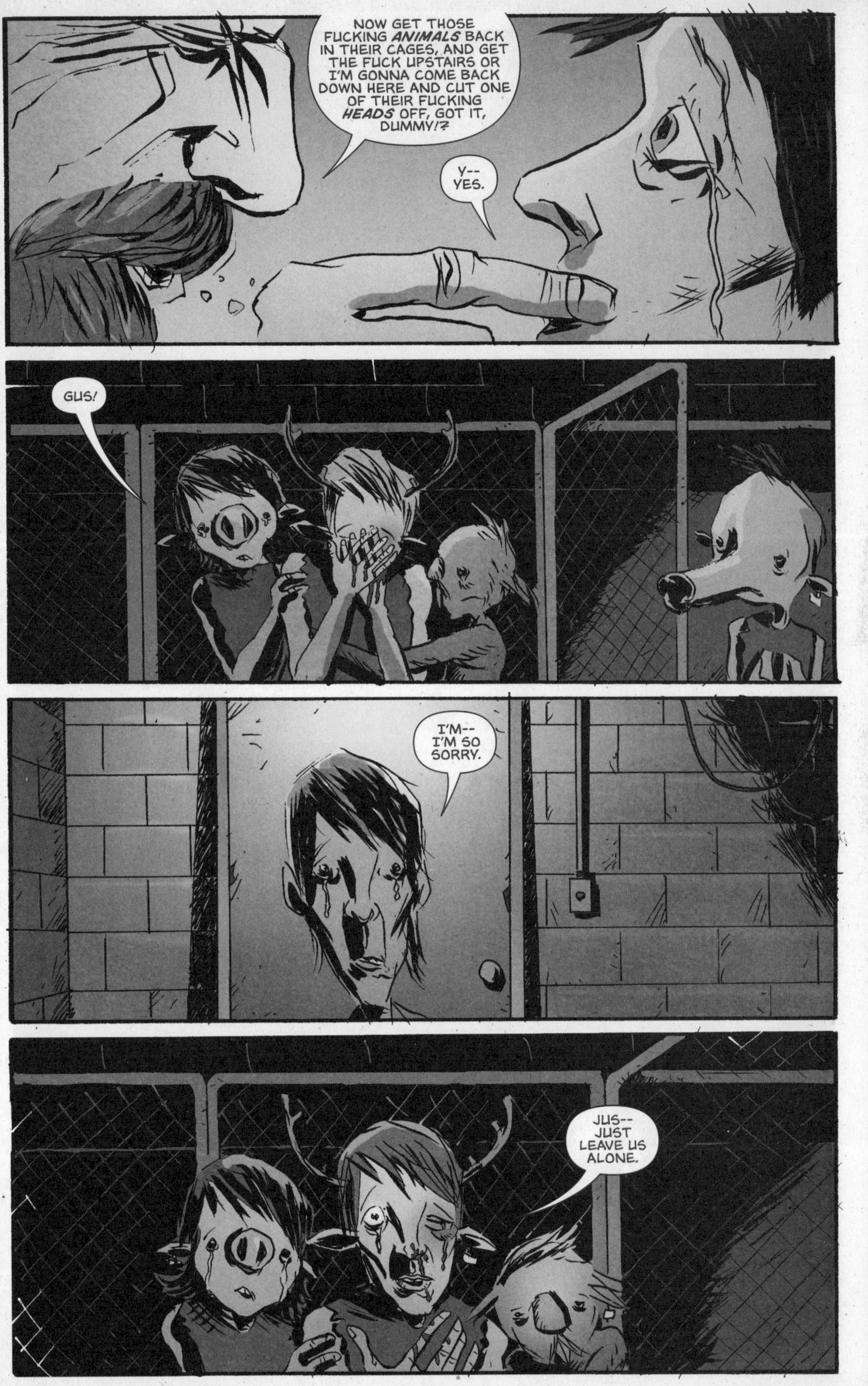
NOW GET THOSE FUCKING *ANIMALS* BACK IN THEIR CAGES, AND GET THE FUCK UPSTAIRS OR I'M GONNA COME BACK DOWN HERE AND CUT ONE OF THEIR FUCKING *HEADS* OFF, GOT IT, DUMMY!?
Y-- YES.
GUS!
I'M-- I'M SO SORRY.
JUS-- JUST LEAVE US ALONE.

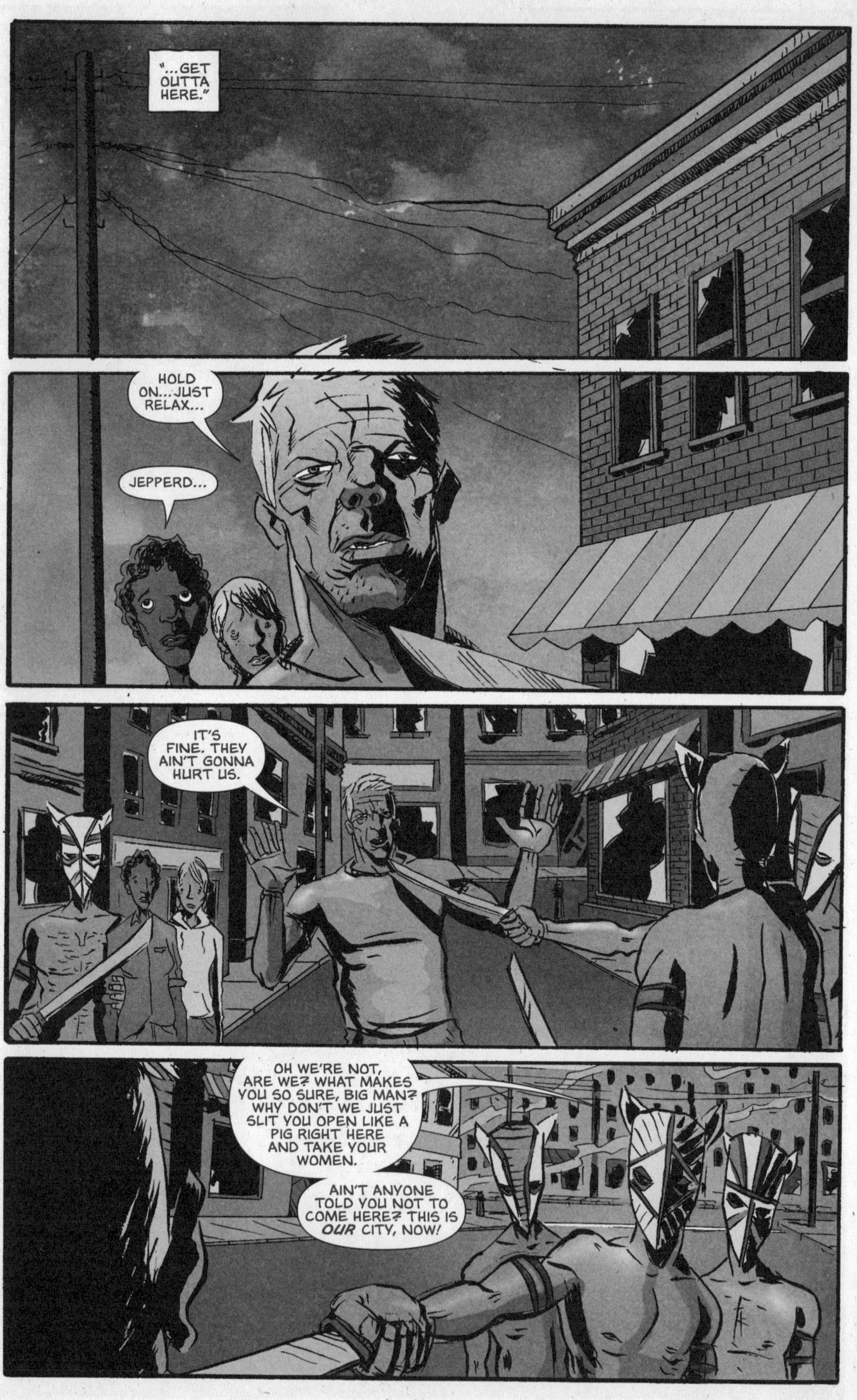
"...GET OUTTA HERE."
HOLD ON...JUST RELAX...
JEPPERD...
IT'S FINE. THEY AIN'T GONNA HURT US.
OH WE'RE NOT, ARE WE? WHAT MAKES YOU SO SURE, BIG MAN? WHY DON'T WE JUST SLIT YOU OPEN LIKE A PIG RIGHT HERE AND TAKE YOUR WOMEN.
AIN'T ANYONE TOLD YOU NOT TO COME HERE? THIS IS *OUR* CITY, NOW!

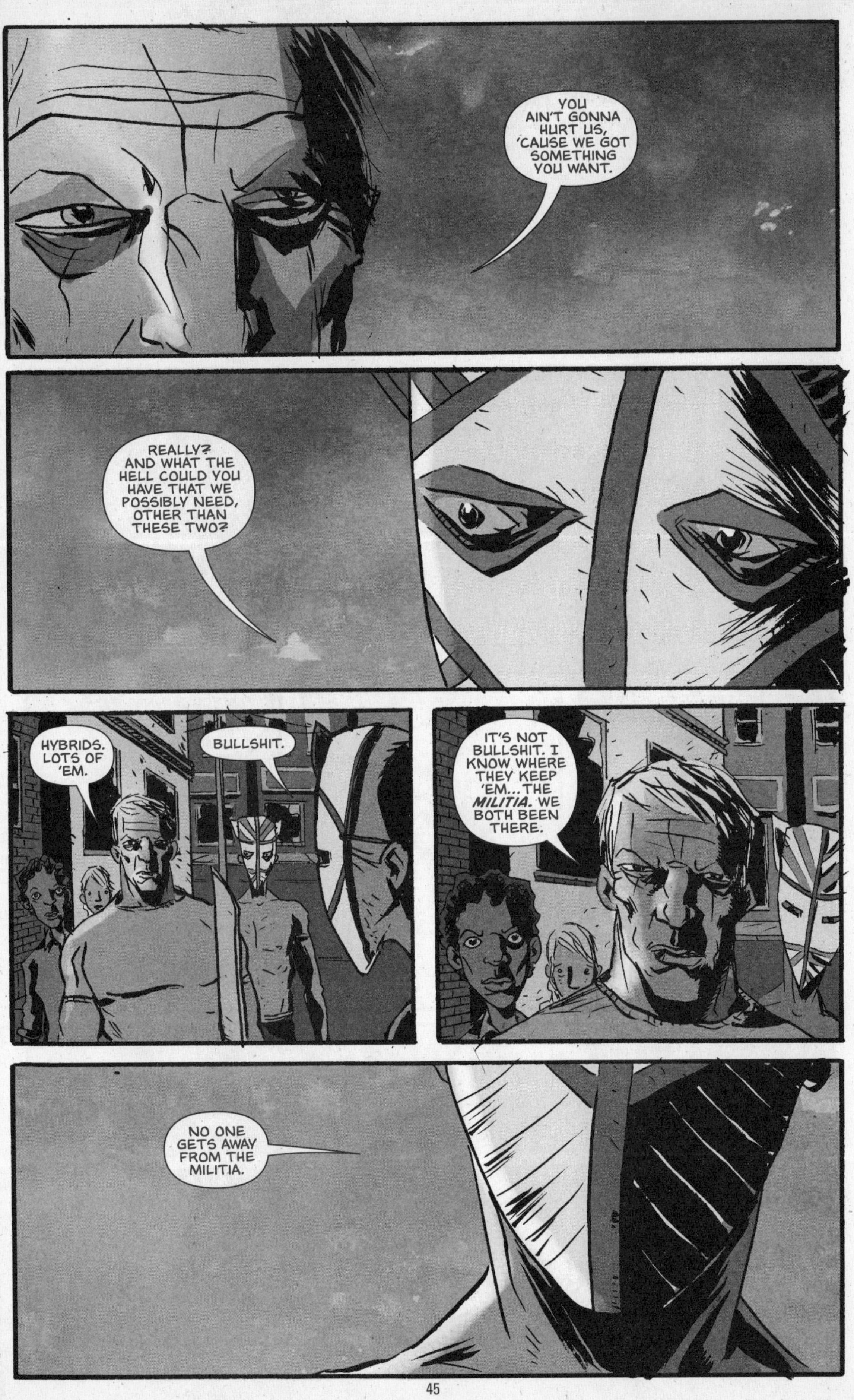
YOU AIN'T GONNA HURT US, 'CAUSE WE GOT SOMETHING YOU WANT.
REALLY? AND WHAT THE HELL COULD YOU HAVE THAT WE POSSIBLY NEED, OTHER THAN THESE TWO?
HYBRIDS. LOTS OF 'EM.
BULLSHIT.
IT'S NOT BULLSHIT. I KNOW WHERE THEY KEEP 'EM... THE *MILITIA.* WE BOTH BEEN THERE.
NO ONE GETS AWAY FROM THE MILITIA.

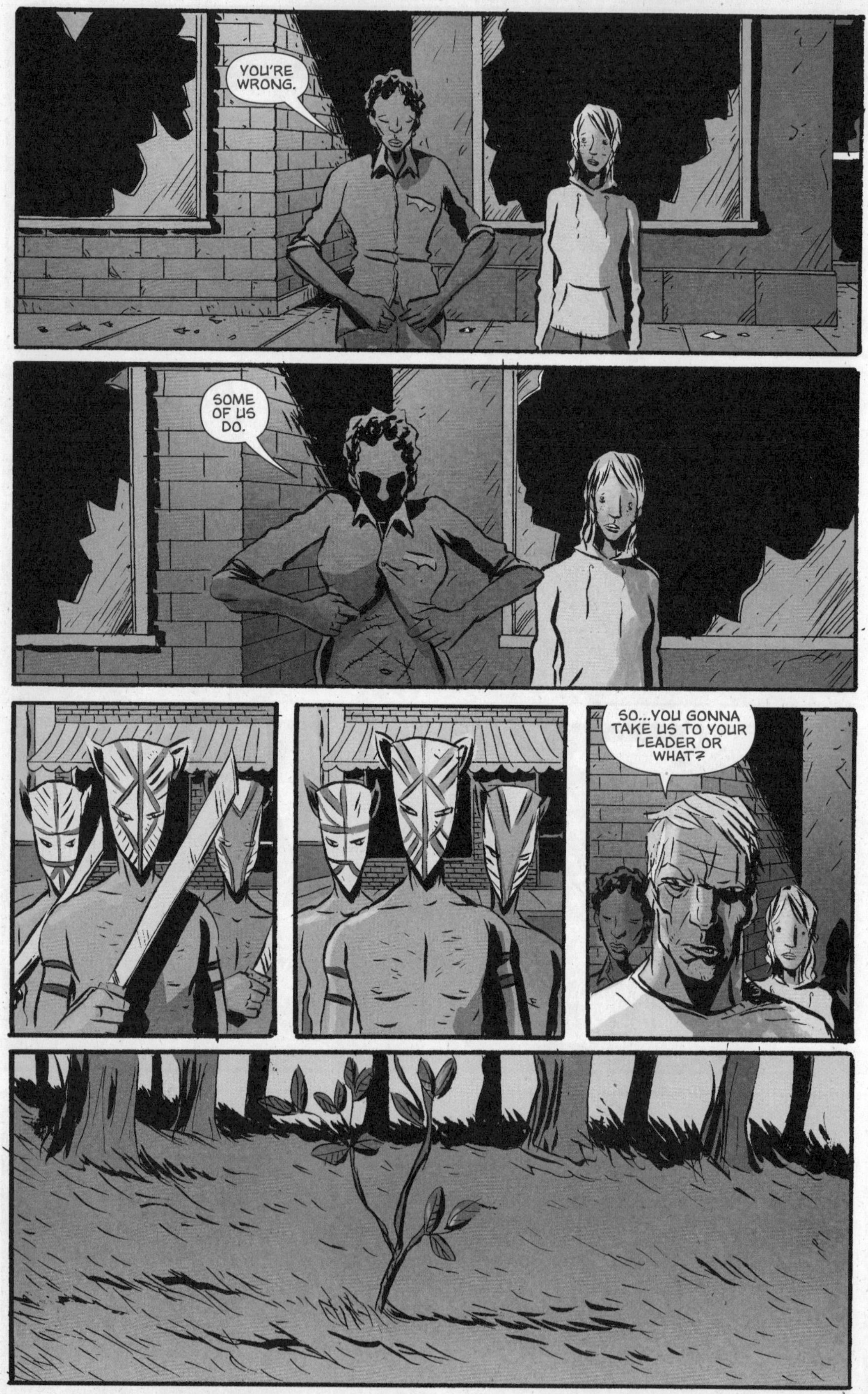
YOU'RE WRONG.
SOME OF US DO.
SO...YOU GONNA TAKE US TO YOUR LEADER OR WHAT?

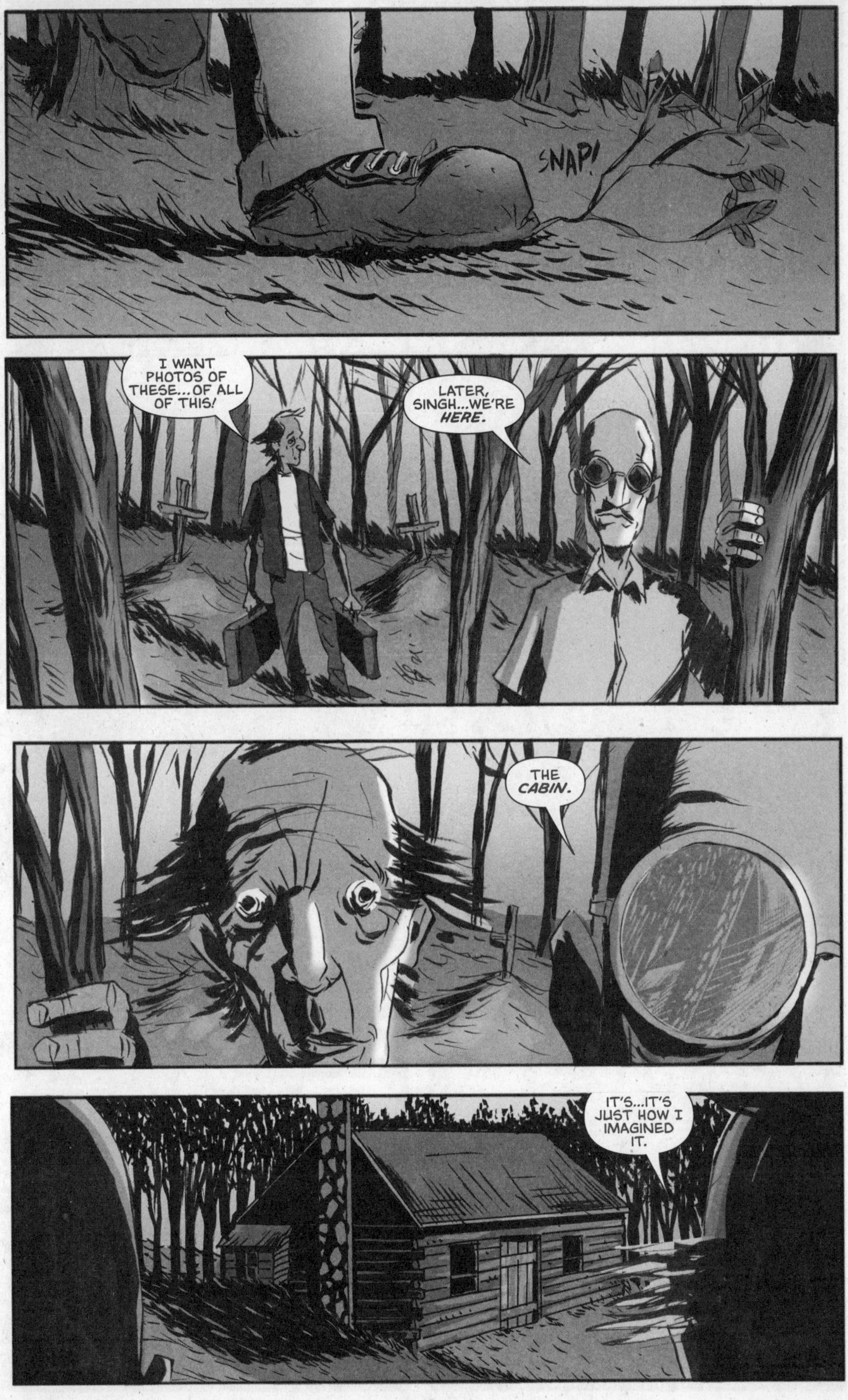
SNAP!
I WANT PHOTOS OF THESE...OF ALL OF THIS!
LATER, SINGH...WE'RE *HERE.*
THE *CABIN.*
IT'S...IT'S JUST HOW I IMAGINED IT.

BZZZZZZZZZ

Johny + Douglas
Summer 1992

WHAT *HAPPENED* TO US?

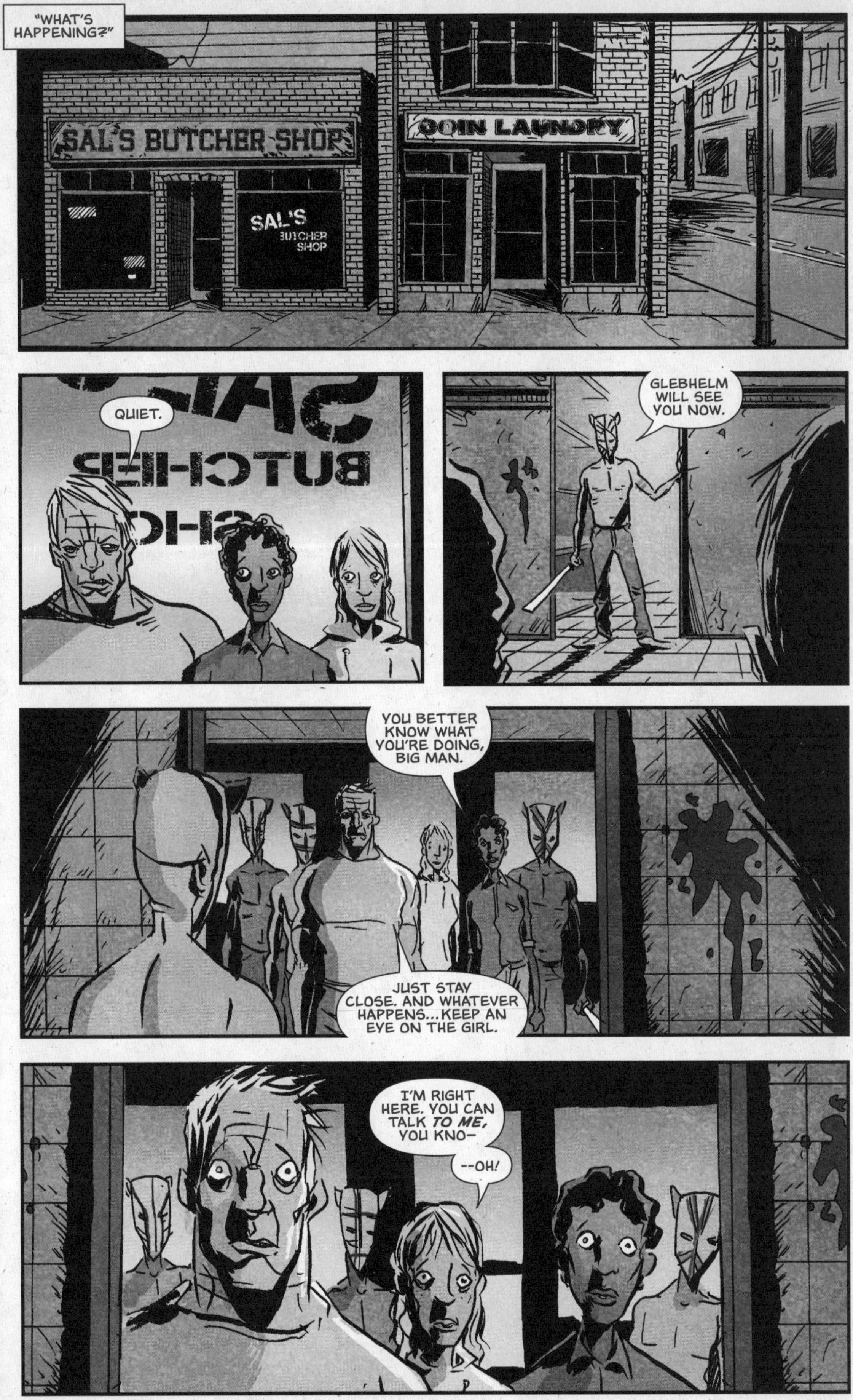
"WHAT'S HAPPENING?"
SAL'S BUTCHER SHOP
COIN LAUNDRY
SAL'S BUTCHER SHOP
QUIET.
GLEBHELM WILL SEE YOU NOW.
YOU BETTER KNOW WHAT YOU'RE DOING, BIG MAN.
JUST STAY CLOSE. AND WHATEVER HAPPENS...KEEP AN EYE ON THE GIRL.
I'M RIGHT HERE. YOU CAN TALK *TO ME,* YOU KNO–
--OH!

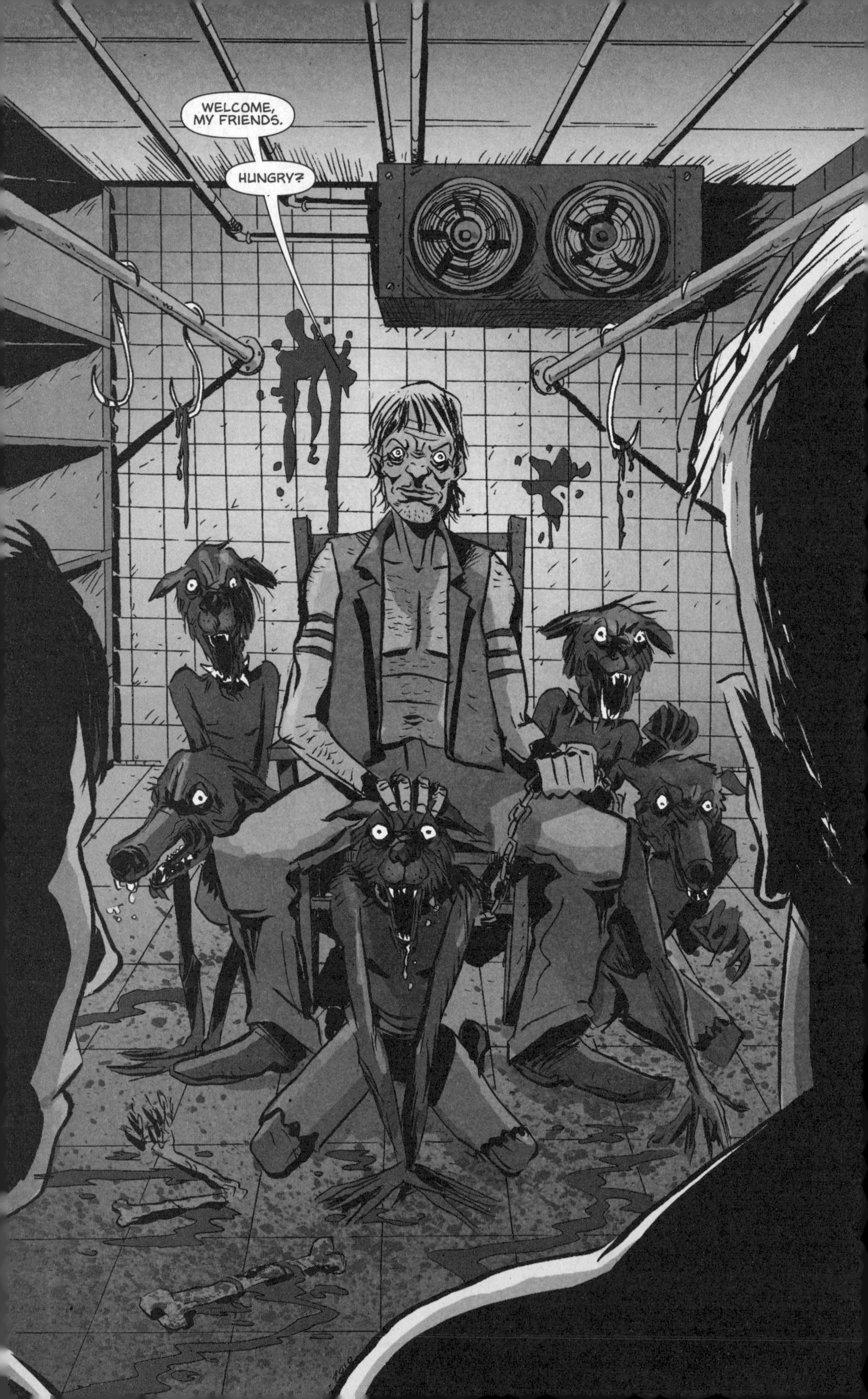
WELCOME, MY FRIENDS.
HUNGRY?

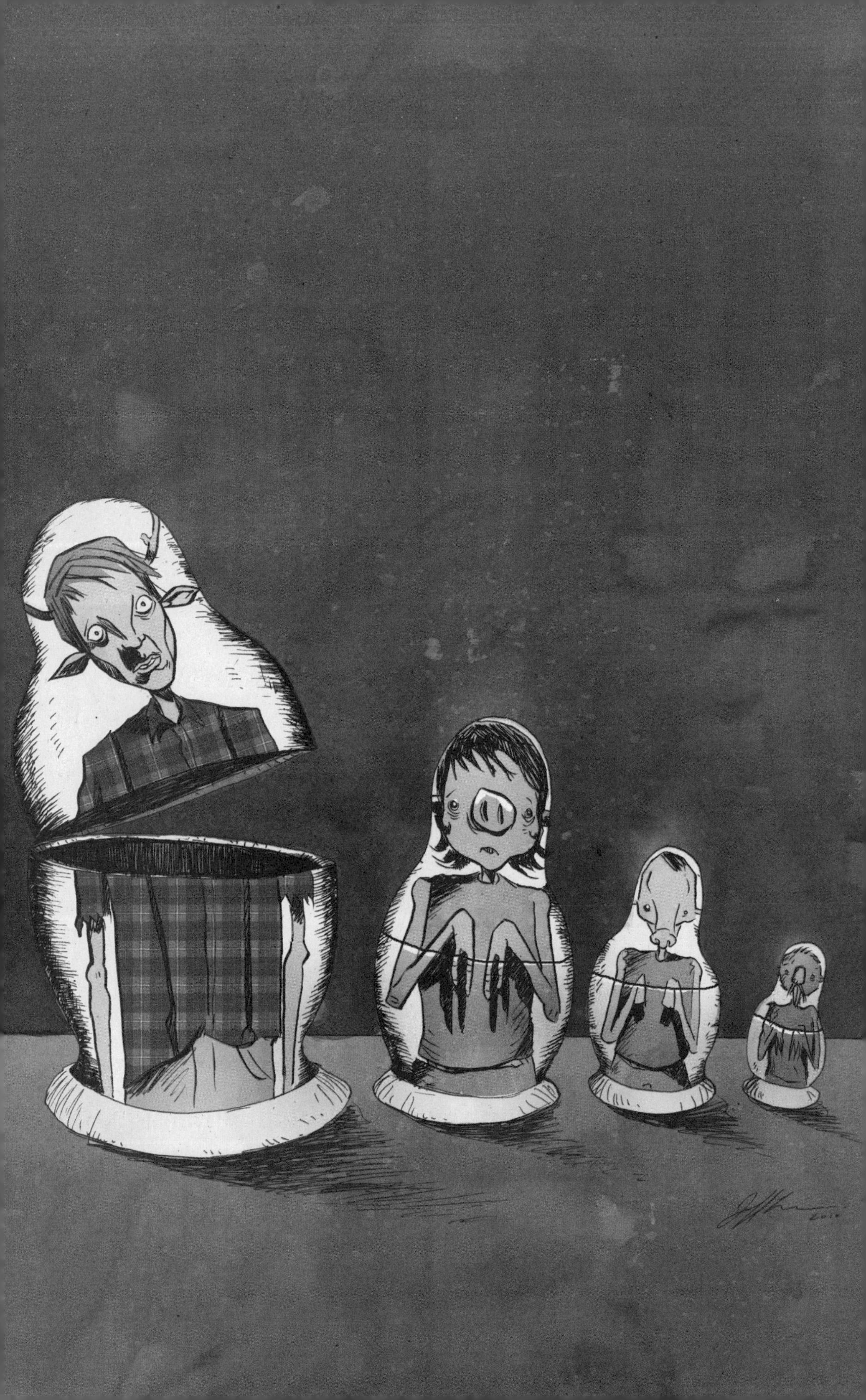

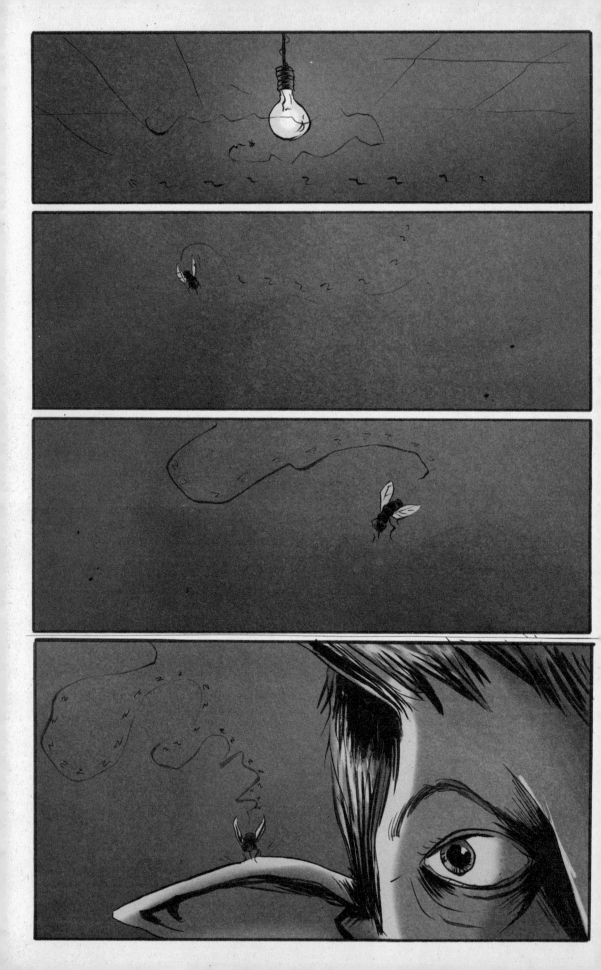

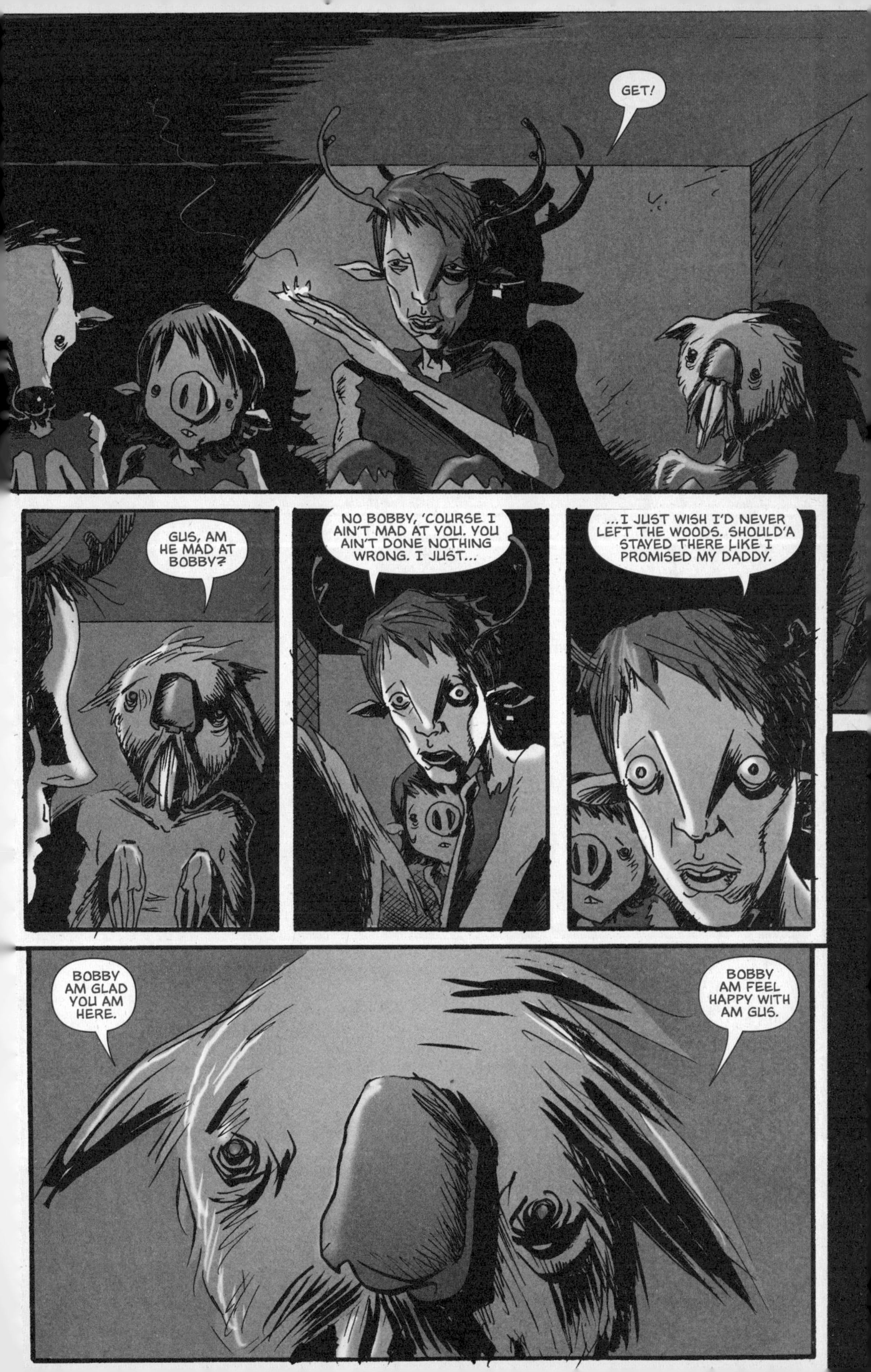
GET!
GUS, AM HE MAD AT BOBBY?
NO BOBBY, 'COURSE I AIN'T MAD AT YOU. YOU AIN'T DONE NOTHING WRONG. I JUST...
...I JUST WISH I'D NEVER LEFT THE WOODS. SHOULD'A STAYED THERE LIKE I PROMISED MY DADDY.
BOBBY AM GLAD YOU AM HERE.
BOBBY AM FEEL HAPPY WITH AM GUS.

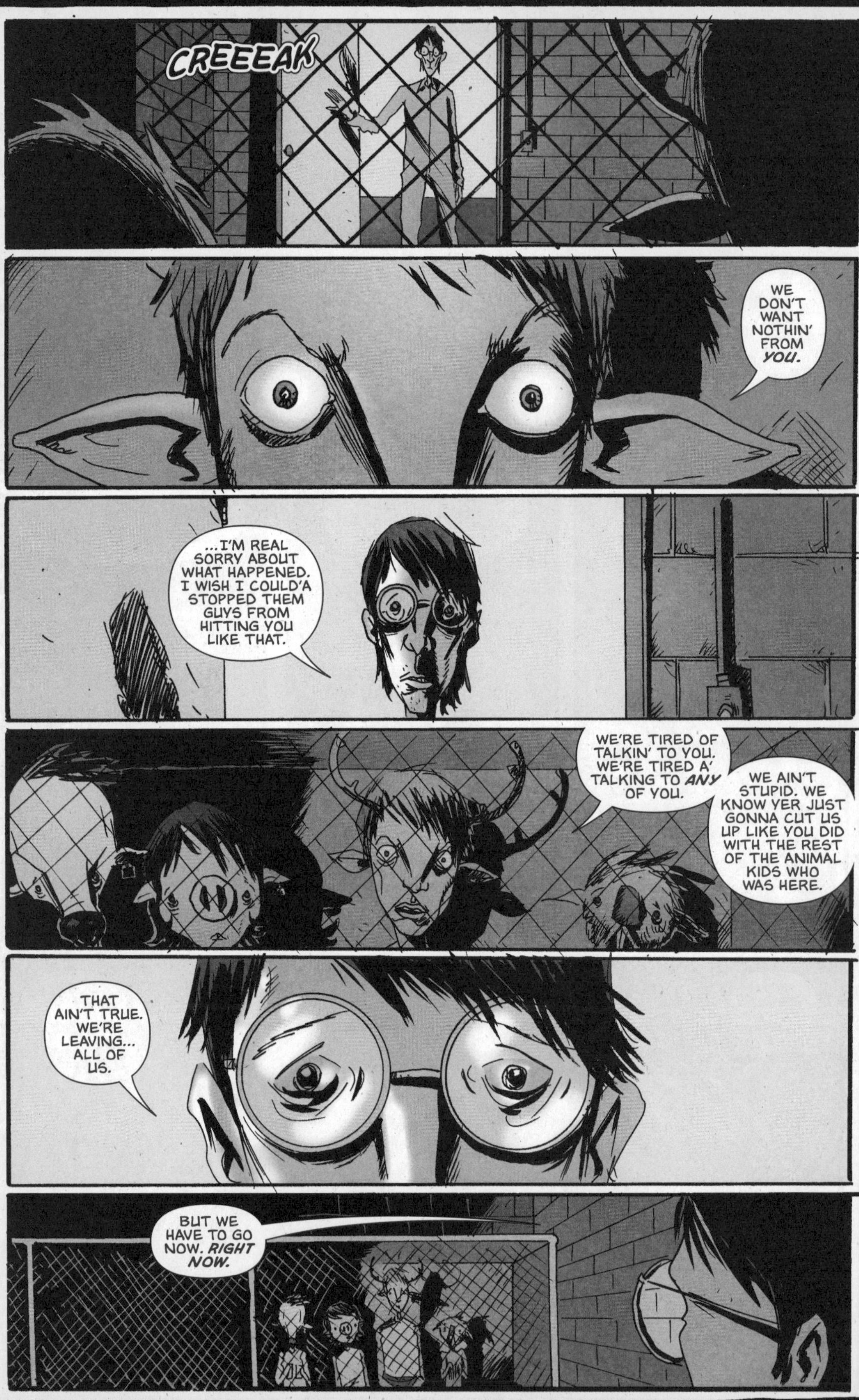
CREEEEAK
WE DON'T WANT NOTHIN' FROM YOU.
...I'M REAL SORRY ABOUT WHAT HAPPENED. I WISH I COULD'A STOPPED THEM GUYS FROM HITTING YOU LIKE THAT.
WE'RE TIRED OF TALKIN' TO YOU. WE'RE TIRED A' TALKING TO ANY OF YOU.
WE AIN'T STUPID. WE KNOW YER JUST GONNA CUT US UP LIKE YOU DID WITH THE REST OF THE ANIMAL KIDS WHO WAS HERE.
THAT AIN'T TRUE. WE'RE LEAVING... ALL OF US.
BUT WE HAVE TO GO NOW. RIGHT NOW.

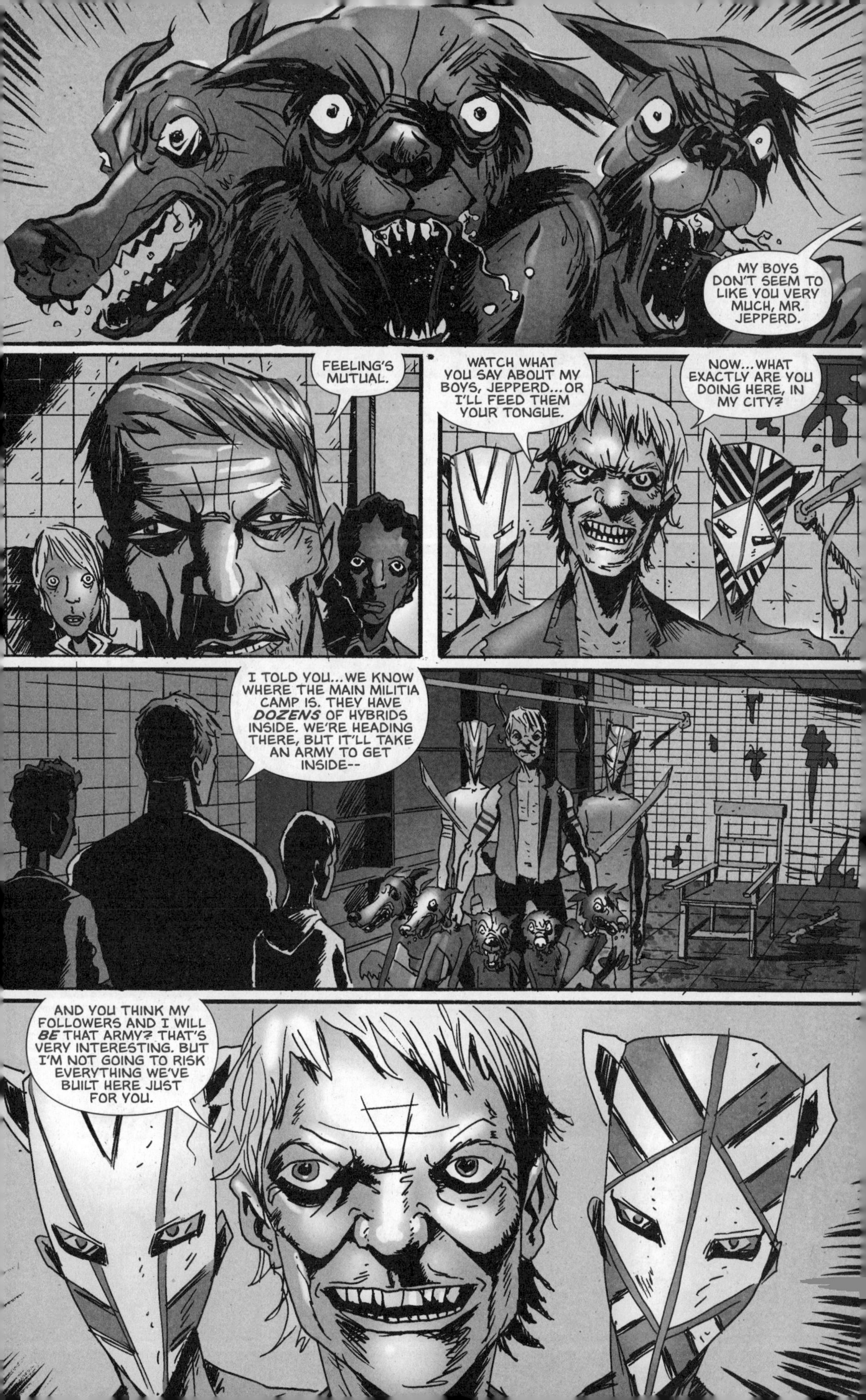
MY BOYS DON'T SEEM TO LIKE YOU VERY MUCH, MR. JEPPERD.
FEELING'S MUTUAL.
WATCH WHAT YOU SAY ABOUT MY BOYS, JEPPERD...OR I'LL FEED THEM YOUR TONGUE.
NOW...WHAT EXACTLY ARE YOU DOING HERE, IN MY CITY?
I TOLD YOU...WE KNOW WHERE THE MAIN MILITIA CAMP IS. THEY HAVE DOZENS OF HYBRIDS INSIDE. WE'RE HEADING THERE, BUT IT'LL TAKE AN ARMY TO GET INSIDE--
AND YOU THINK MY FOLLOWERS AND I WILL BE THAT ARMY? THAT'S VERY INTERESTING. BUT I'M NOT GOING TO RISK EVERYTHING WE'VE BUILT HERE JUST FOR YOU.

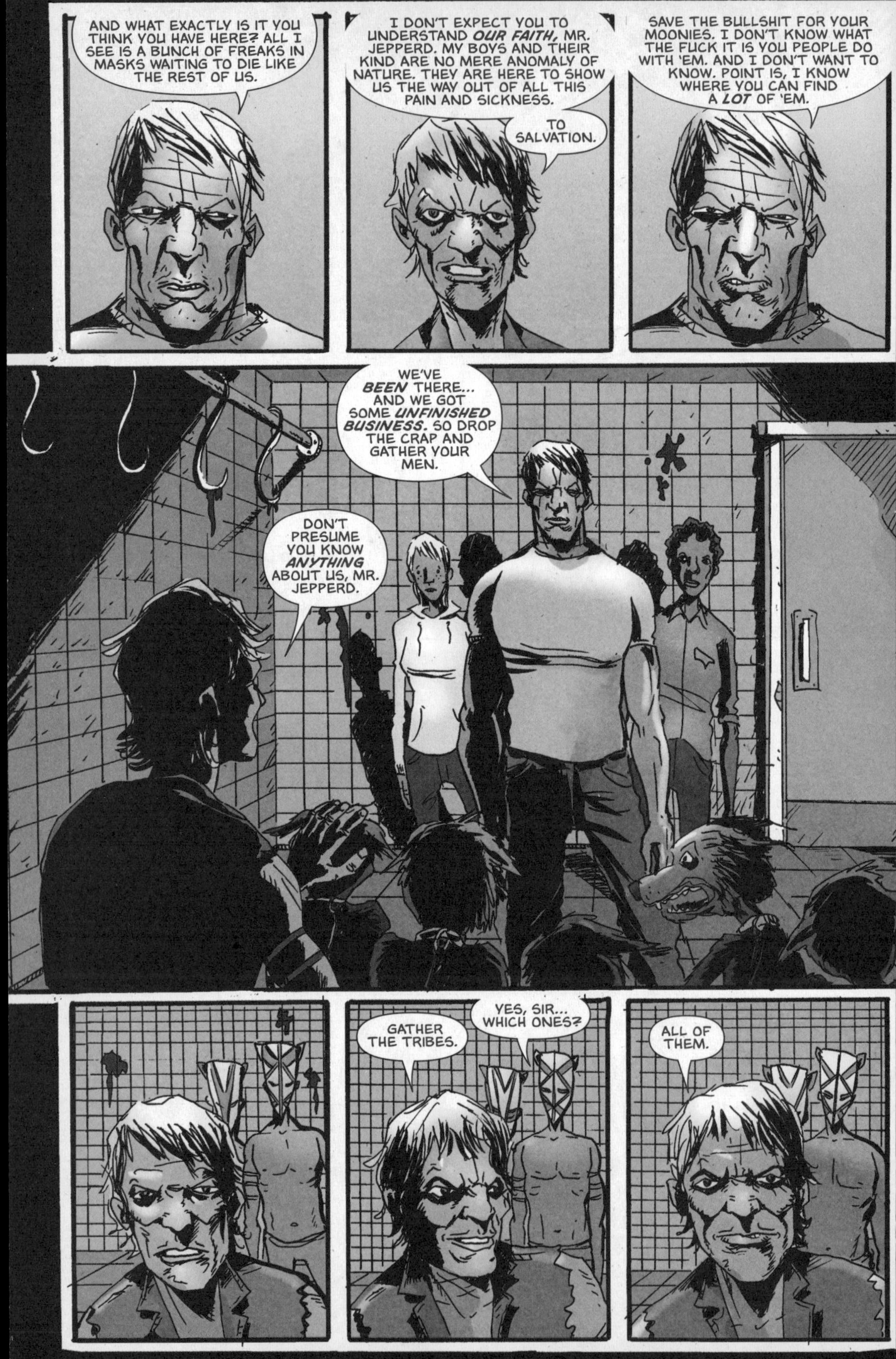
AND WHAT EXACTLY IS IT YOU THINK YOU HAVE HERE? ALL I SEE IS A BUNCH OF FREAKS IN MASKS WAITING TO DIE LIKE THE REST OF US.
I DON'T EXPECT YOU TO UNDERSTAND OUR FAITH, MR. JEPPERD. MY BOYS AND THEIR KIND ARE NO MERE ANOMALY OF NATURE. THEY ARE HERE TO SHOW US THE WAY OUT OF ALL THIS PAIN AND SICKNESS.
TO SALVATION.
SAVE THE BULLSHIT FOR YOUR MOONIES. I DON'T KNOW WHAT THE FUCK IT IS YOU PEOPLE DO WITH 'EM. AND I DON'T WANT TO KNOW. POINT IS, I KNOW WHERE YOU CAN FIND A LOT OF 'EM.
WE'VE BEEN THERE... AND WE GOT SOME UNFINISHED BUSINESS. SO DROP THE CRAP AND GATHER YOUR MEN.
DON'T PRESUME YOU KNOW ANYTHING ABOUT US, MR. JEPPERD.
GATHER THE TRIBES.
YES, SIR... WHICH ONES?
ALL OF THEM.

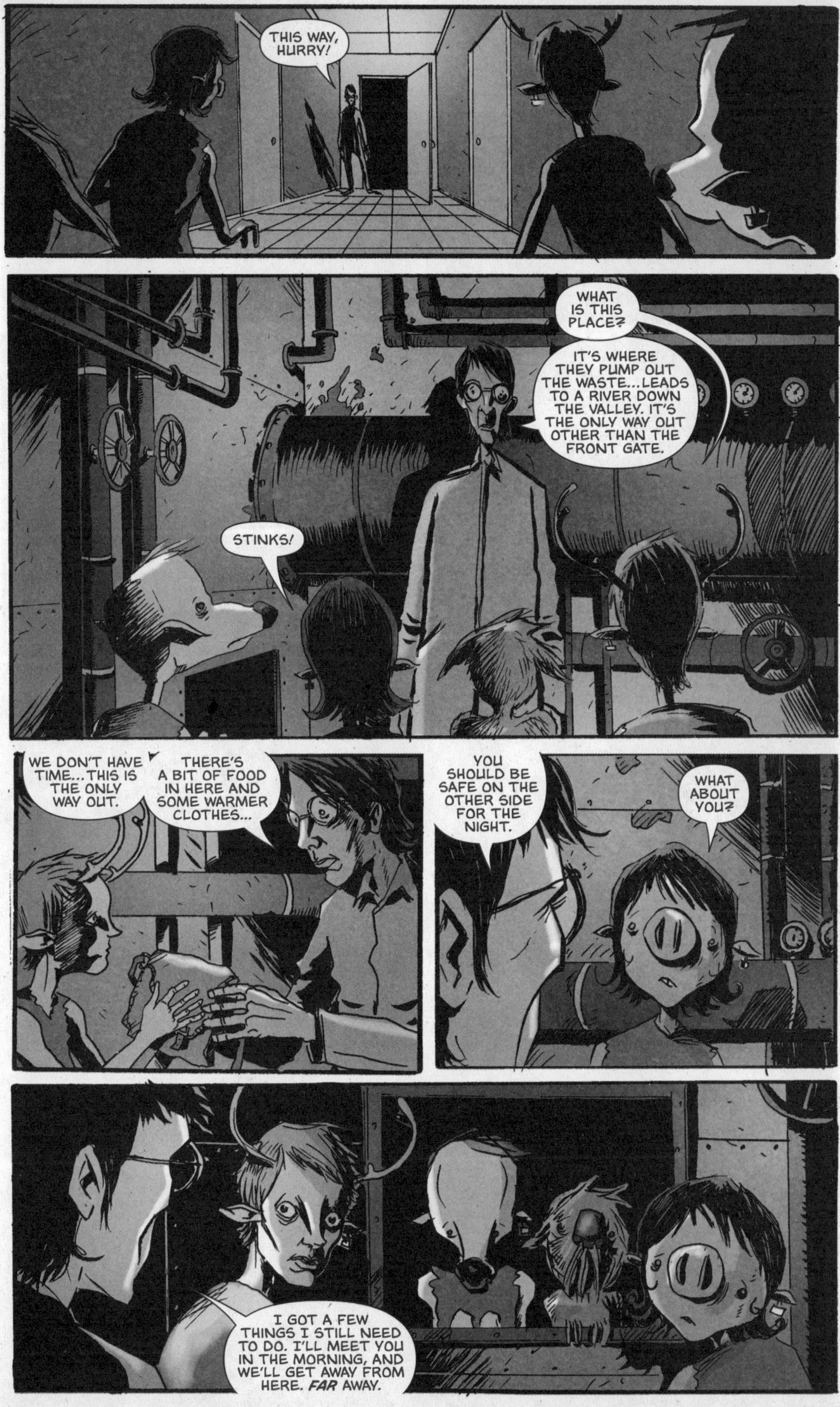
THIS WAY, HURRY!
WHAT IS THIS PLACE?
IT'S WHERE THEY PUMP OUT THE WASTE...LEADS TO A RIVER DOWN THE VALLEY. IT'S THE ONLY WAY OUT OTHER THAN THE FRONT GATE.
STINKS!
WE DON'T HAVE TIME...THIS IS THE ONLY WAY OUT.
THERE'S A BIT OF FOOD IN HERE AND SOME WARMER CLOTHES...
YOU SHOULD BE SAFE ON THE OTHER SIDE FOR THE NIGHT.
WHAT ABOUT YOU?
I GOT A FEW THINGS I STILL NEED TO DO. I'LL MEET YOU IN THE MORNING, AND WE'LL GET AWAY FROM HERE. FAR AWAY.

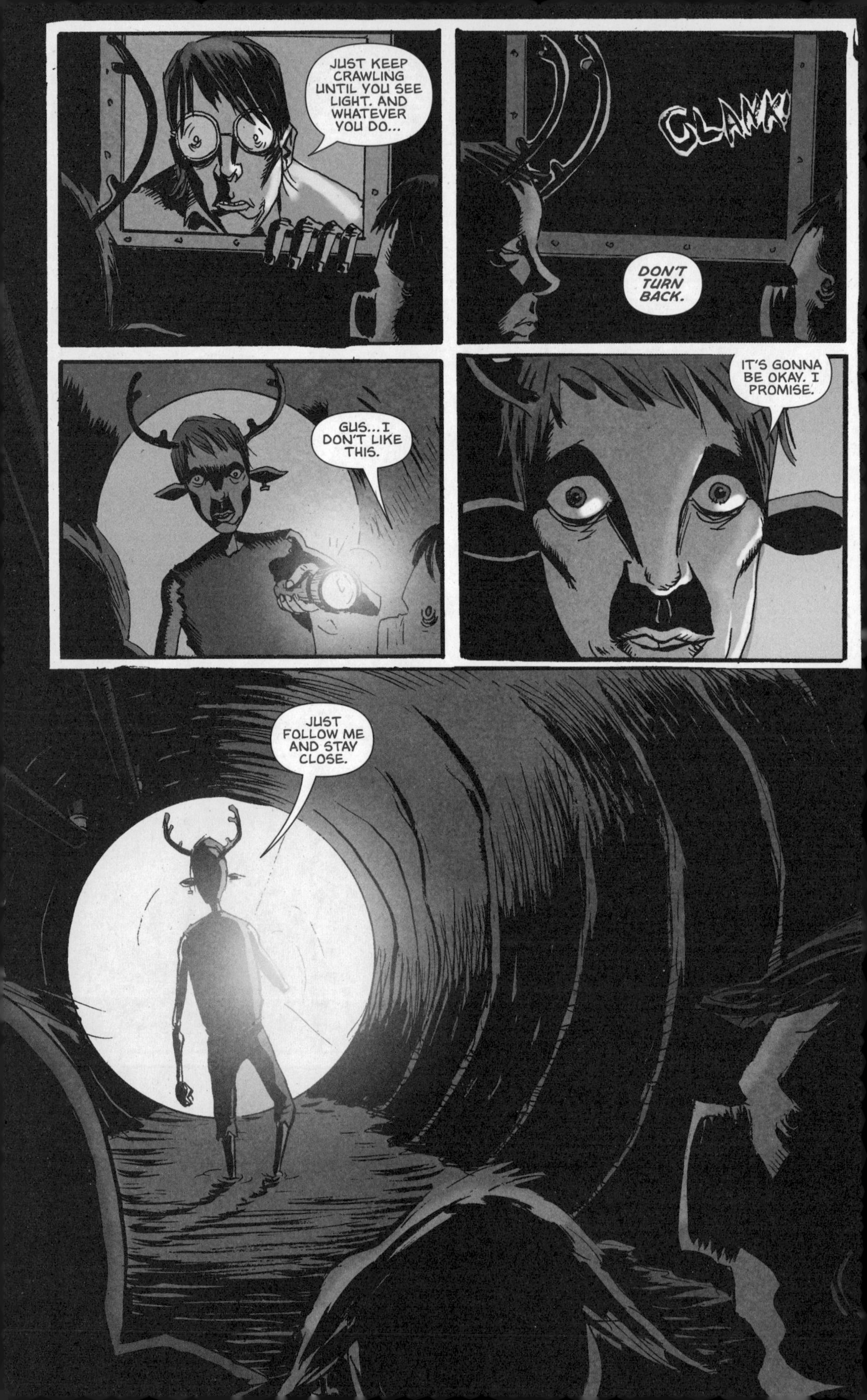
JUST KEEP CRAWLING UNTIL YOU SEE LIGHT. AND WHATEVER YOU DO...
CLANK!
DON'T TURN BACK.
GUS...I DON'T LIKE THIS.
IT'S GONNA BE OKAY. I PROMISE.
JUST FOLLOW ME AND STAY CLOSE.

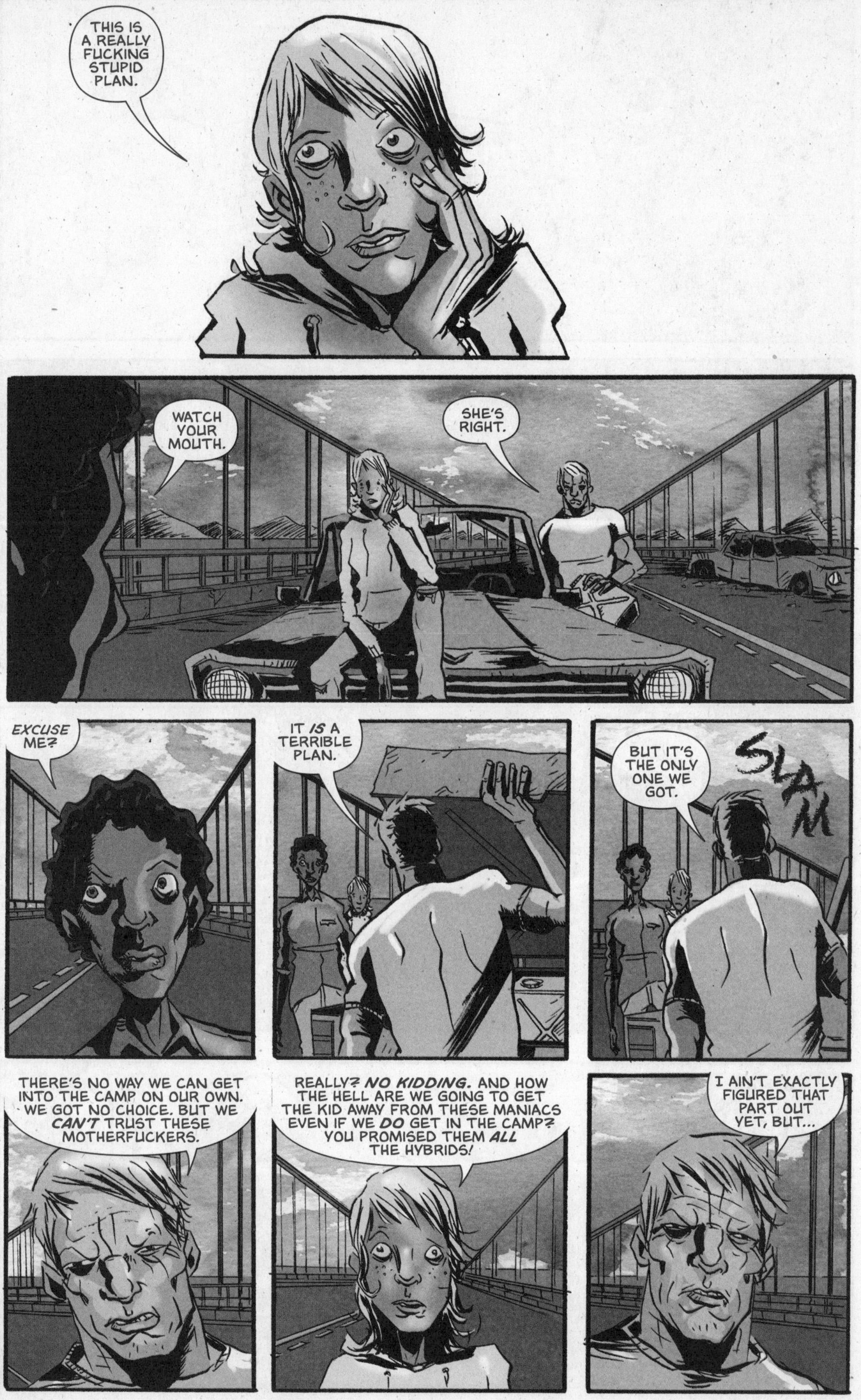
THIS IS A REALLY FUCKING STUPID PLAN.
WATCH YOUR MOUTH.
SHE'S RIGHT.
EXCUSE ME?
IT IS A TERRIBLE PLAN.
BUT IT'S THE ONLY ONE WE GOT.
SLAM
THERE'S NO WAY WE CAN GET INTO THE CAMP ON OUR OWN. WE GOT NO CHOICE. BUT WE CAN'T TRUST THESE MOTHERFUCKERS.
REALLY? NO KIDDING. AND HOW THE HELL ARE WE GOING TO GET THE KID AWAY FROM THESE MANIACS EVEN IF WE DO GET IN THE CAMP? YOU PROMISED THEM ALL THE HYBRIDS!
I AIN'T EXACTLY FIGURED THAT PART OUT YET, BUT...

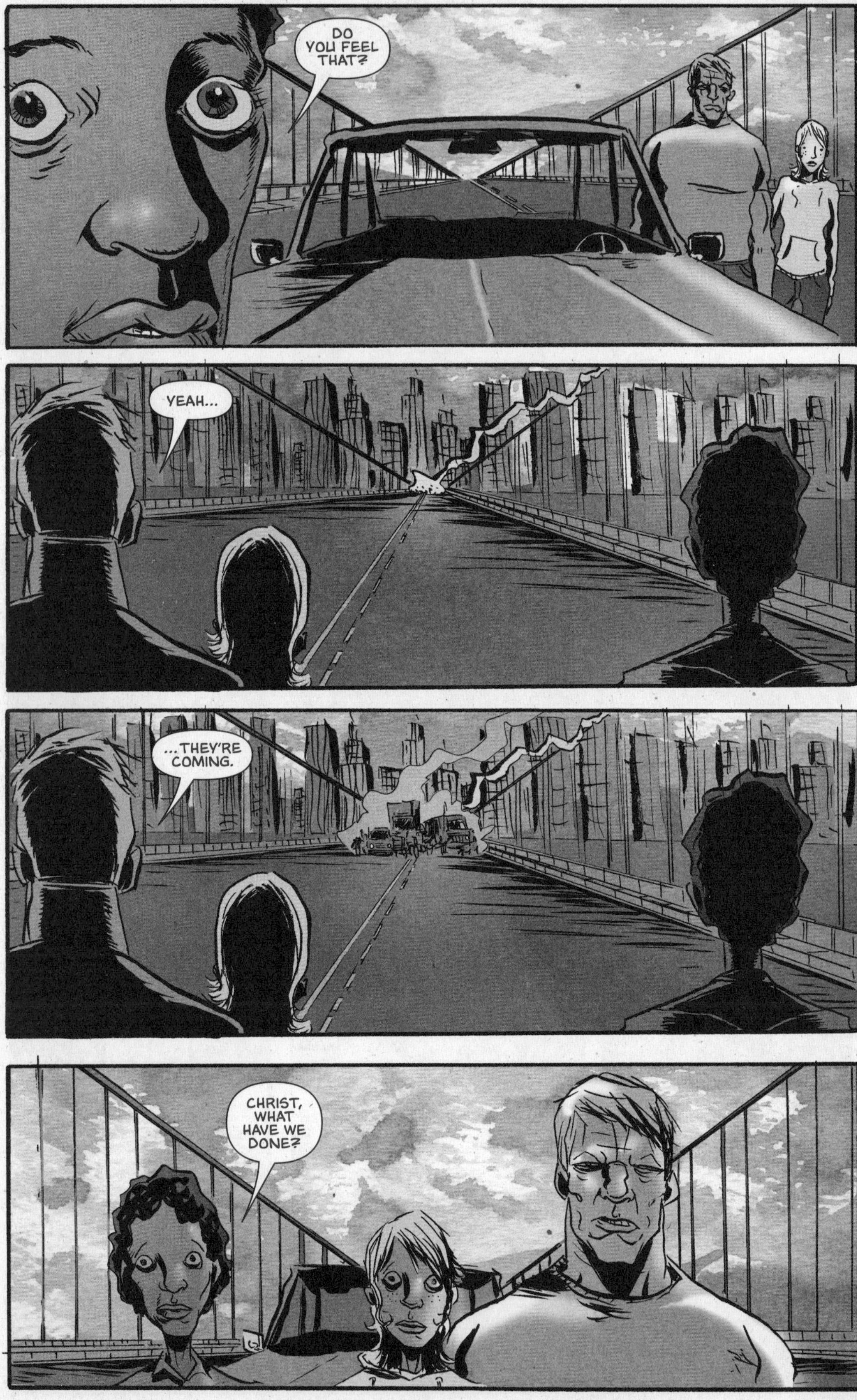
DO YOU FEEL THAT?
YEAH...
...THEY'RE COMING.
CHRIST, WHAT HAVE WE DONE?

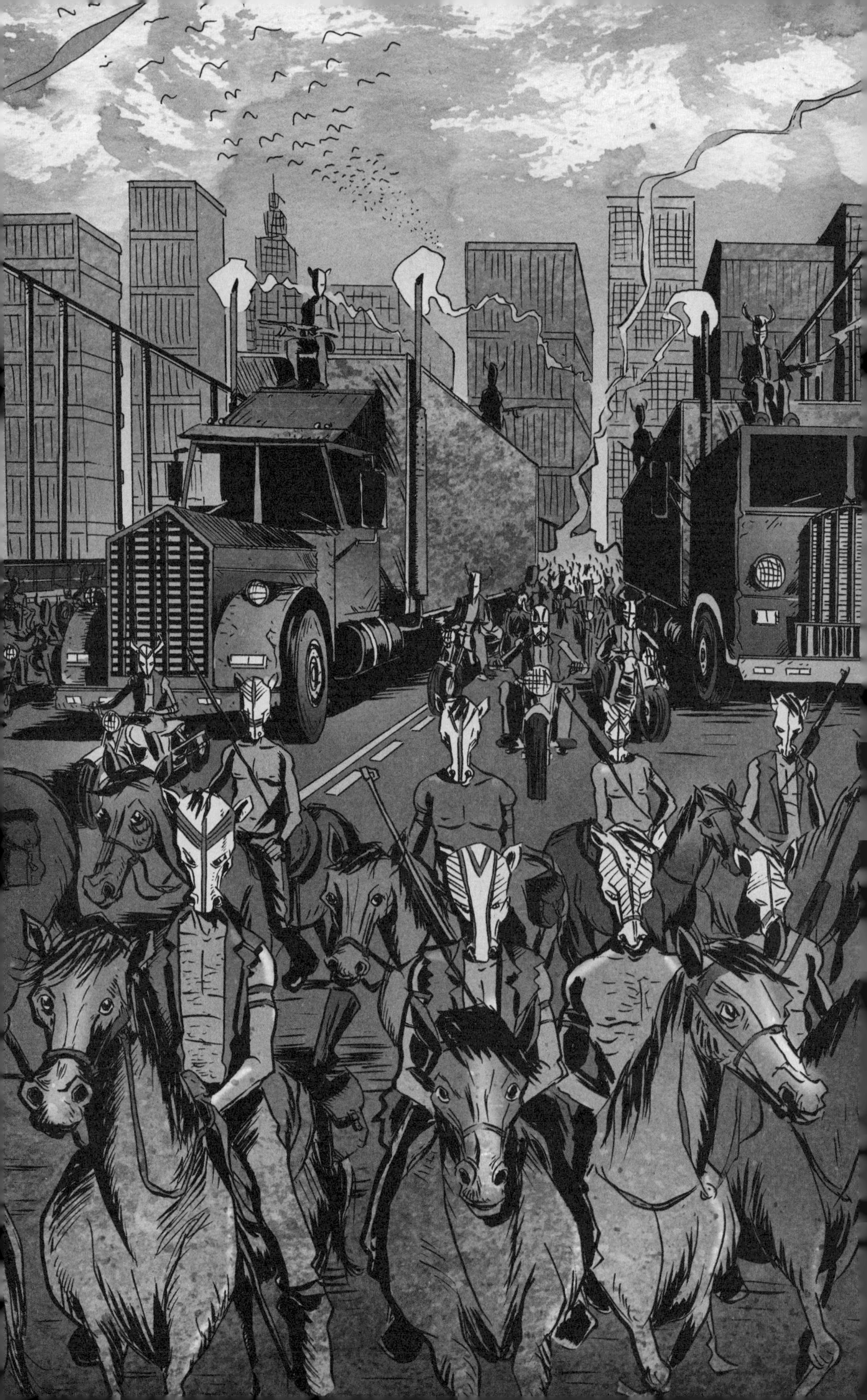

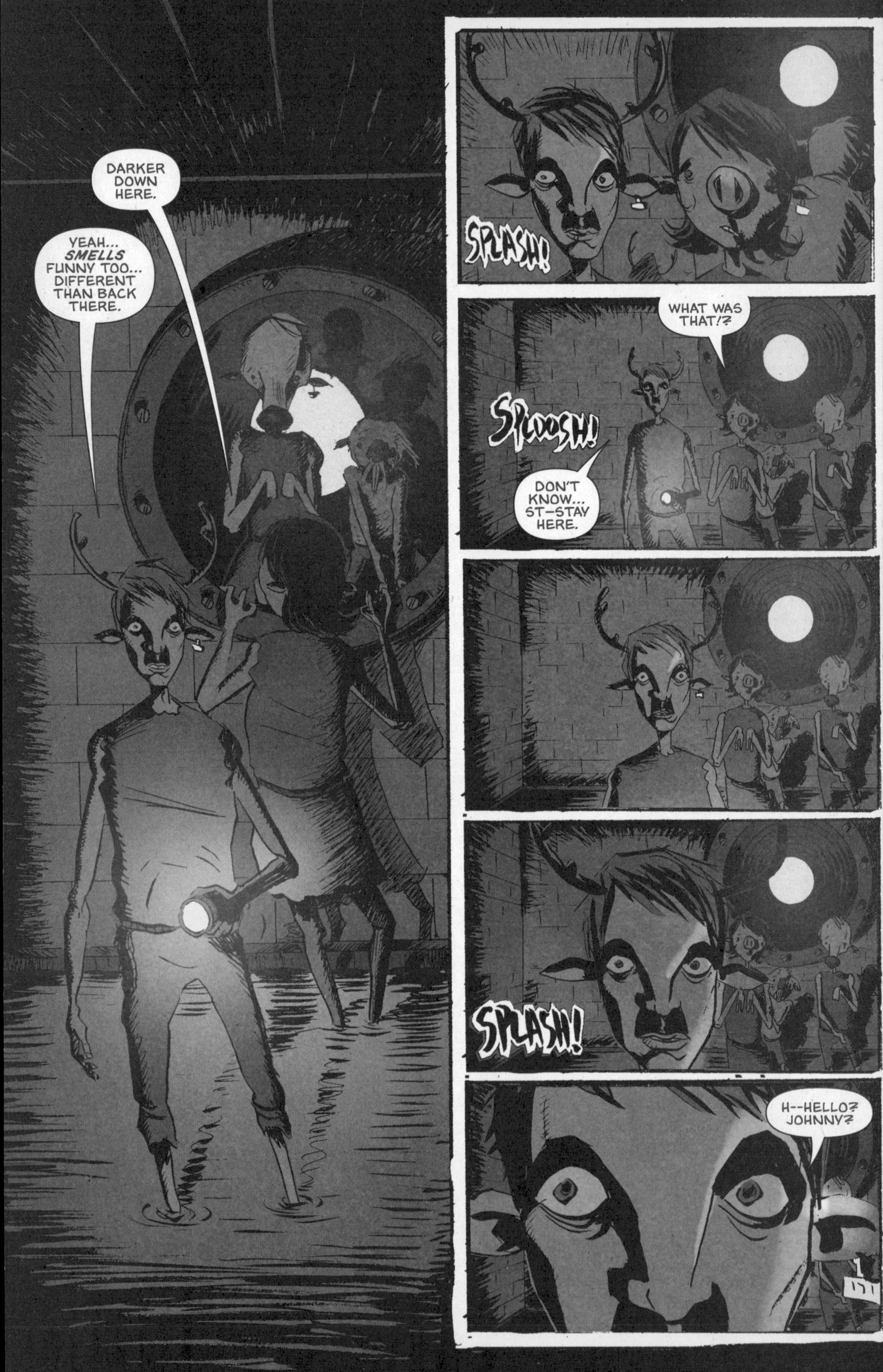
DARKER DOWN HERE.
YEAH... SMELLS FUNNY TOO... DIFFERENT THAN BACK THERE.
SPLASH!
WHAT WAS THAT!?
SPLOOSH!
DON'T KNOW... ST-STAY HERE.
SPLASH!
H--HELLO? JOHNNY?

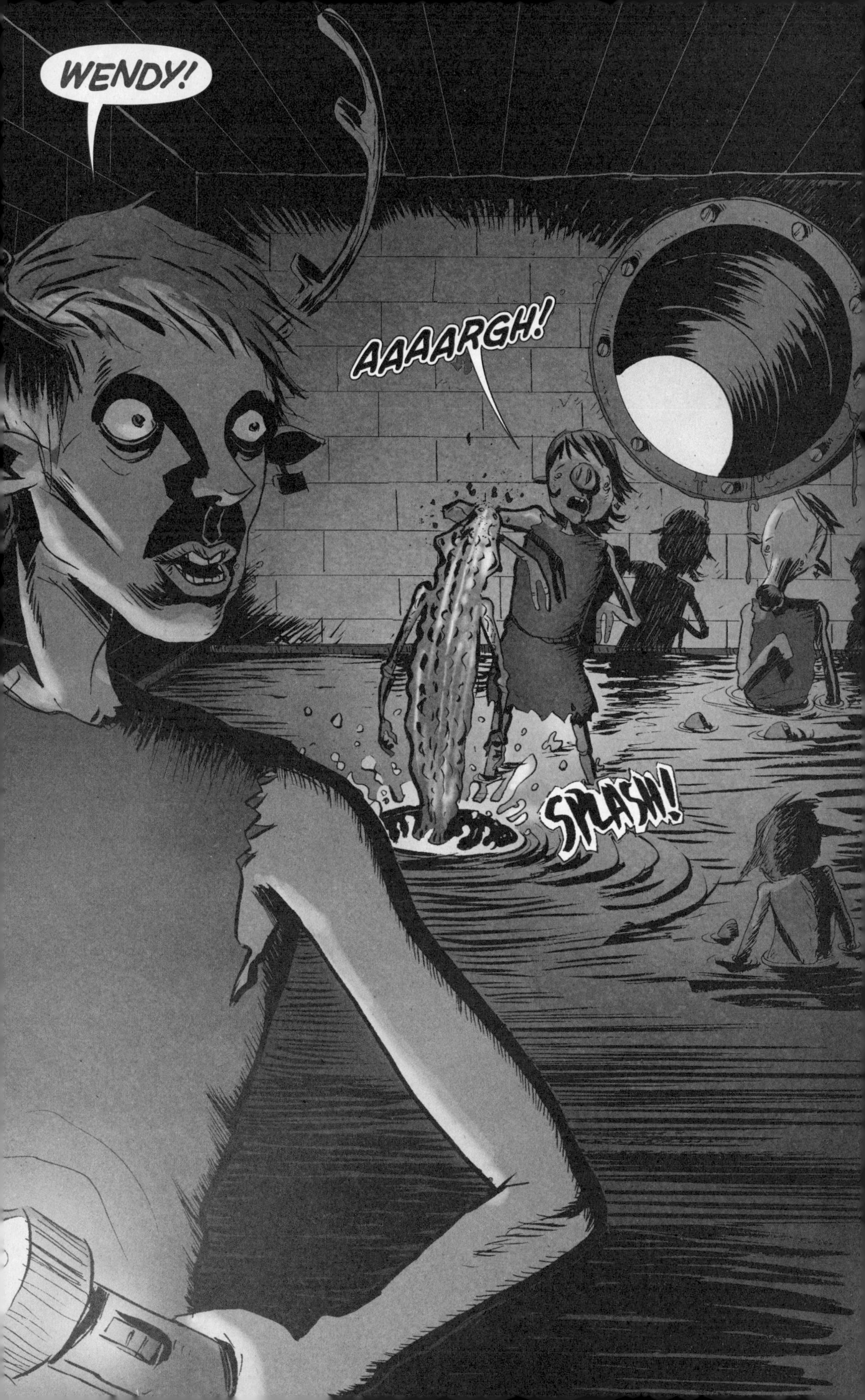
WENDY!
AAAARGH!
SPLASH!

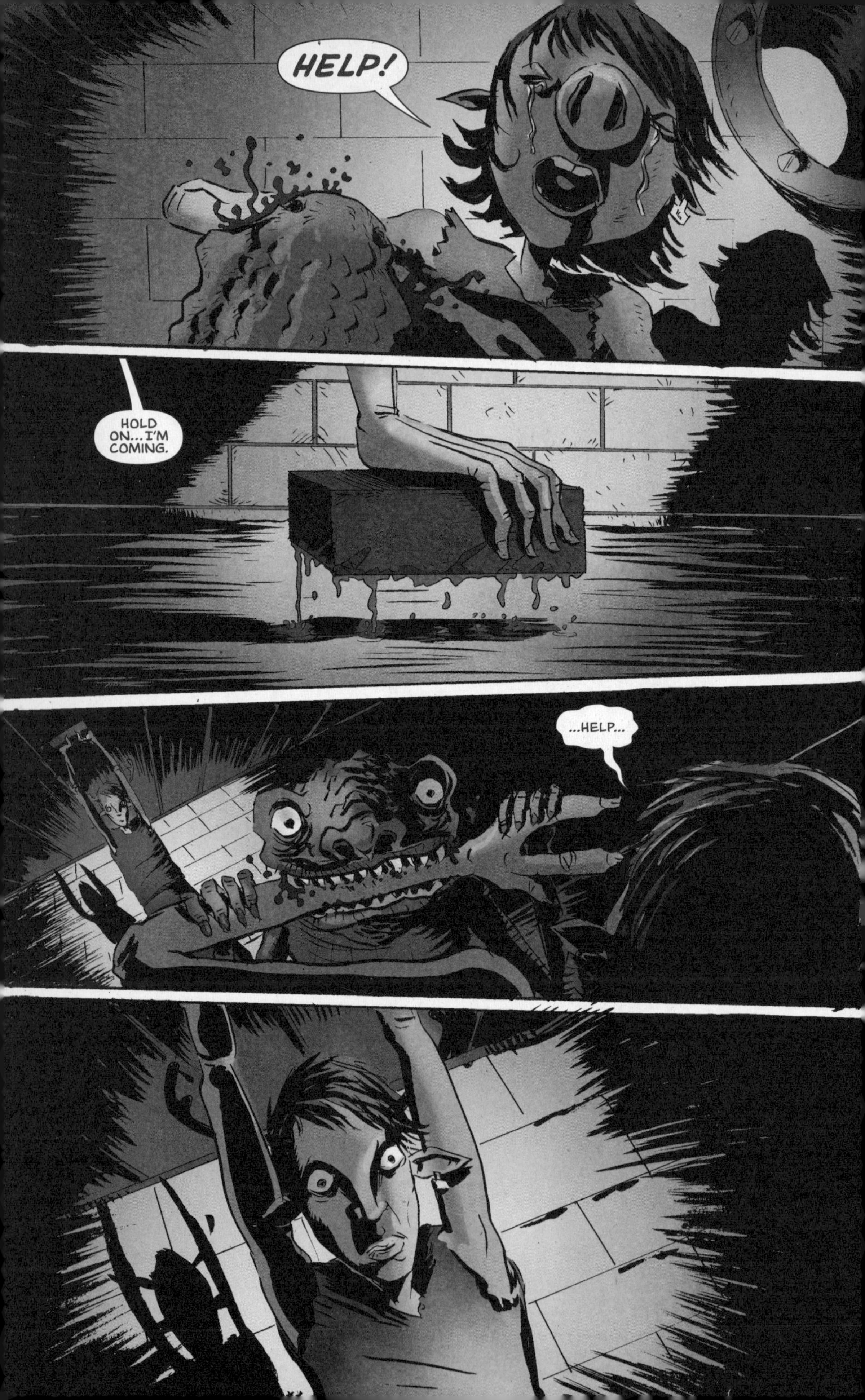
HELP!
HOLD ON... I'M COMING.
...HELP...

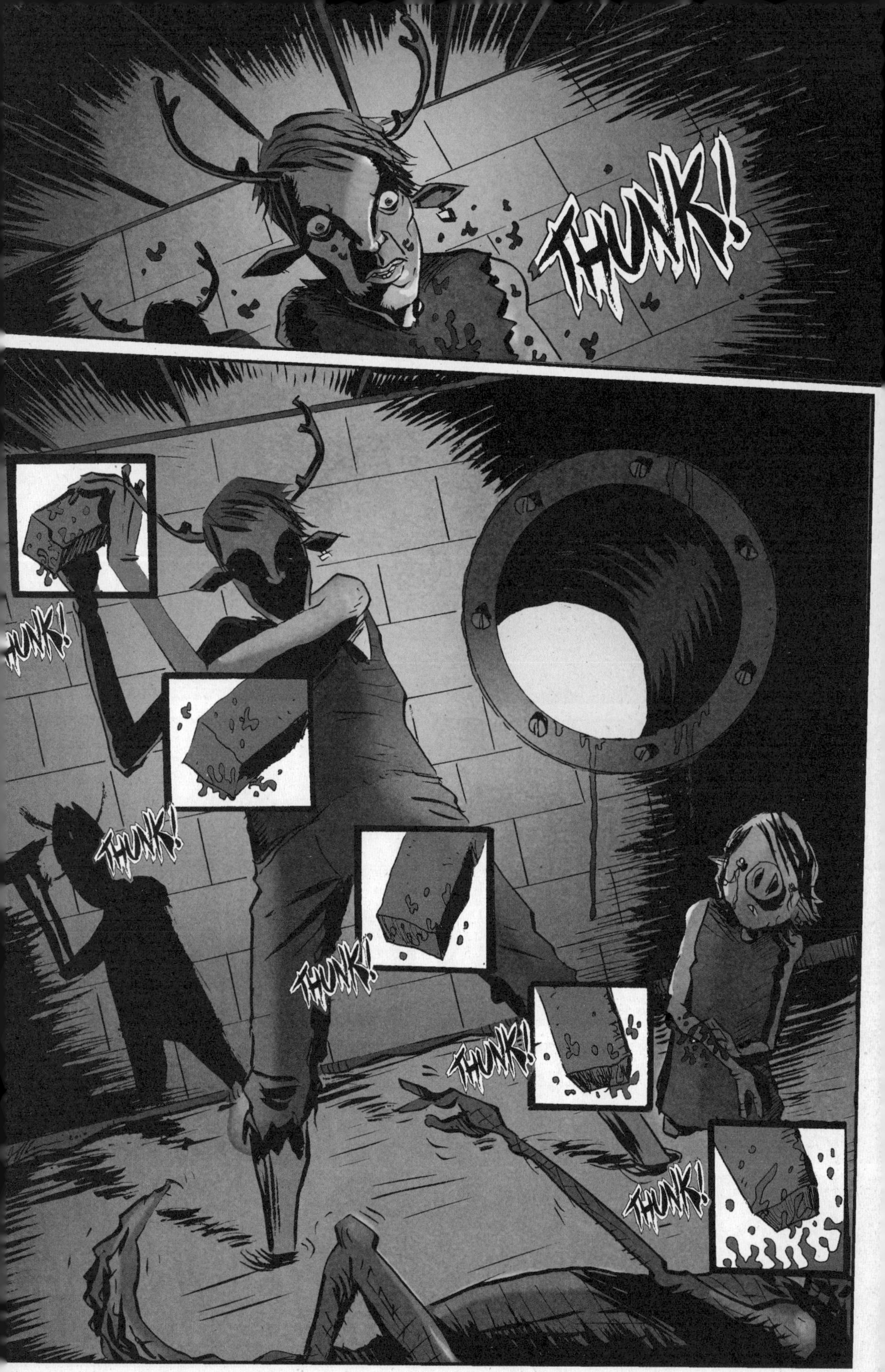
THUNK!
HUNK!
THUNK!
THUNK!
THUNK!
THUNK!

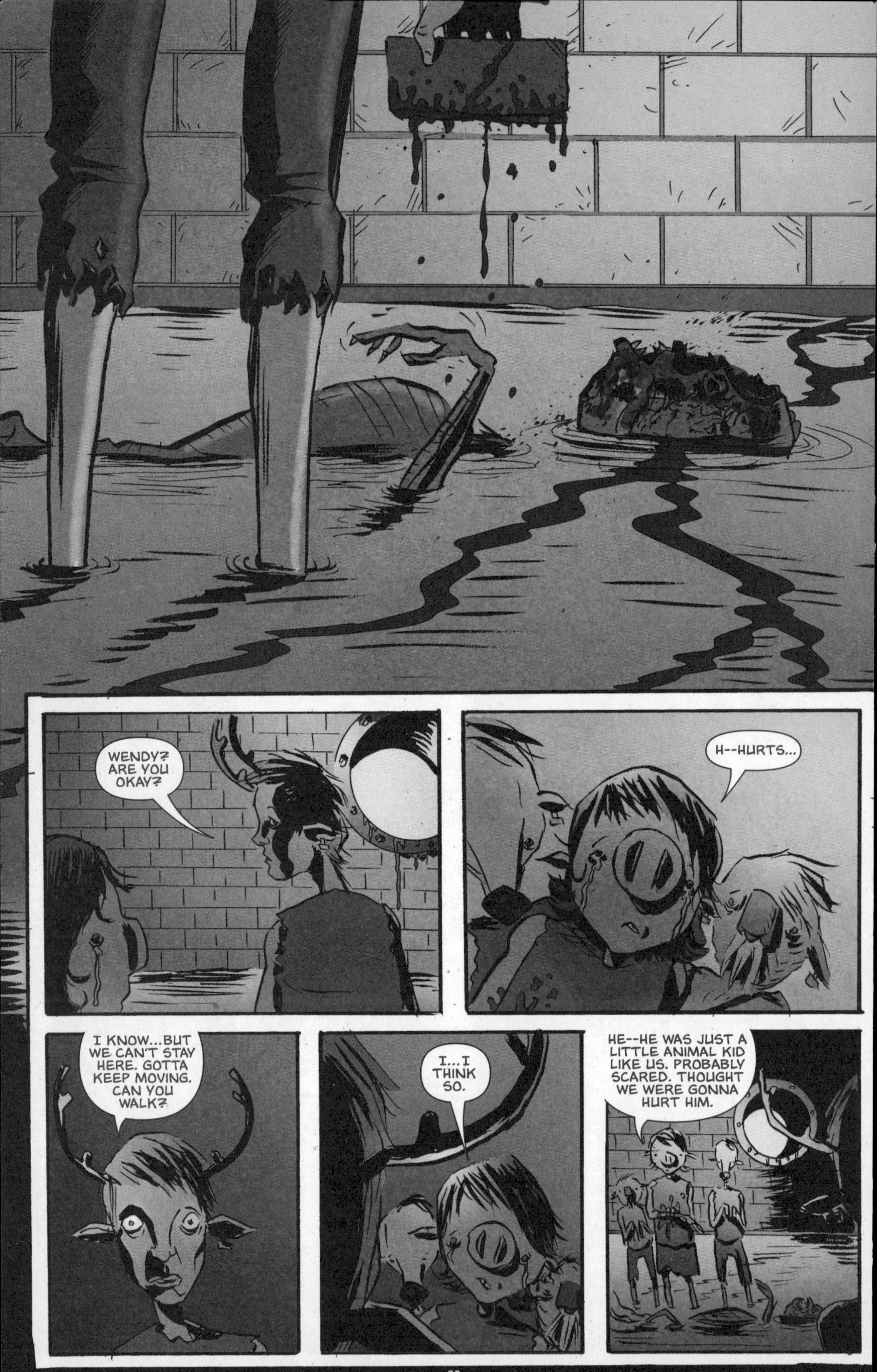
WENDY? ARE YOU OKAY?
H--HURTS...
I KNOW...BUT WE CAN'T STAY HERE. GOTTA KEEP MOVING. CAN YOU WALK?
I...I THINK SO.
HE--HE WAS JUST A LITTLE ANIMAL KID LIKE US. PROBABLY SCARED. THOUGHT WE WERE GONNA HURT HIM.

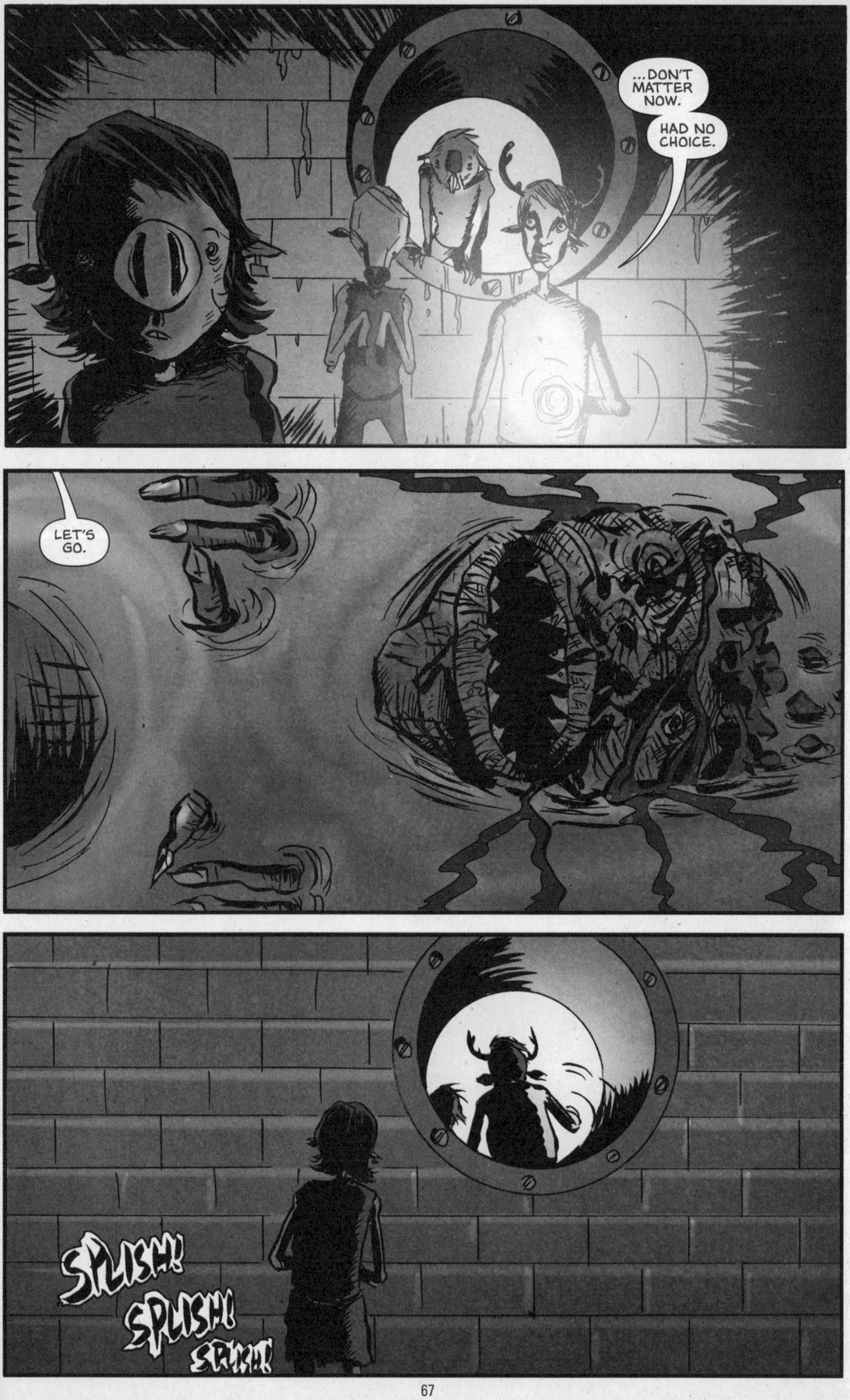
...DON'T MATTER NOW.
HAD NO CHOICE.
LET'S GO.
SPLISH!
SPLISH!
SPLISH!

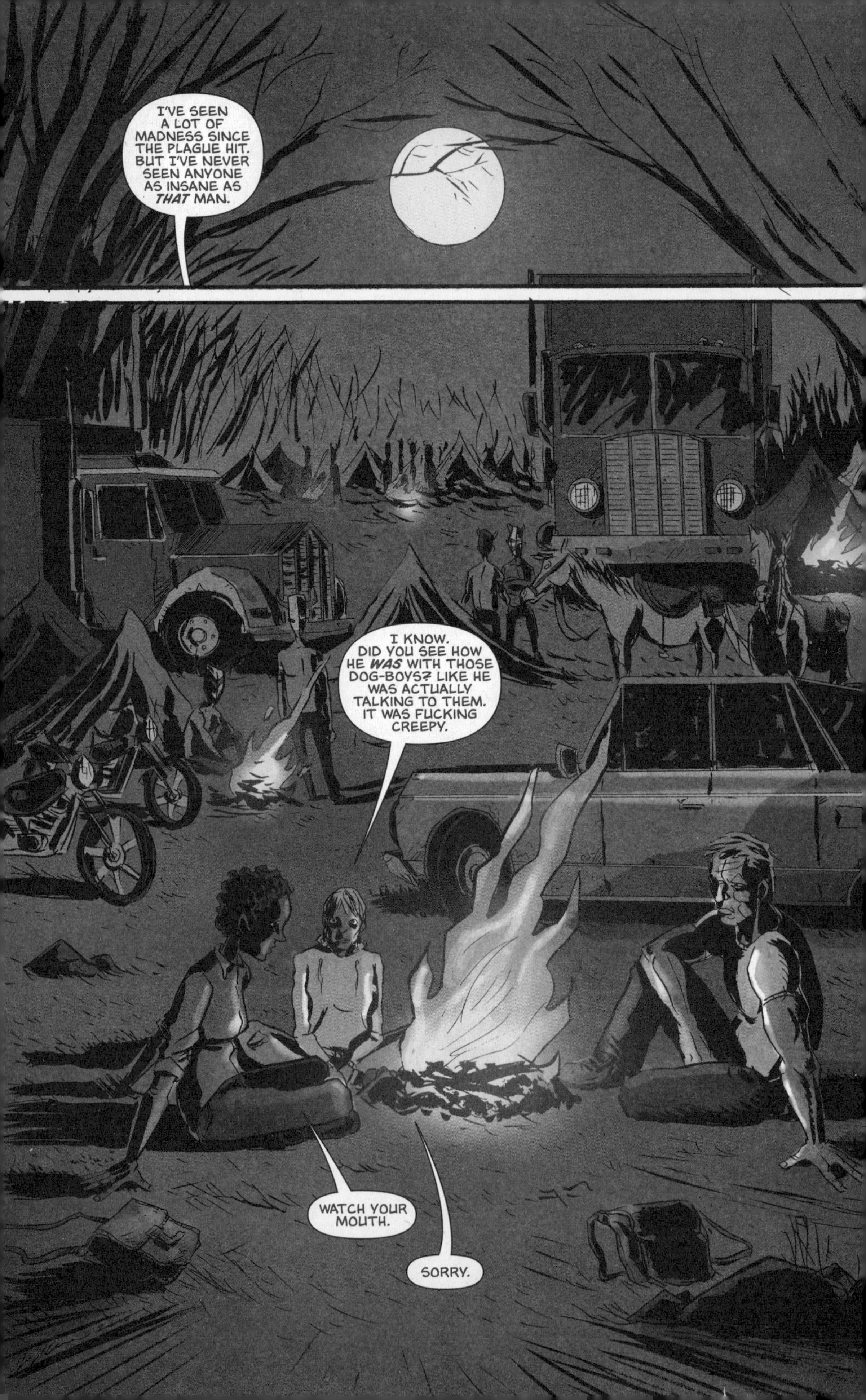
I'VE SEEN A LOT OF MADNESS SINCE THE PLAGUE HIT. BUT I'VE NEVER SEEN ANYONE AS INSANE AS *THAT* MAN.
I KNOW. DID YOU SEE HOW HE *WAS* WITH THOSE DOG-BOYS? LIKE HE WAS ACTUALLY TALKING TO THEM. IT WAS FUCKING CREEPY.
WATCH YOUR MOUTH.
SORRY.

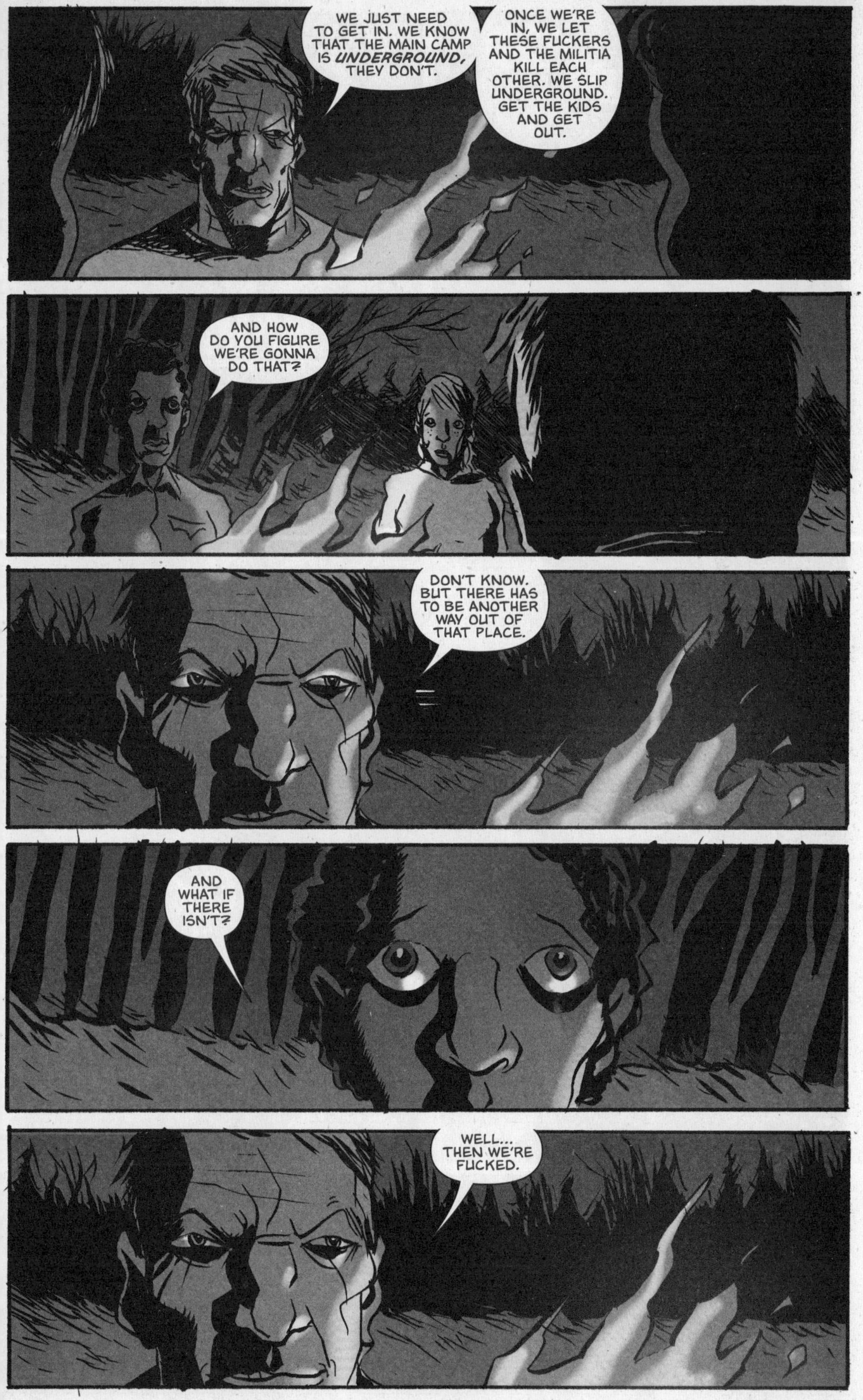
WE JUST NEED TO GET IN. WE KNOW THAT THE MAIN CAMP IS *UNDERGROUND,* THEY DON'T.
ONCE WE'RE IN, WE LET THESE FUCKERS AND THE MILITIA KILL EACH OTHER. WE SLIP UNDERGROUND. GET THE KIDS AND GET OUT.
AND HOW DO YOU FIGURE WE'RE GONNA DO THAT?
DON'T KNOW. BUT THERE HAS TO BE ANOTHER WAY OUT OF THAT PLACE.
AND WHAT IF THERE ISN'T?
WELL... THEN WE'RE FUCKED.

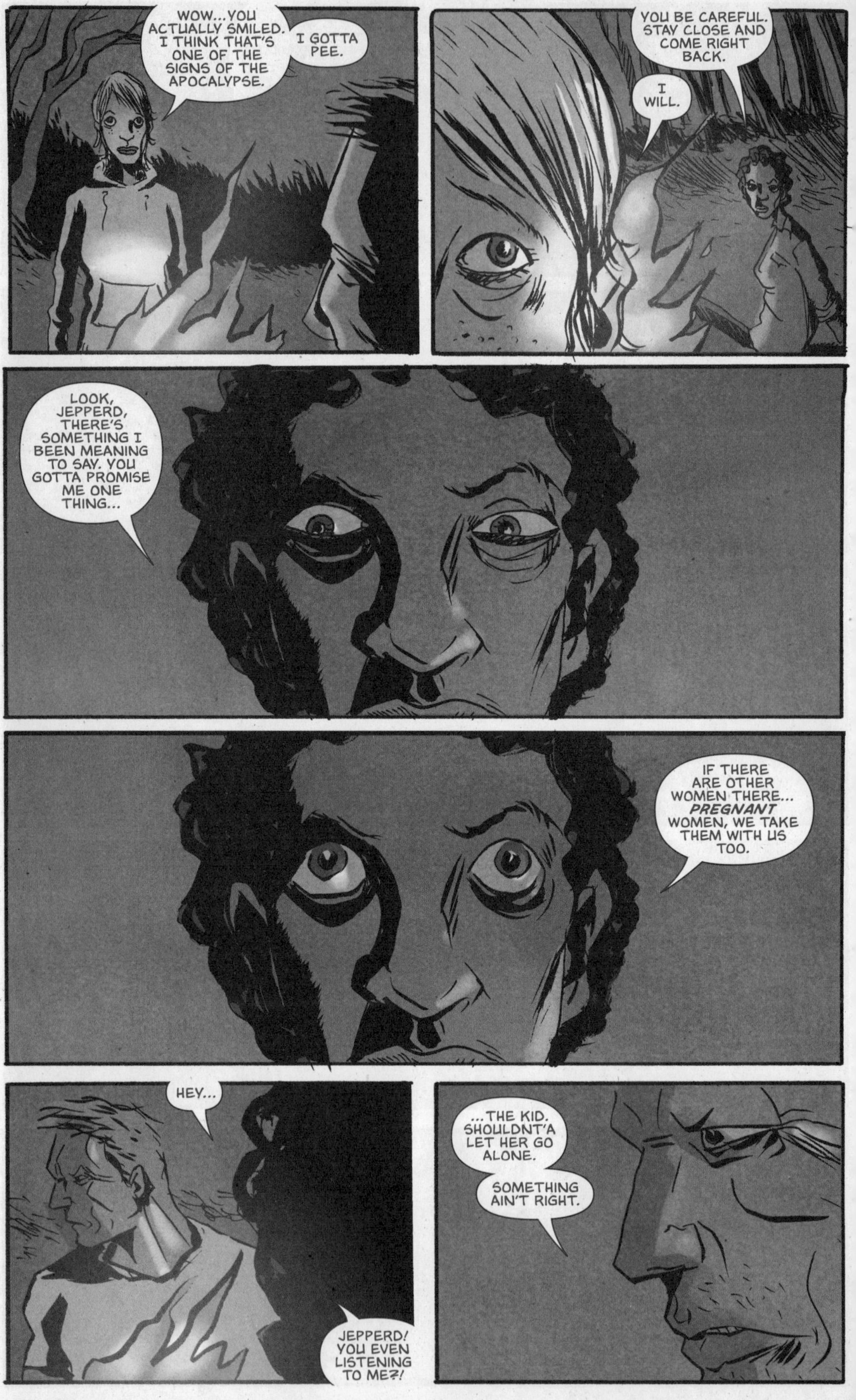
WOW...YOU ACTUALLY SMILED. I THINK THAT'S ONE OF THE SIGNS OF THE APOCALYPSE.
I GOTTA PEE.
YOU BE CAREFUL. STAY CLOSE AND COME RIGHT BACK.
I WILL.
LOOK, JEPPERD, THERE'S SOMETHING I BEEN MEANING TO SAY. YOU GOTTA PROMISE ME ONE THING...
IF THERE ARE OTHER WOMEN THERE... *PREGNANT* WOMEN, WE TAKE THEM WITH US TOO.
HEY...
JEPPERD! YOU EVEN LISTENING TO ME?!
...THE KID. SHOULDNT'A LET HER GO ALONE.
SOMETHING AIN'T RIGHT.

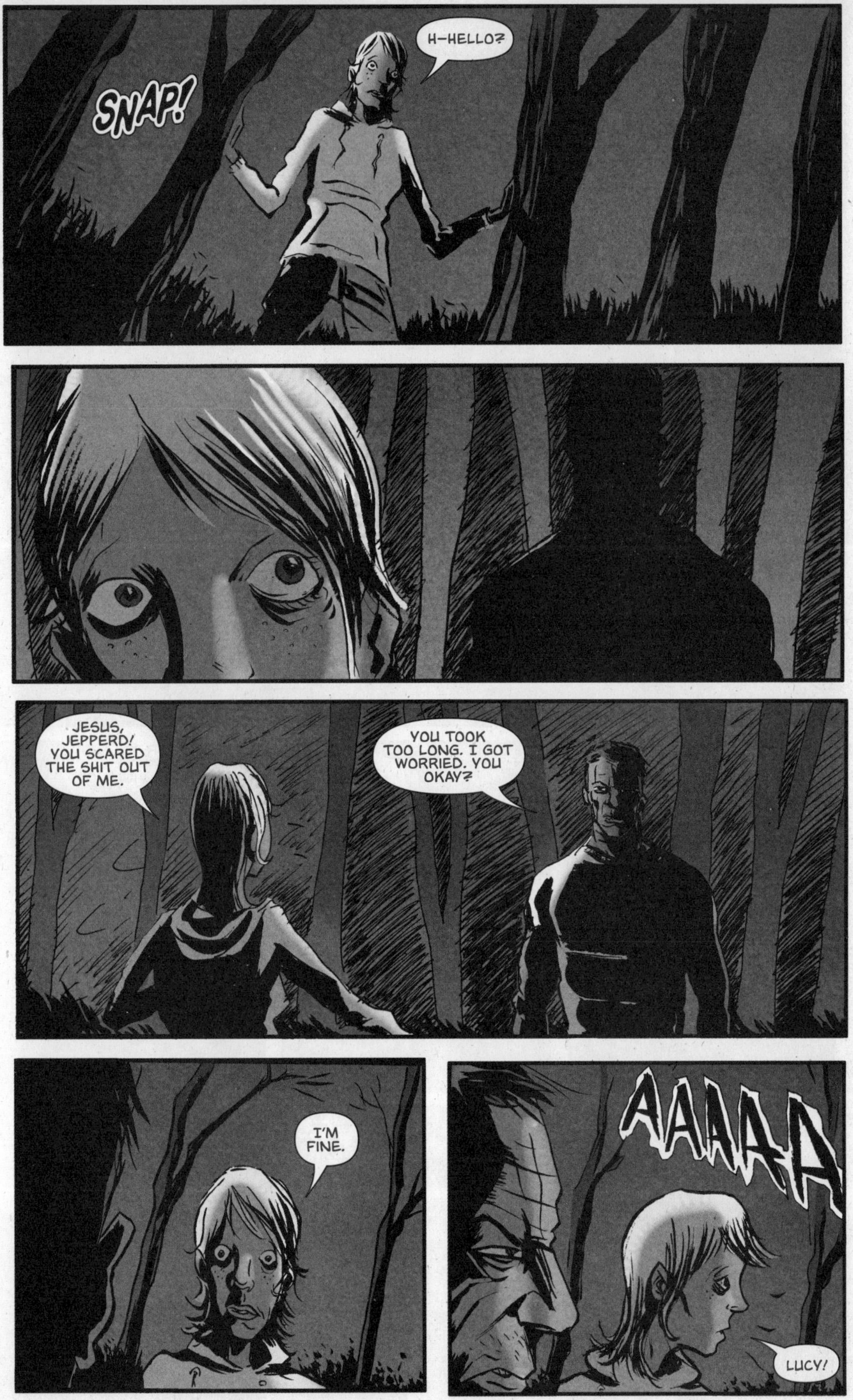
SNAP!
H-HELLO?
JESUS, JEPPERD! YOU SCARED THE SHIT OUT OF ME.
YOU TOOK TOO LONG. I GOT WORRIED. YOU OKAY?
I'M FINE.
AAAAA
LUCY!

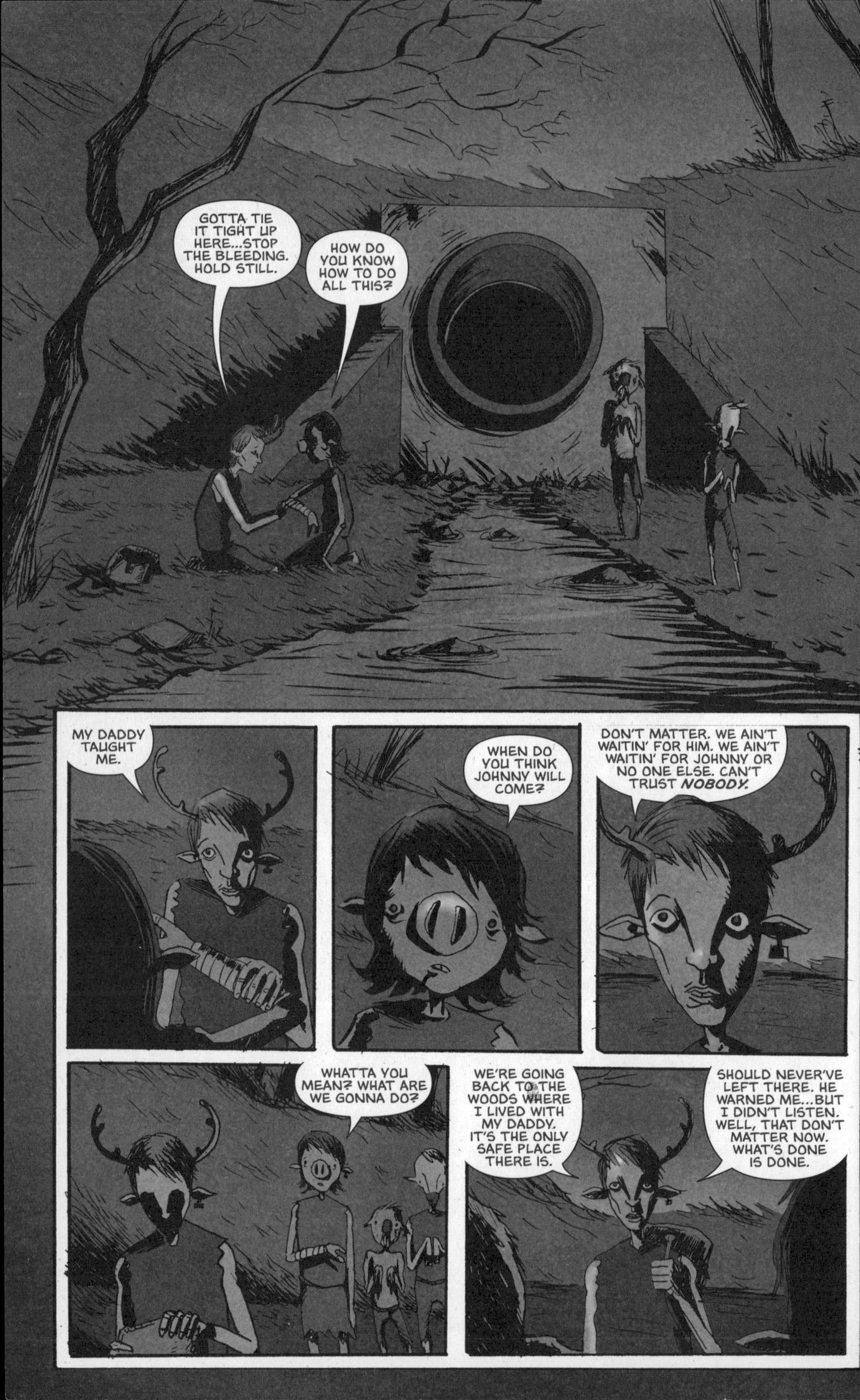
GOTTA TIE IT TIGHT UP HERE...STOP THE BLEEDING. HOLD STILL.
HOW DO YOU KNOW HOW TO DO ALL THIS?
MY DADDY TAUGHT ME.
WHEN DO YOU THINK JOHNNY WILL COME?
DON'T MATTER. WE AIN'T WAITIN' FOR HIM. WE AIN'T WAITIN' FOR JOHNNY OR NO ONE ELSE. CAN'T TRUST *NOBODY.*
WHATTA YOU MEAN? WHAT ARE WE GONNA DO?
WE'RE GOING BACK TO THE WOODS WHERE I LIVED WITH MY DADDY. IT'S THE ONLY SAFE PLACE THERE IS.
SHOULD NEVER'VE LEFT THERE. HE WARNED ME...BUT I DIDN'T LISTEN. WELL, THAT DON'T MATTER NOW. WHAT'S DONE IS DONE.

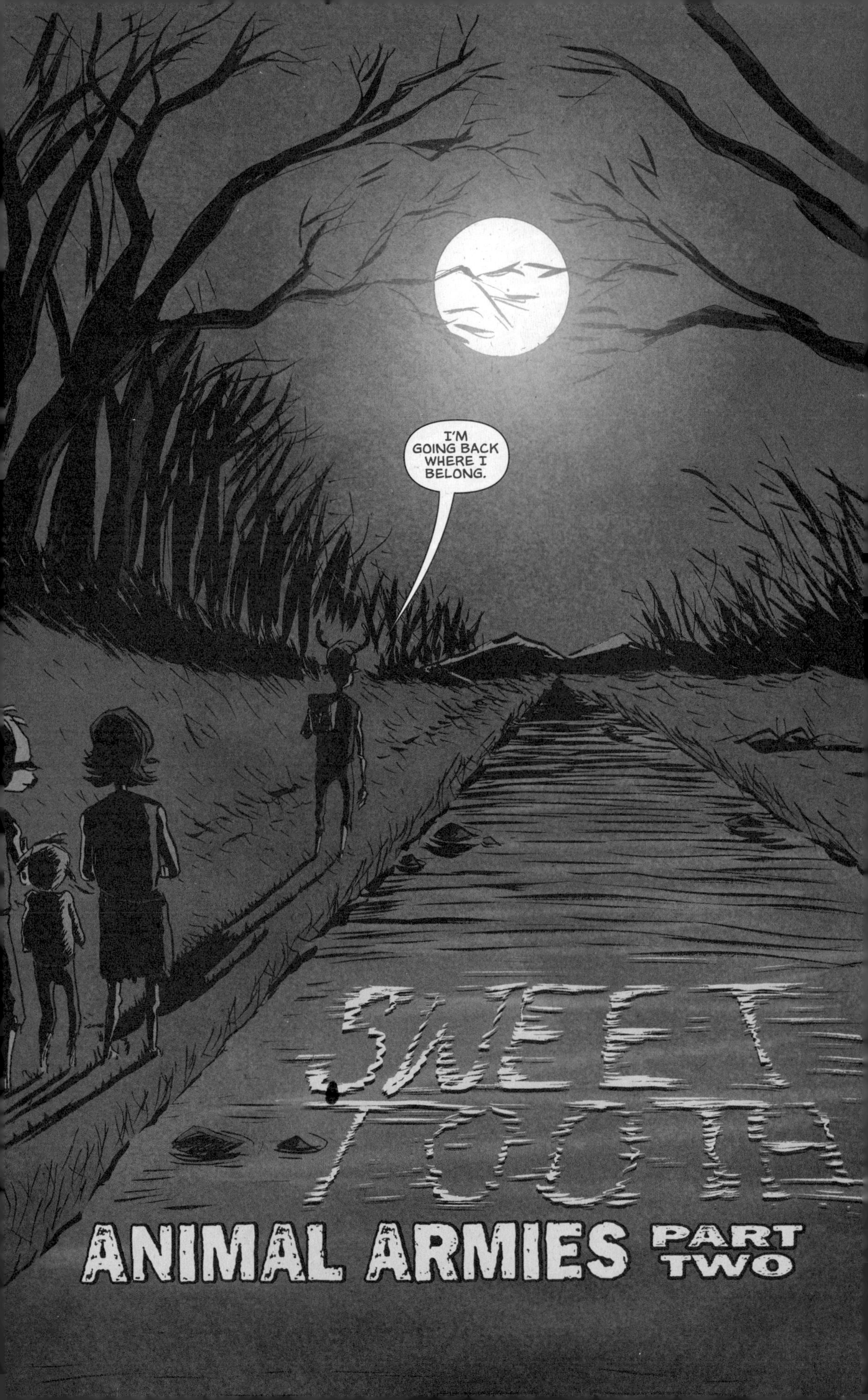
I'M GOING BACK WHERE I BELONG.
SWEET TOOTH
ANIMAL ARMIES PART TWO

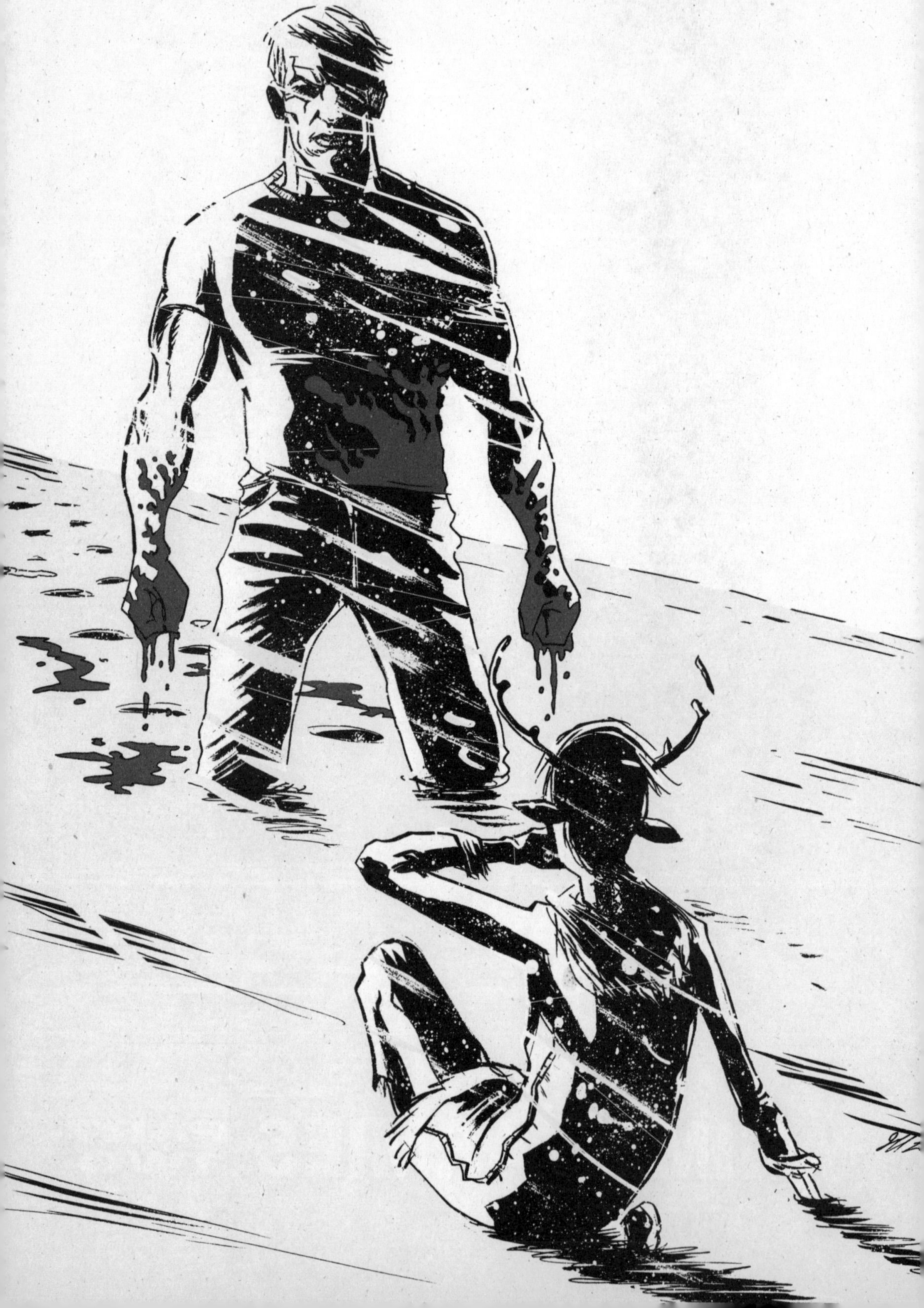

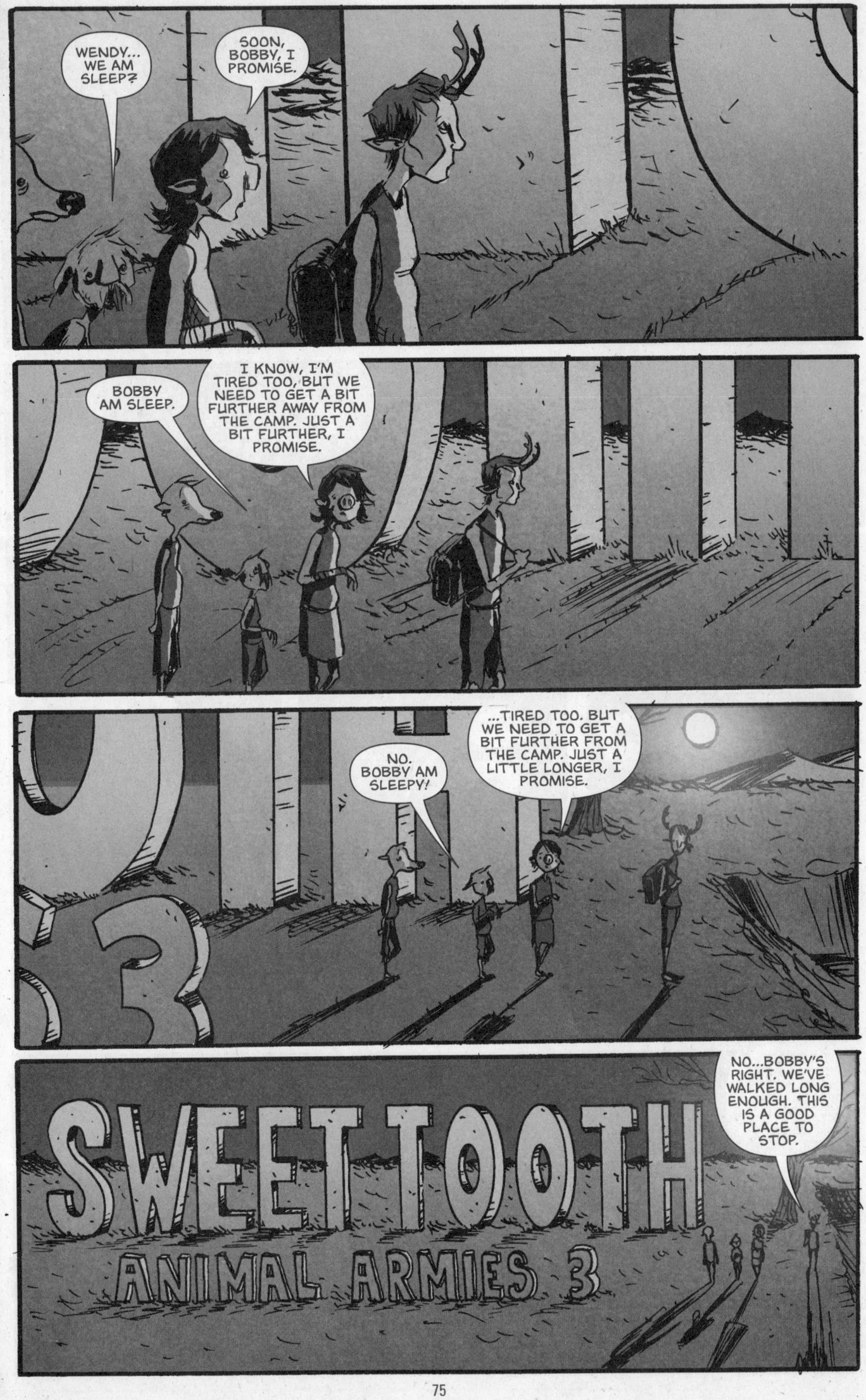
WENDY... WE AM SLEEP?
SOON, BOBBY, I PROMISE.
BOBBY AM SLEEP.
I KNOW, I'M TIRED TOO, BUT WE NEED TO GET A BIT FURTHER AWAY FROM THE CAMP. JUST A BIT FURTHER, I PROMISE.
NO. BOBBY AM SLEEPY!
...TIRED TOO. BUT WE NEED TO GET A BIT FURTHER FROM THE CAMP. JUST A LITTLE LONGER, I PROMISE.
SWEET TOOTH
ANIMAL ARMIES 3
NO...BOBBY'S RIGHT. WE'VE WALKED LONG ENOUGH. THIS IS A GOOD PLACE TO STOP.

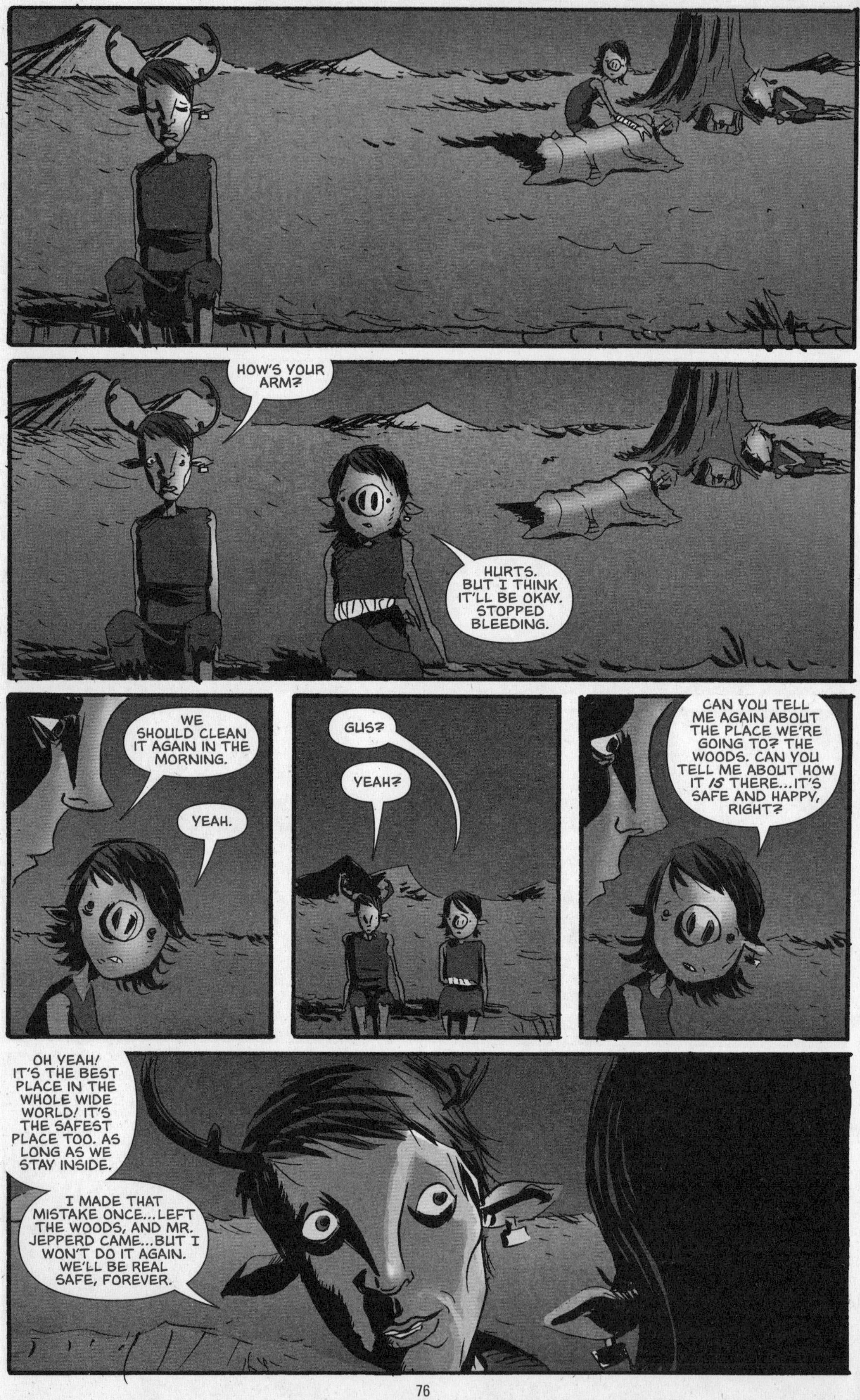
HOW'S YOUR ARM?
HURTS. BUT I THINK IT'LL BE OKAY. STOPPED BLEEDING.
WE SHOULD CLEAN IT AGAIN IN THE MORNING.
YEAH.
GUS?
YEAH?
CAN YOU TELL ME AGAIN ABOUT THE PLACE WE'RE GOING TO? THE WOODS. CAN YOU TELL ME ABOUT HOW IT *IS* THERE...IT'S SAFE AND HAPPY, RIGHT?
OH YEAH! IT'S THE BEST PLACE IN THE WHOLE WIDE WORLD! IT'S THE SAFEST PLACE TOO. AS LONG AS WE STAY INSIDE.
I MADE THAT MISTAKE ONCE...LEFT THE WOODS, AND MR. JEPPERD CAME...BUT I WON'T DO IT AGAIN. WE'LL BE REAL SAFE, FOREVER.

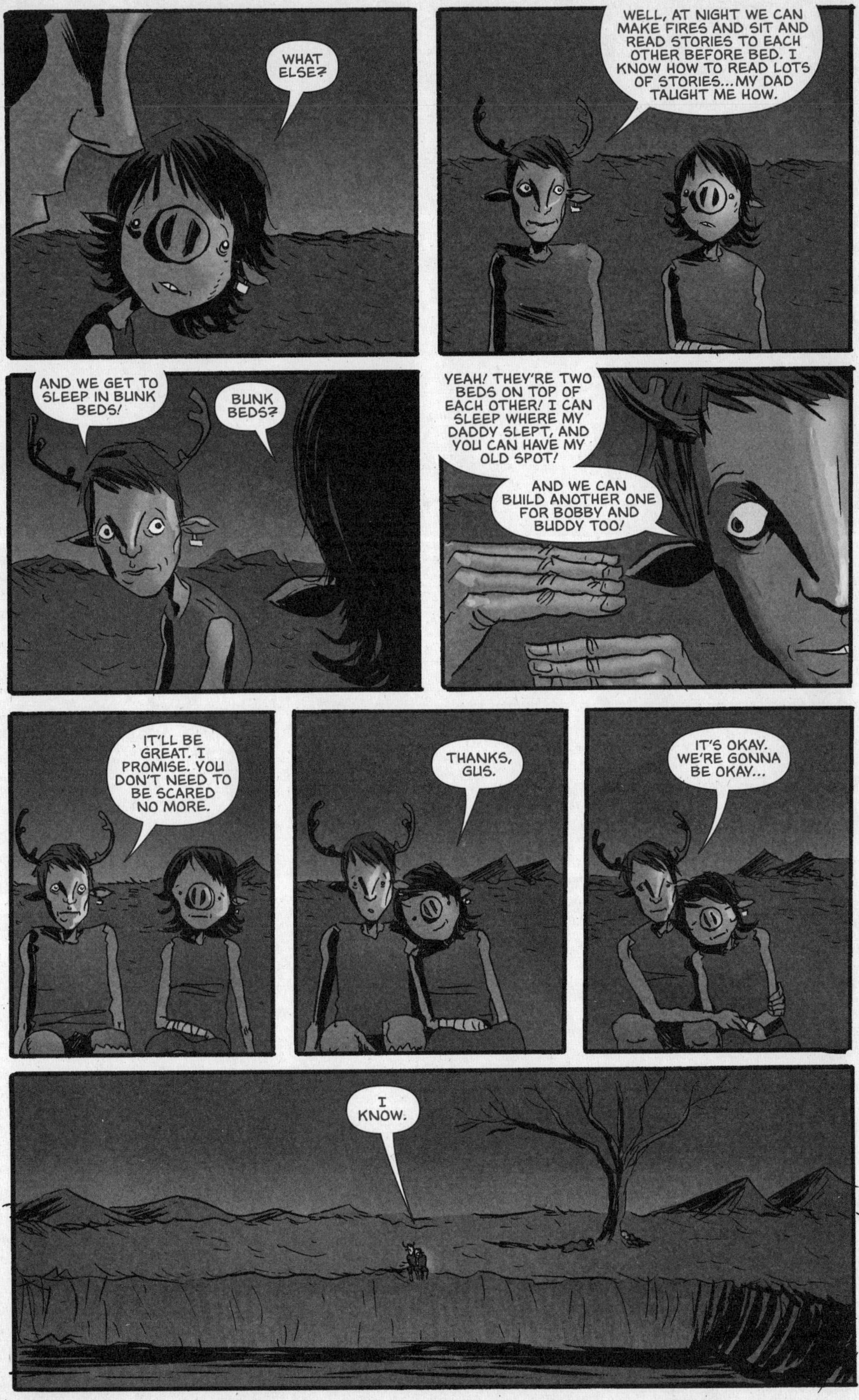
WHAT ELSE?
WELL, AT NIGHT WE CAN MAKE FIRES AND SIT AND READ STORIES TO EACH OTHER BEFORE BED. I KNOW HOW TO READ LOTS OF STORIES... MY DAD TAUGHT ME HOW.
AND WE GET TO SLEEP IN BUNK BEDS!
BUNK BEDS?
YEAH! THEY'RE TWO BEDS ON TOP OF EACH OTHER! I CAN SLEEP WHERE MY DADDY SLEPT, AND YOU CAN HAVE MY OLD SPOT!
AND WE CAN BUILD ANOTHER ONE FOR BOBBY AND BUDDY TOO!
IT'LL BE GREAT. I PROMISE. YOU DON'T NEED TO BE SCARED NO MORE.
THANKS, GUS.
IT'S OKAY. WE'RE GONNA BE OKAY...
I KNOW.

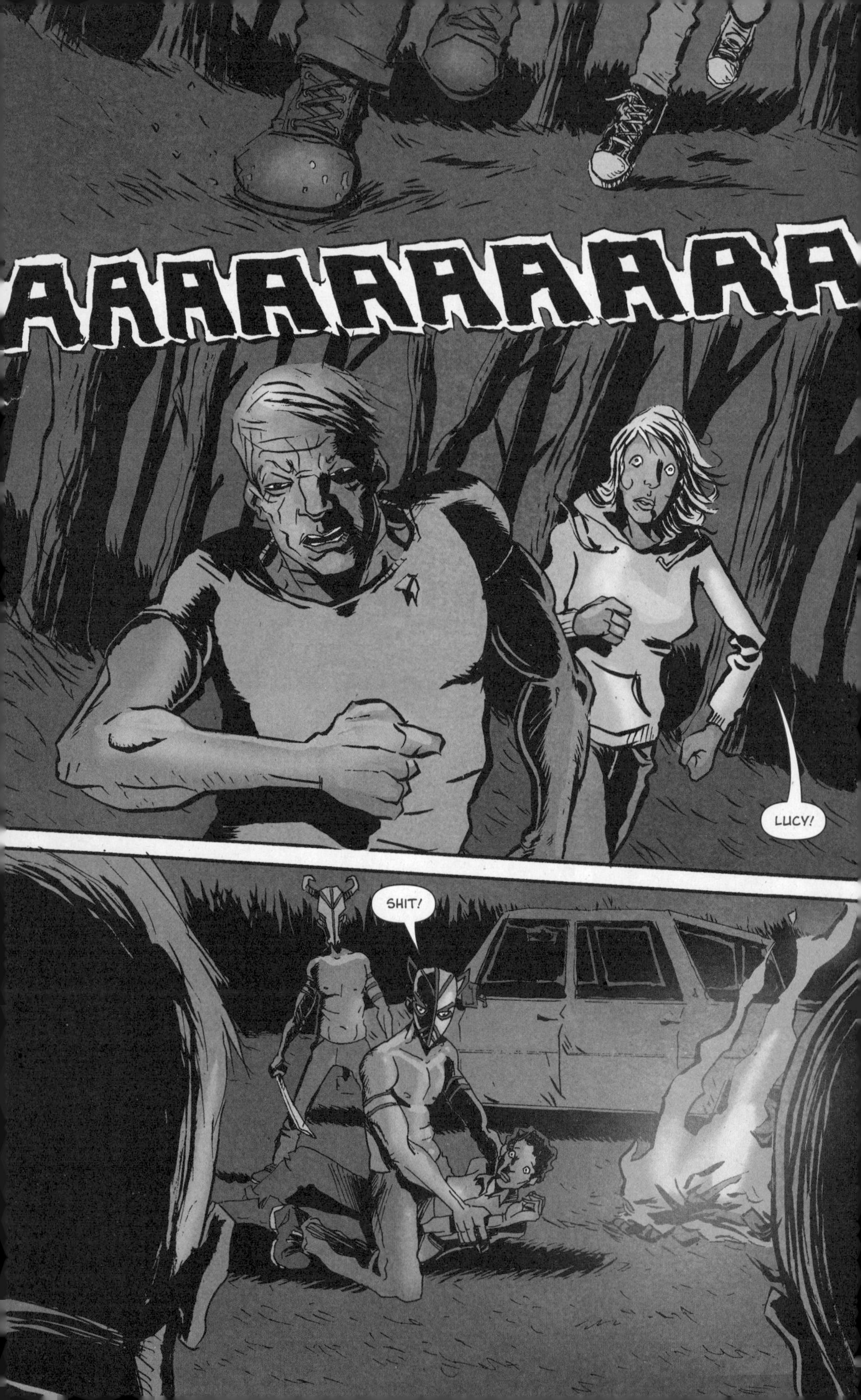
AAAAAAAAAAA
LUCY!
SHIT!

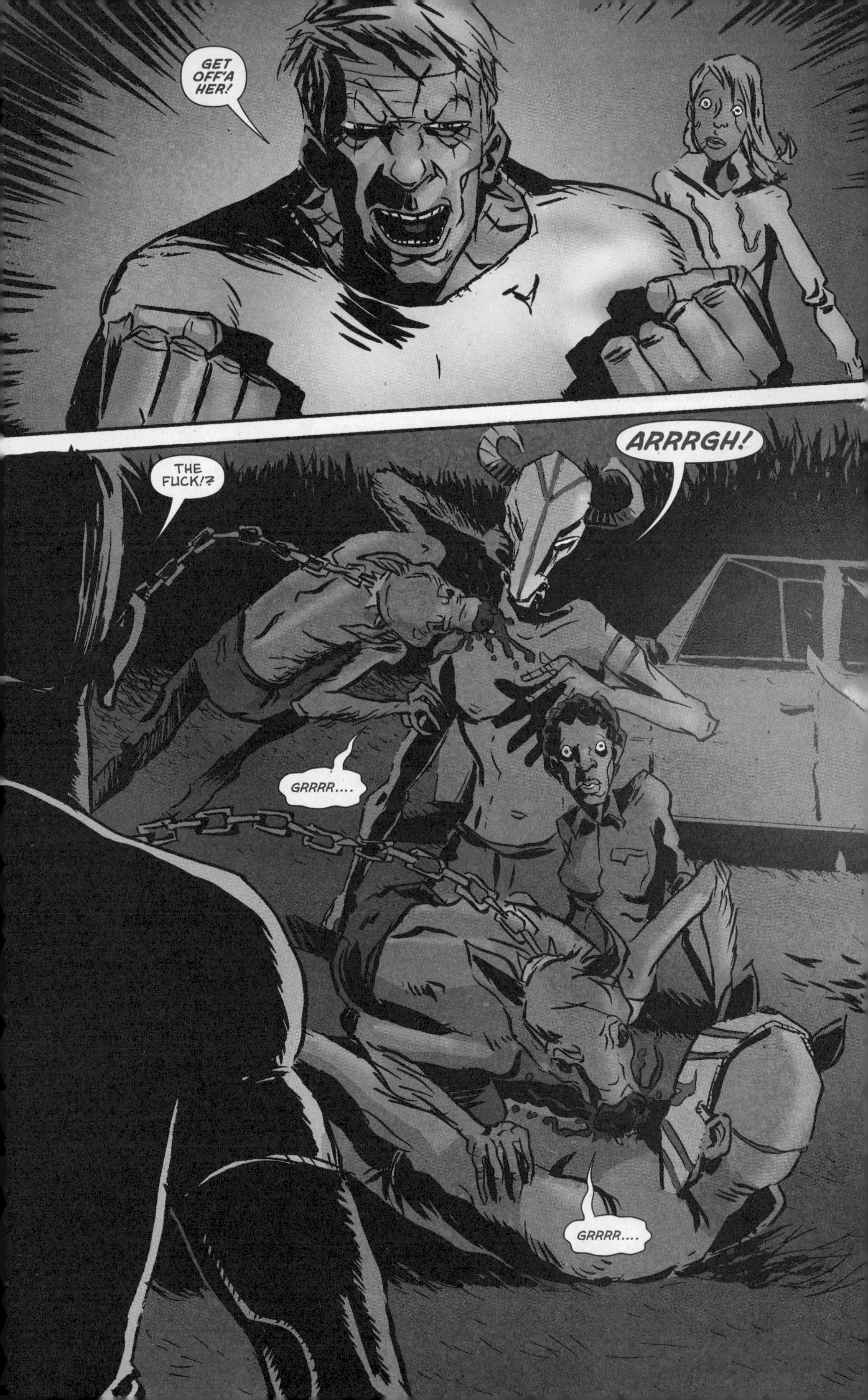

GET OFF'A HER!
THE FUCK!?
ARRRGH!
GRRRR....
GRRRR....

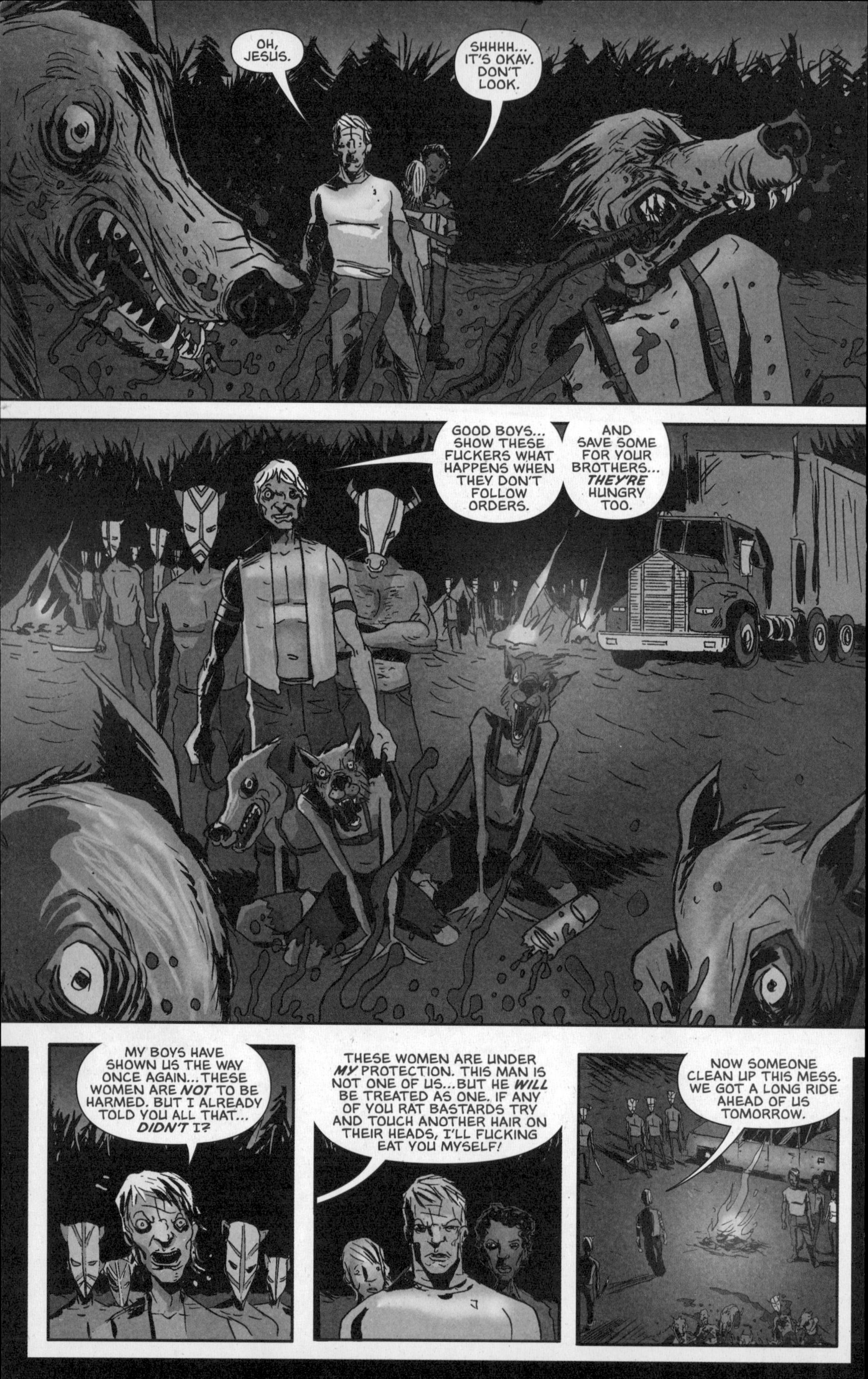
OH, JESUS.
SHHHH... IT'S OKAY. DON'T LOOK.
GOOD BOYS... SHOW THESE FUCKERS WHAT HAPPENS WHEN THEY DON'T FOLLOW ORDERS.
AND SAVE SOME FOR YOUR BROTHERS... *THEY'RE* HUNGRY TOO.
MY BOYS HAVE SHOWN US THE WAY ONCE AGAIN... THESE WOMEN ARE *NOT* TO BE HARMED. BUT I ALREADY TOLD YOU ALL THAT... *DIDN'T* I?
THESE WOMEN ARE UNDER *MY* PROTECTION. THIS MAN IS NOT ONE OF US... BUT HE *WILL* BE TREATED AS ONE. IF ANY OF YOU RAT BASTARDS TRY AND TOUCH ANOTHER HAIR ON THEIR HEADS, I'LL FUCKING EAT YOU MYSELF!
NOW SOMEONE CLEAN UP THIS MESS. WE GOT A LONG RIDE AHEAD OF US TOMORROW.

The sickness is in me now. I don't have much time left. But when I'm very quiet at night, when I lie listening to my boy's breath above me...I hear it. The voice of God.

He tells me truths. And as horrible as they are, I must listen. I cannot bury these secrets like I buried those of my past....like I buried the man I was.

I came here looking for answers. I don't know what I expected to find...a laboratory...medical equipment? Something that would tell me how the boy was "grown." Something that would tell me how his father created him.

Instead all we've found is his "Bible." Abbot thinks it's utter nonsense. The rantings of a madman.

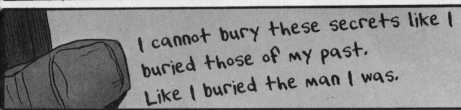

I cannot bury these secrets like I buried those of my past. Like I buried the man I was.

But the more I read, the more I begin to understand. This is a map. A map to unseen places...a map to the answers we so desperately seek.

Like I buried the man I was.

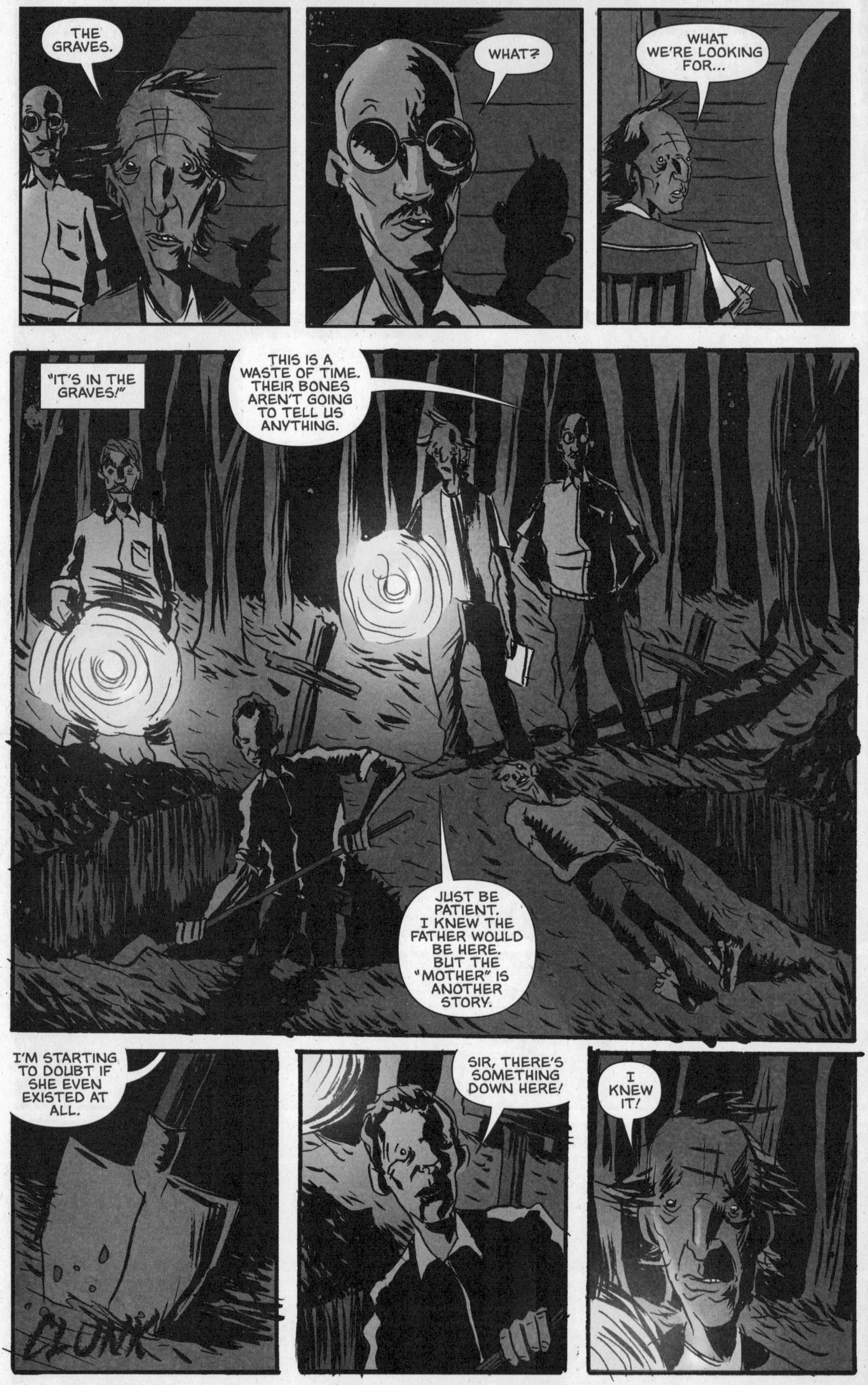
THE GRAVES.
WHAT?
WHAT WE'RE LOOKING FOR...
"IT'S IN THE GRAVES!"
THIS IS A WASTE OF TIME. THEIR BONES AREN'T GOING TO TELL US ANYTHING.
JUST BE PATIENT. I KNEW THE FATHER WOULD BE HERE. BUT THE "MOTHER" IS ANOTHER STORY.
I'M STARTING TO DOUBT IF SHE EVEN EXISTED AT ALL.
CLUNK
SIR, THERE'S SOMETHING DOWN HERE!
I KNEW IT!

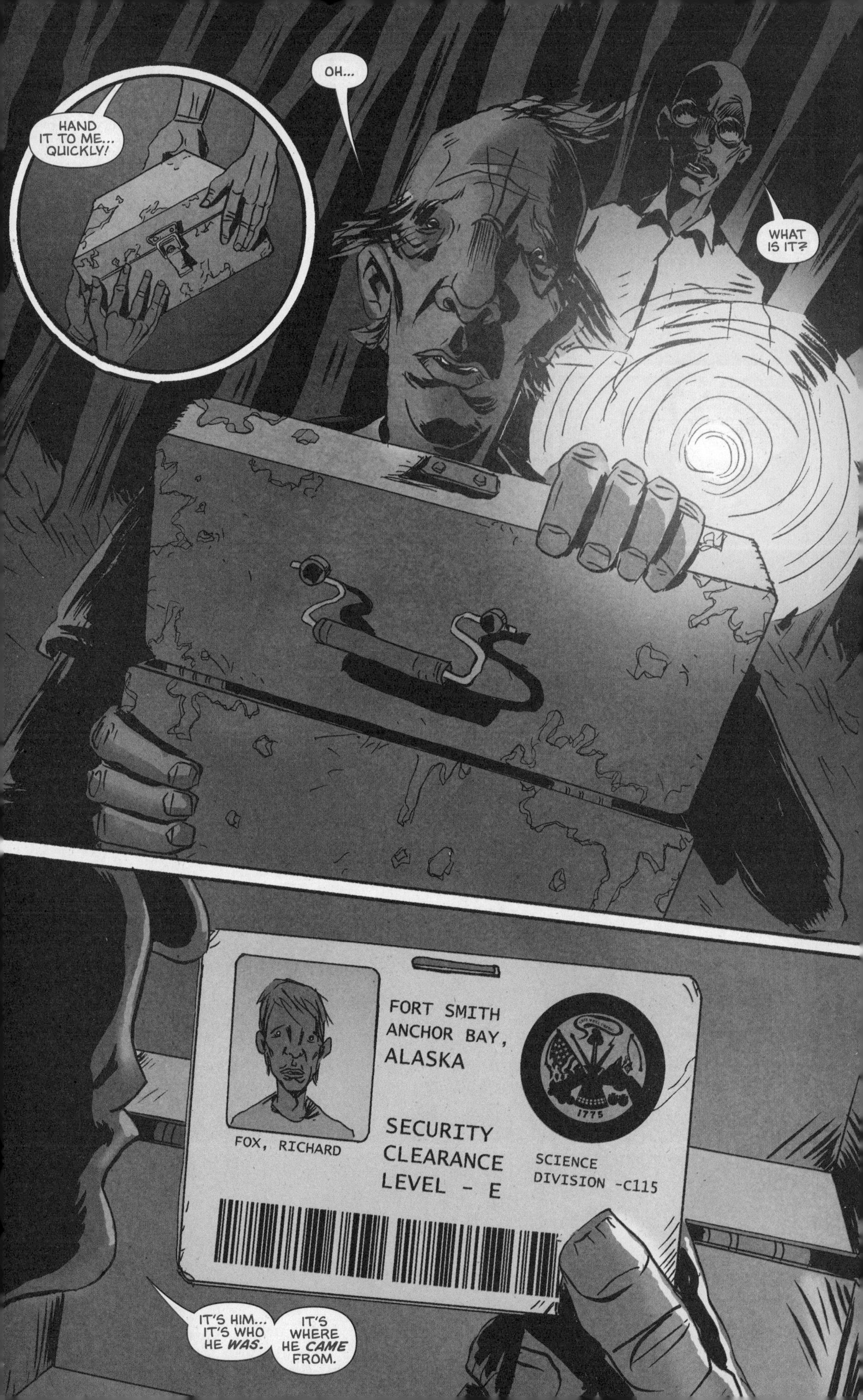
HAND IT TO ME... QUICKLY!
OH...
WHAT IS IT?
FORT SMITH
ANCHOR BAY,
ALASKA
SECURITY
CLEARANCE
LEVEL - E
FOX, RICHARD
SCIENCE
DIVISION -C115
1775
IT'S HIM... IT'S WHO HE *WAS.*
IT'S WHERE HE *CAME* FROM.

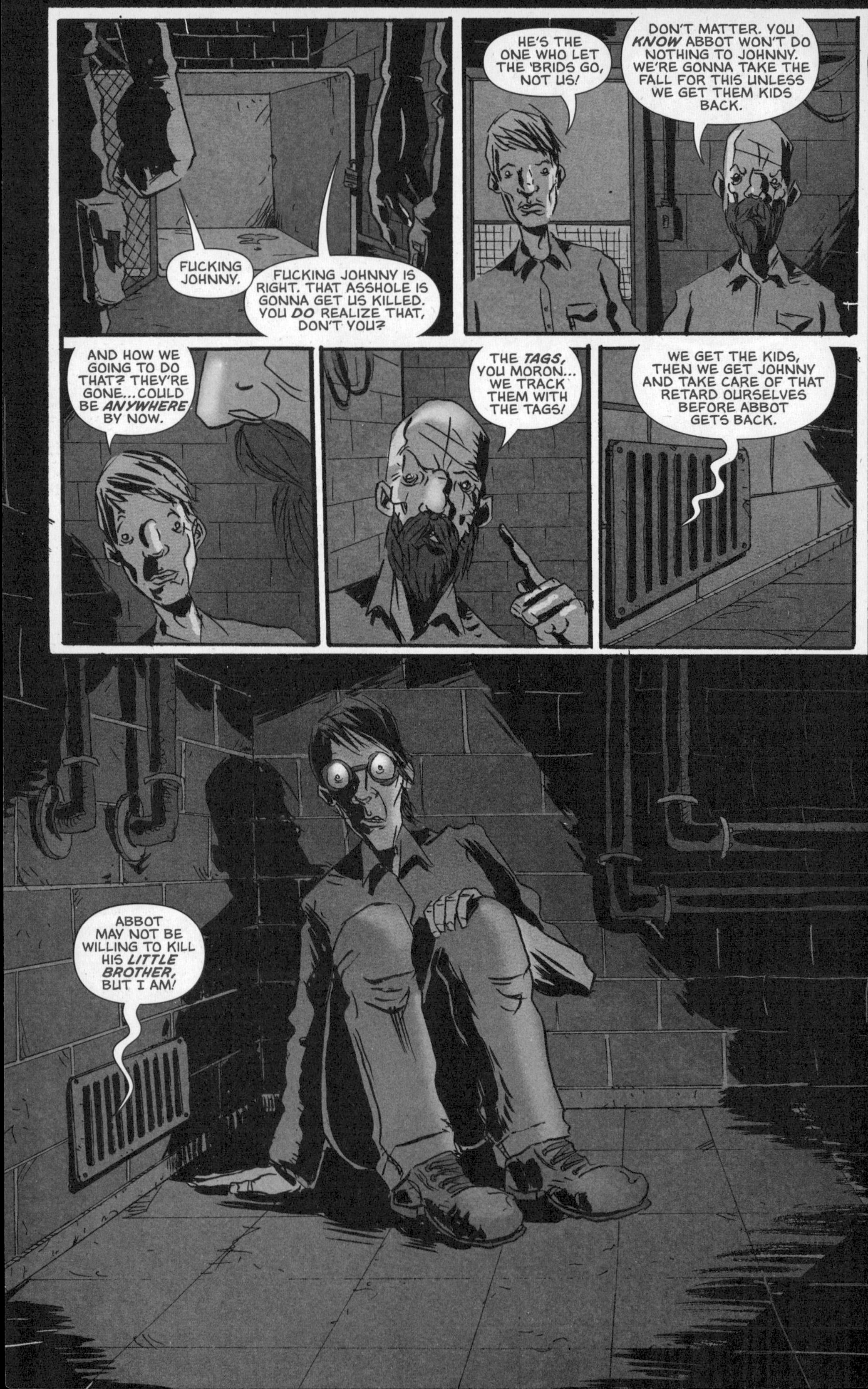
FUCKING JOHNNY.
FUCKING JOHNNY IS RIGHT. THAT ASSHOLE IS GONNA GET US KILLED. YOU DO REALIZE THAT, DON'T YOU?
HE'S THE ONE WHO LET THE 'BRIDS GO, NOT US!
DON'T MATTER. YOU KNOW ABBOT WON'T DO NOTHING TO JOHNNY. WE'RE GONNA TAKE THE FALL FOR THIS UNLESS WE GET THEM KIDS BACK.
AND HOW WE GOING TO DO THAT? THEY'RE GONE...COULD BE ANYWHERE BY NOW.
THE TAGS, YOU MORON... WE TRACK THEM WITH THE TAGS!
WE GET THE KIDS, THEN WE GET JOHNNY AND TAKE CARE OF THAT RETARD OURSELVES BEFORE ABBOT GETS BACK.
ABBOT MAY NOT BE WILLING TO KILL HIS LITTLE BROTHER, BUT I AM!

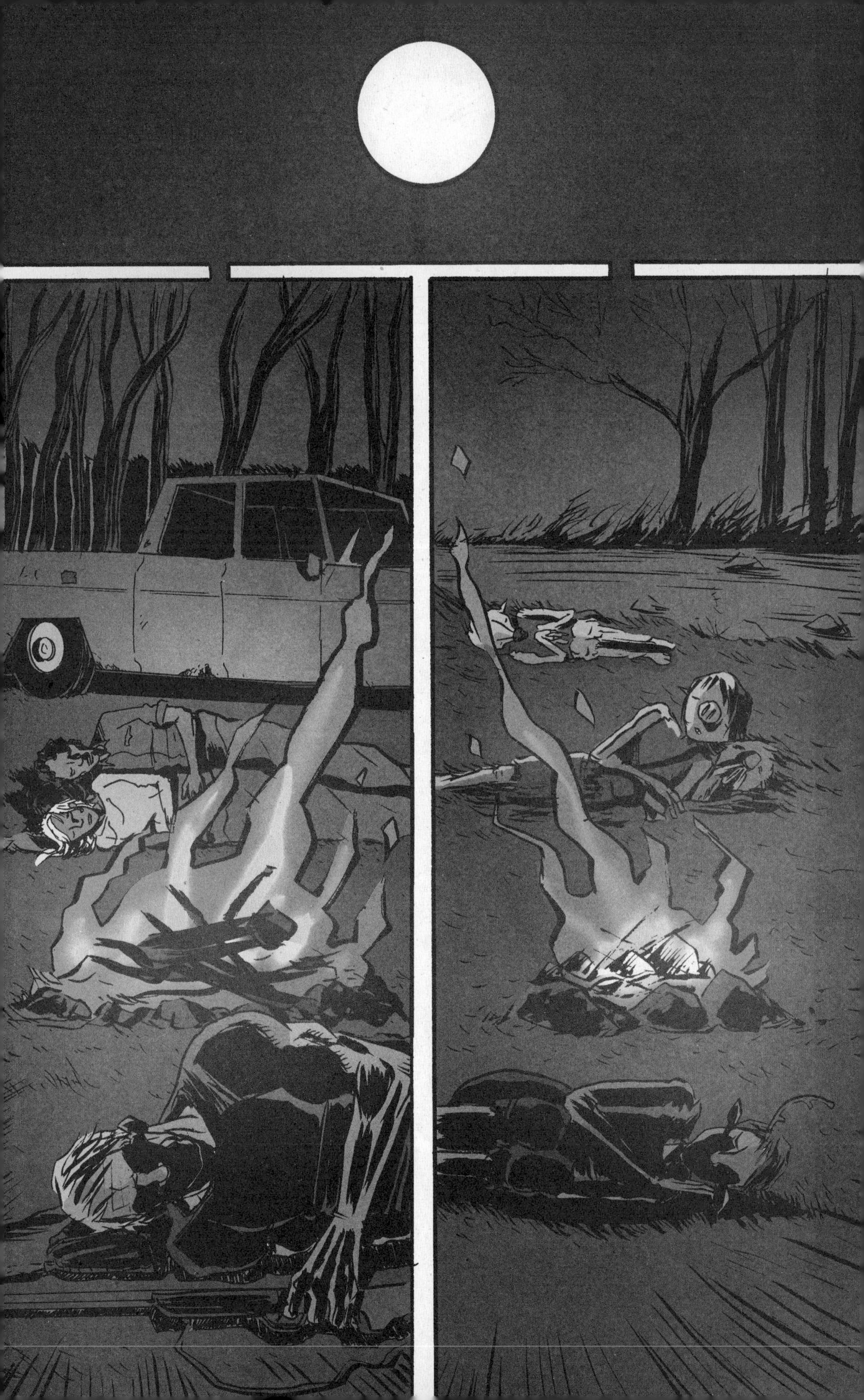

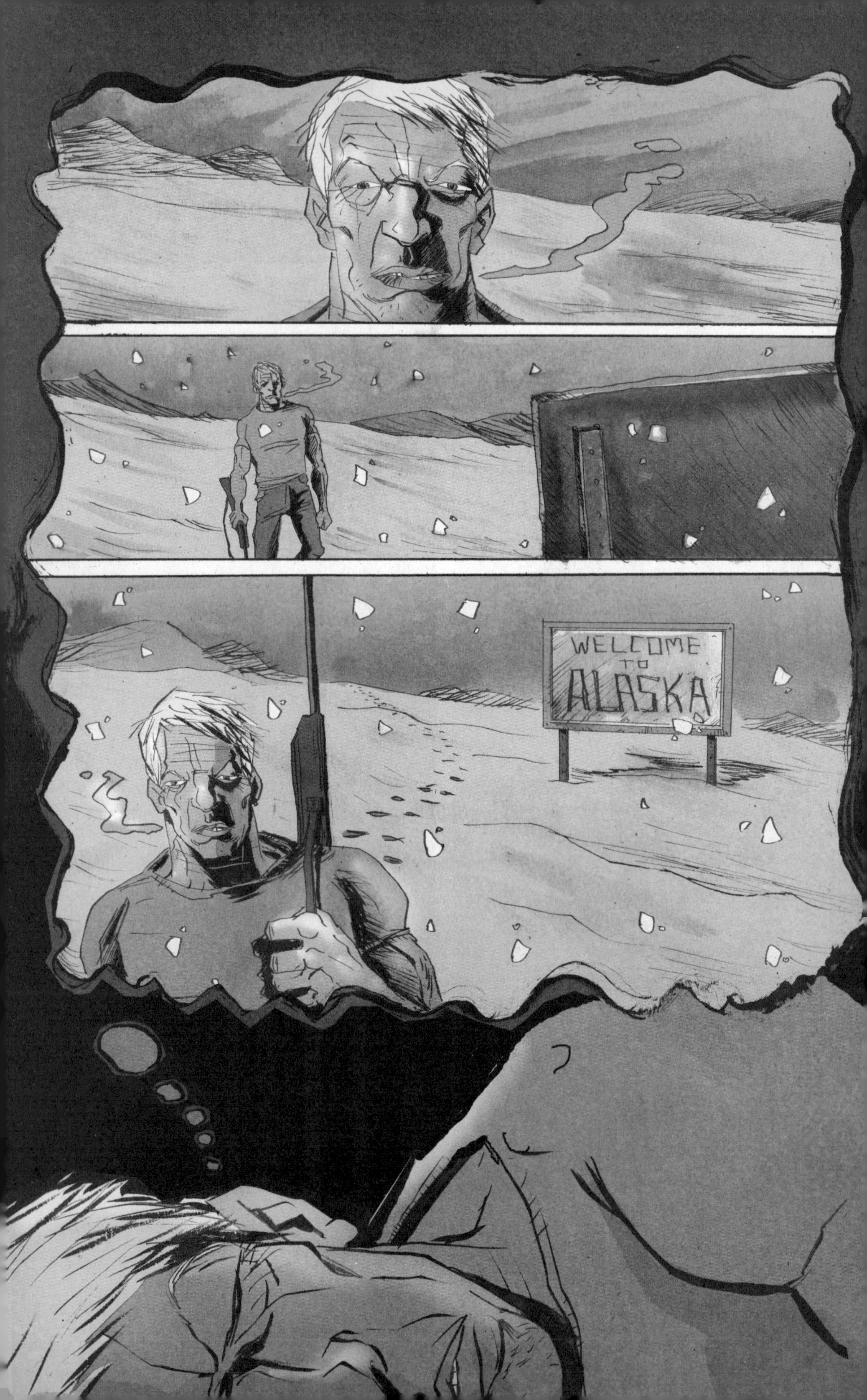
WELCOME TO ALASKA

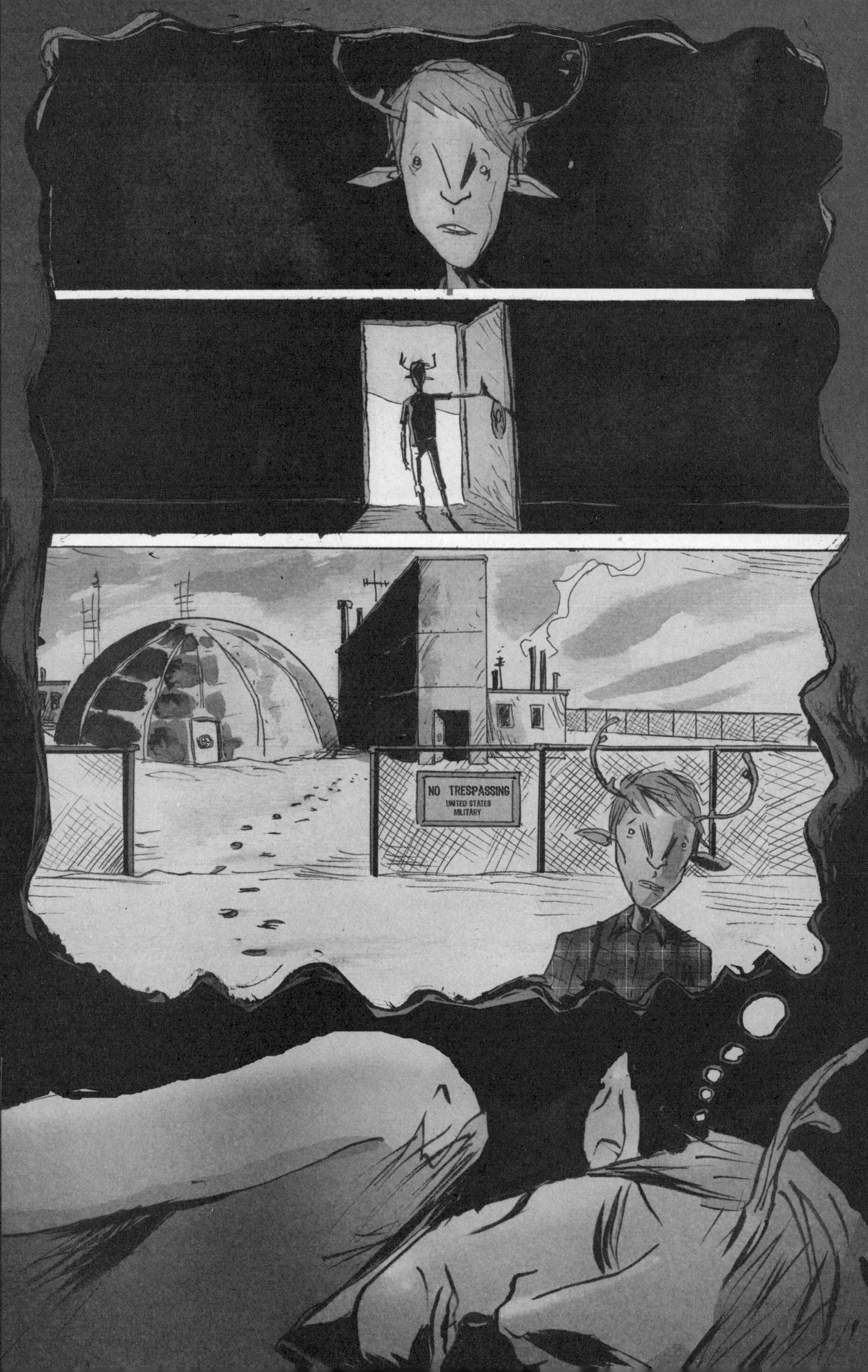
NO TRESPASSING
UNITED STATES
MILITARY

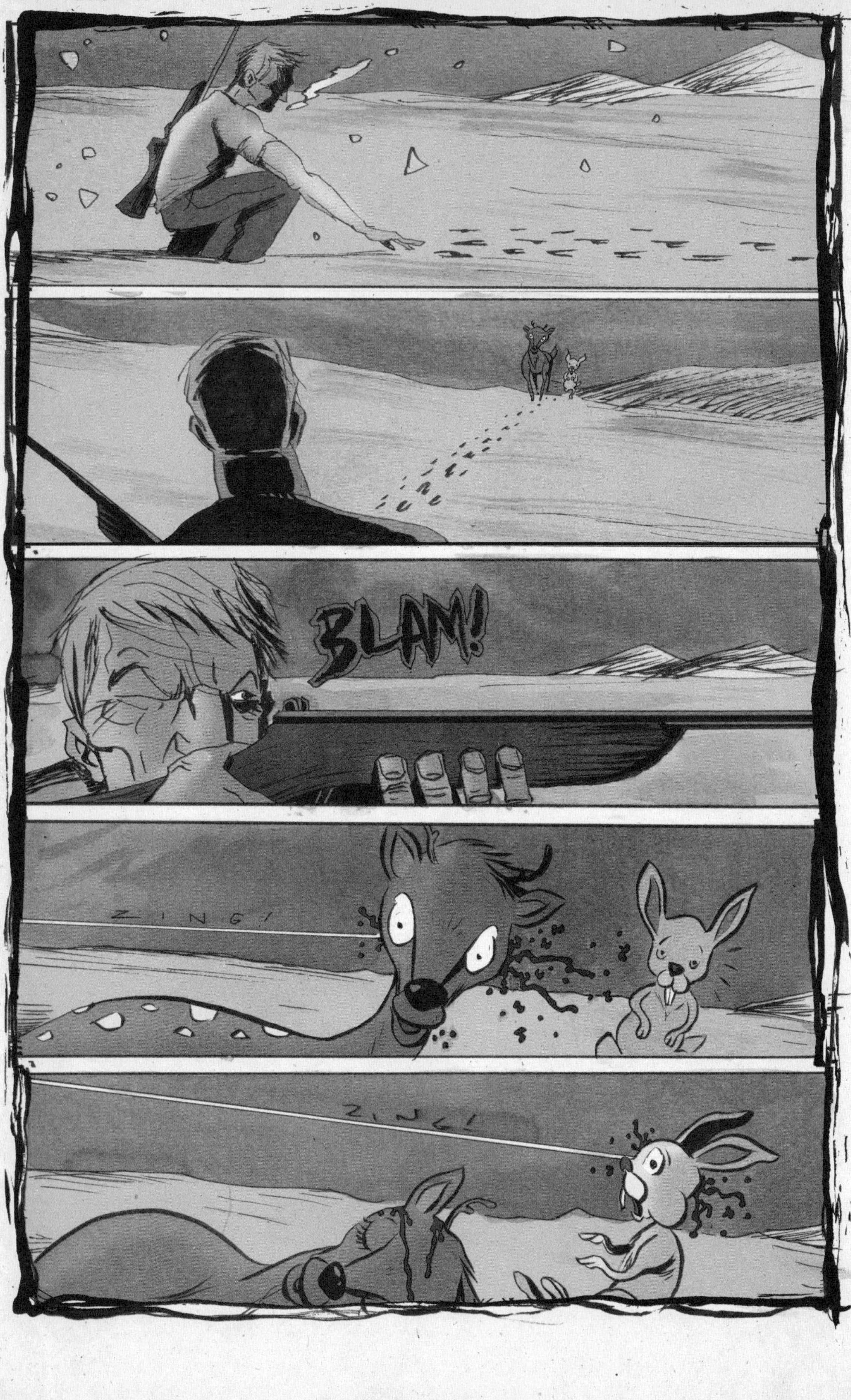
BLAM!
ZING!
ZING!

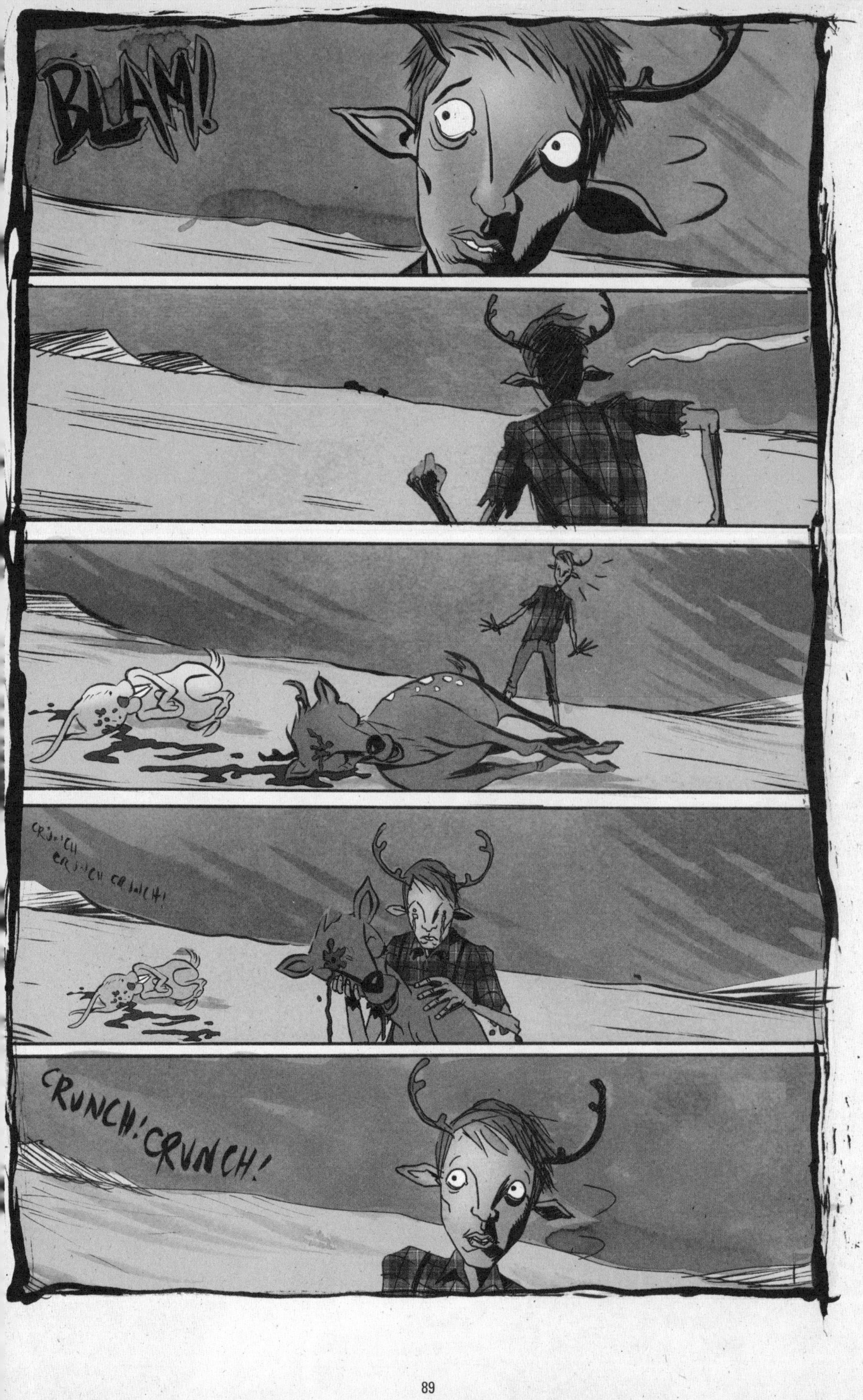
BLAM!
CRUNCH
CRUNCH CRUNCH!
CRUNCH! CRUNCH!

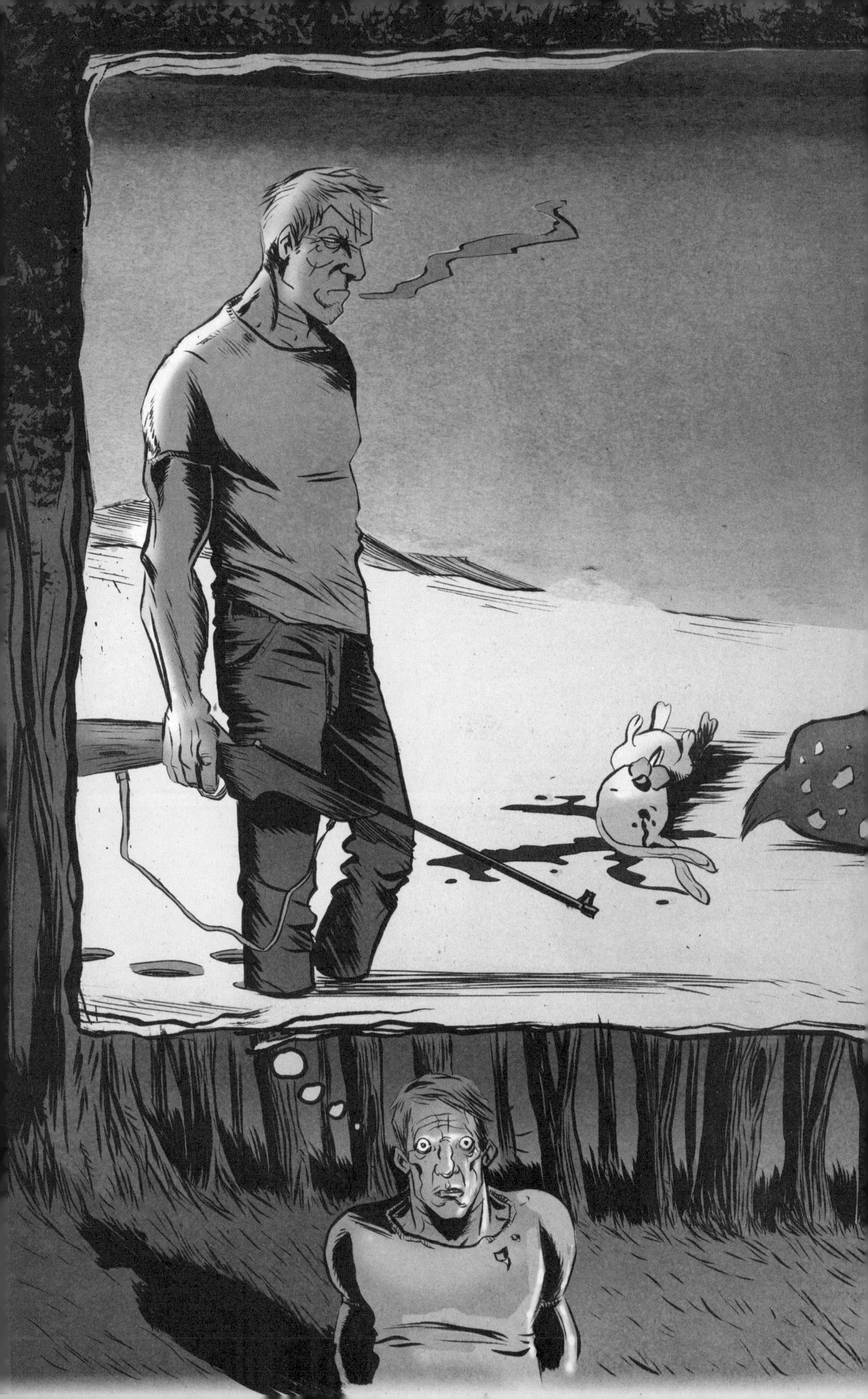

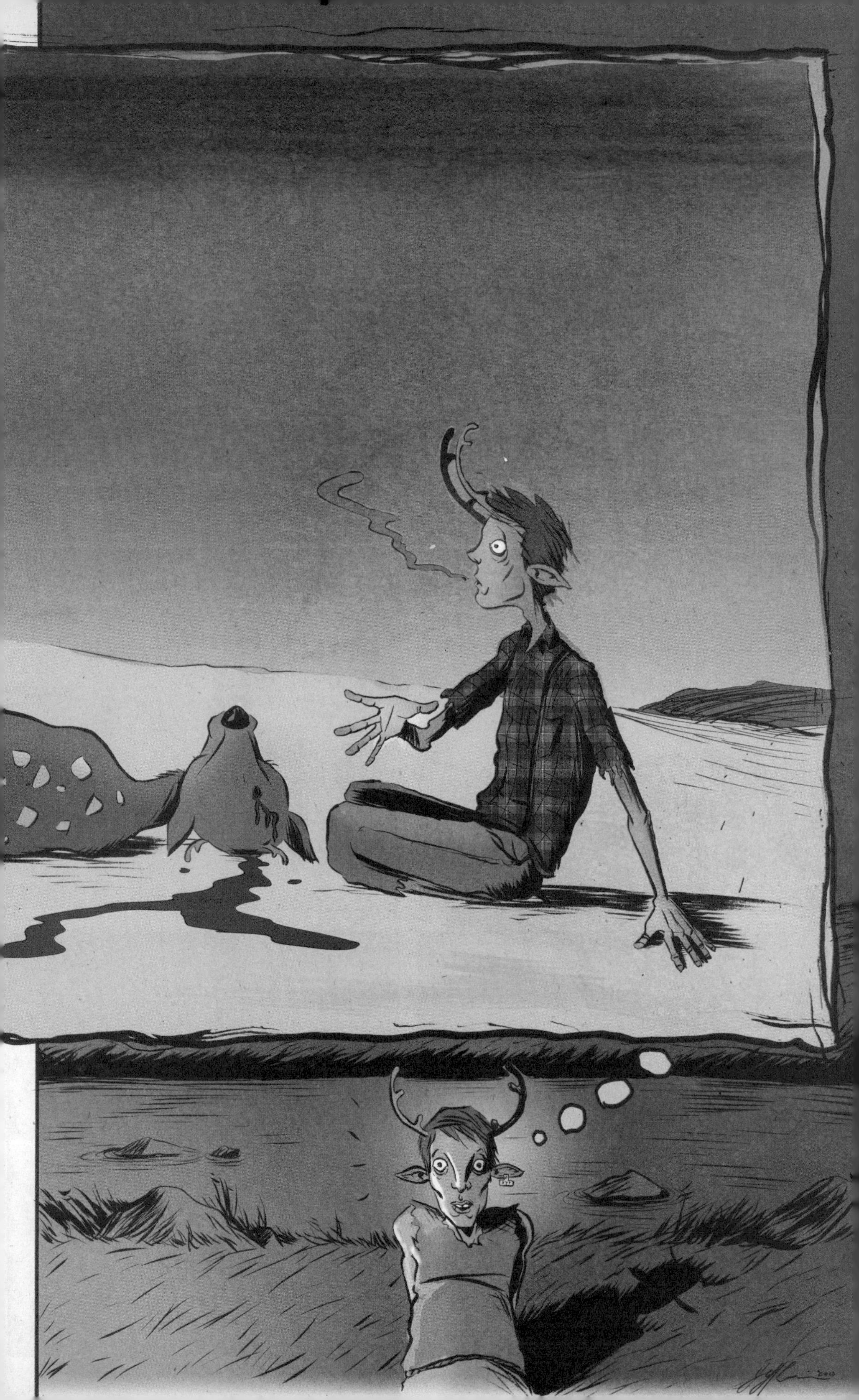

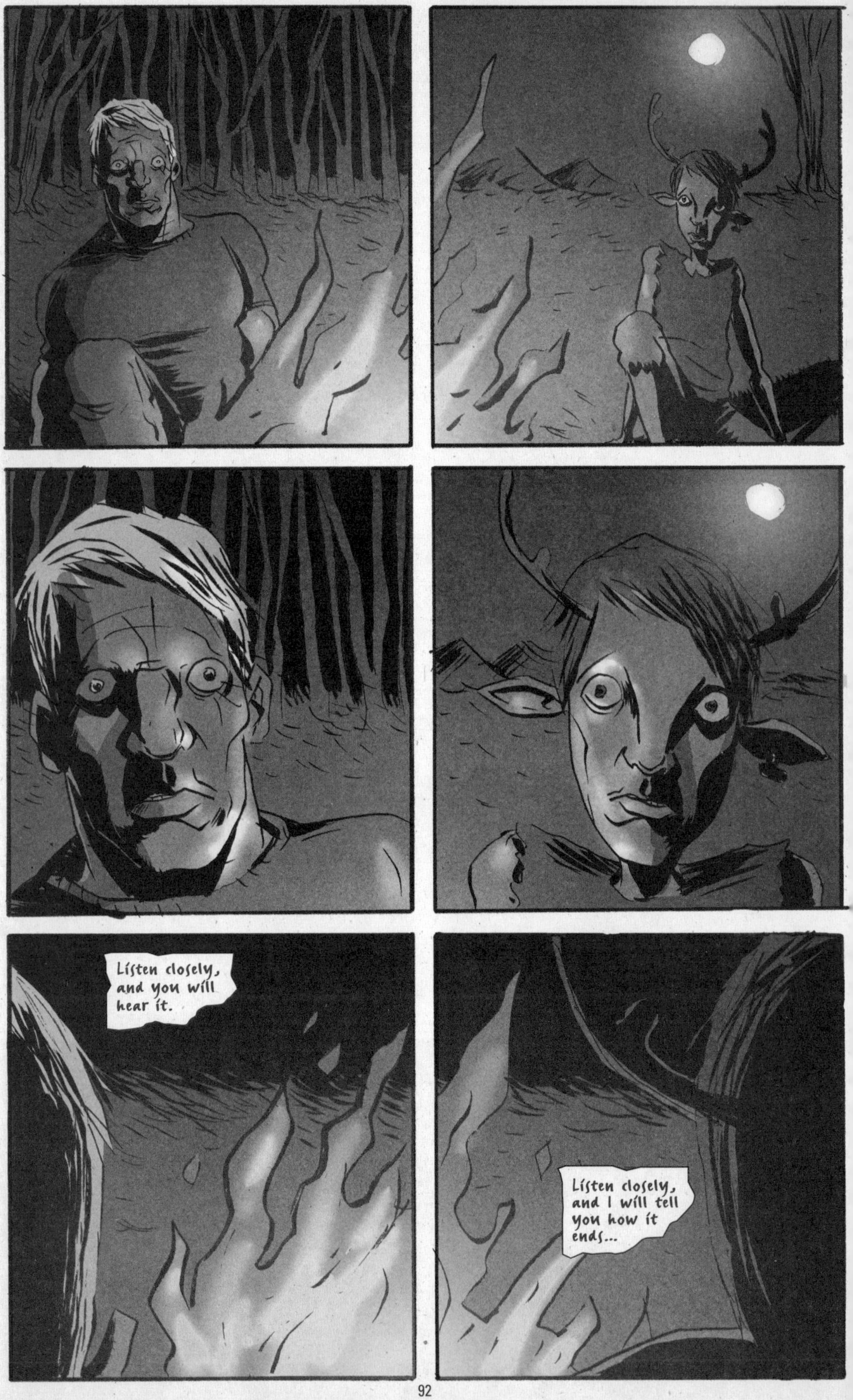
Listen closely, and you will hear it.
Listen closely, and I will tell you how it ends...

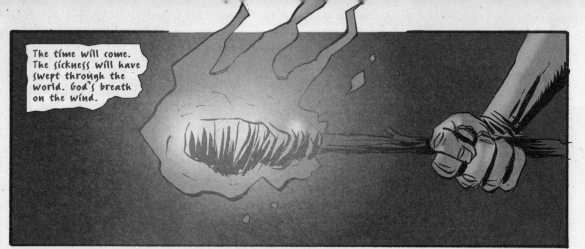

The time will come. The sickness will have swept through the world. God's breath on the wind.

And the prophet's house will burn to ashes. And the ash will ignite the air, filling the lungs of the sinners...filling their black souls.

These things I have seen in my dreams. These are the things I know. These things will happen.

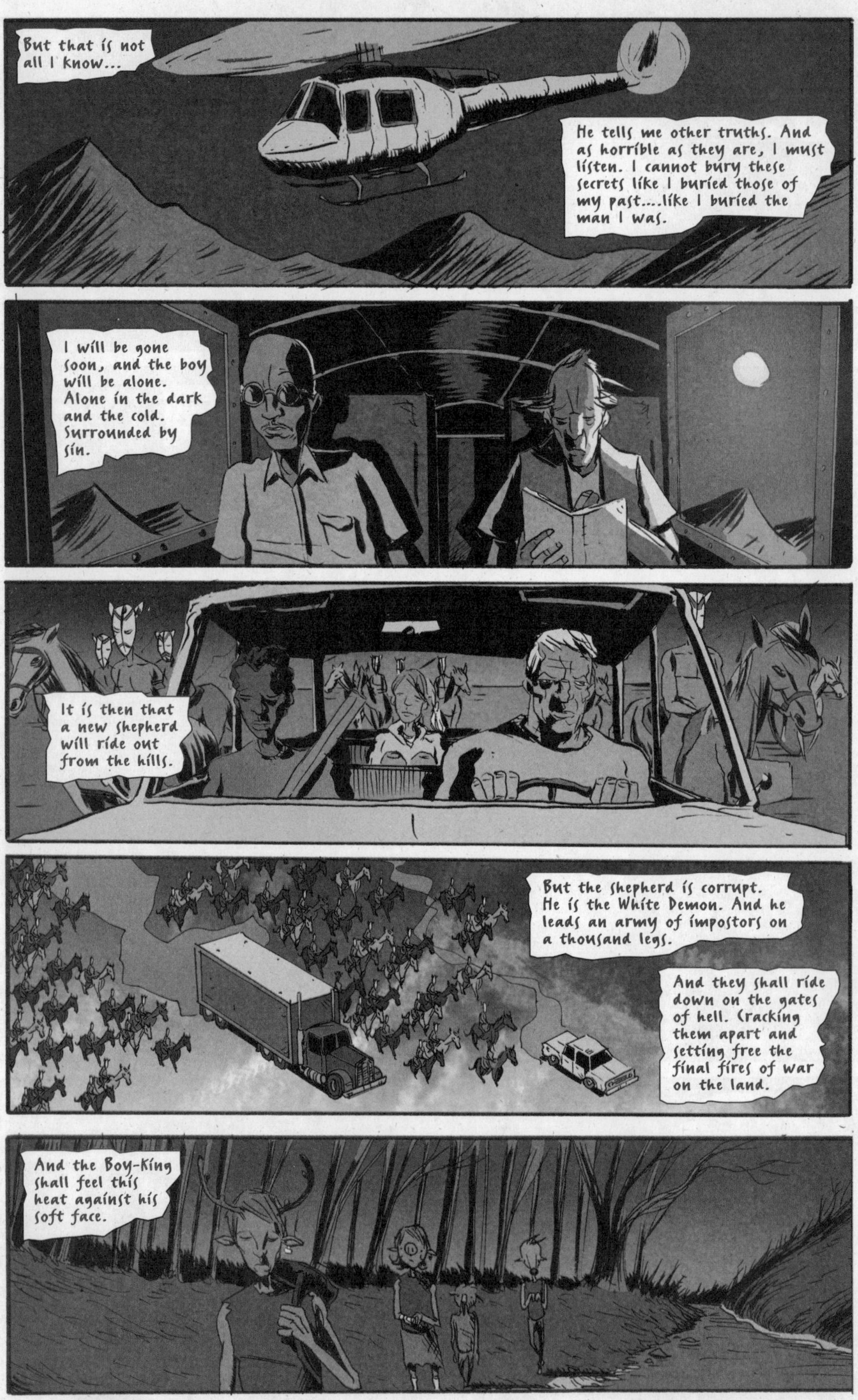

But that is not all I know...
He tells me other truths. And as horrible as they are, I must listen. I cannot bury these secrets like I buried those of my past....like I buried the man I was.
I will be gone soon, and the boy will be alone. Alone in the dark and the cold. Surrounded by sin.
It is then that a new shepherd will ride out from the hills.
But the shepherd is corrupt. He is the White Demon. And he leads an army of impostors on a thousand legs.
And they shall ride down on the gates of hell. Cracking them apart and setting free the final fires of war on the land.
And the Boy-King shall feel this heat against his soft face.

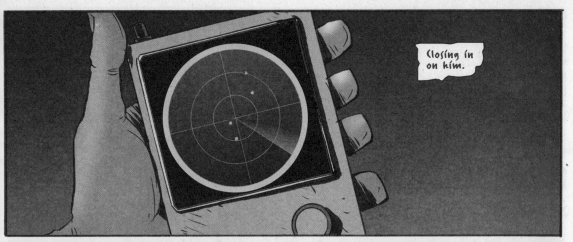

Closing in on him.

Threatening to burn his pure soul forever.

But this is not all that tries to take him from God's grace.

The black-eyed monster waits in the fire as well.

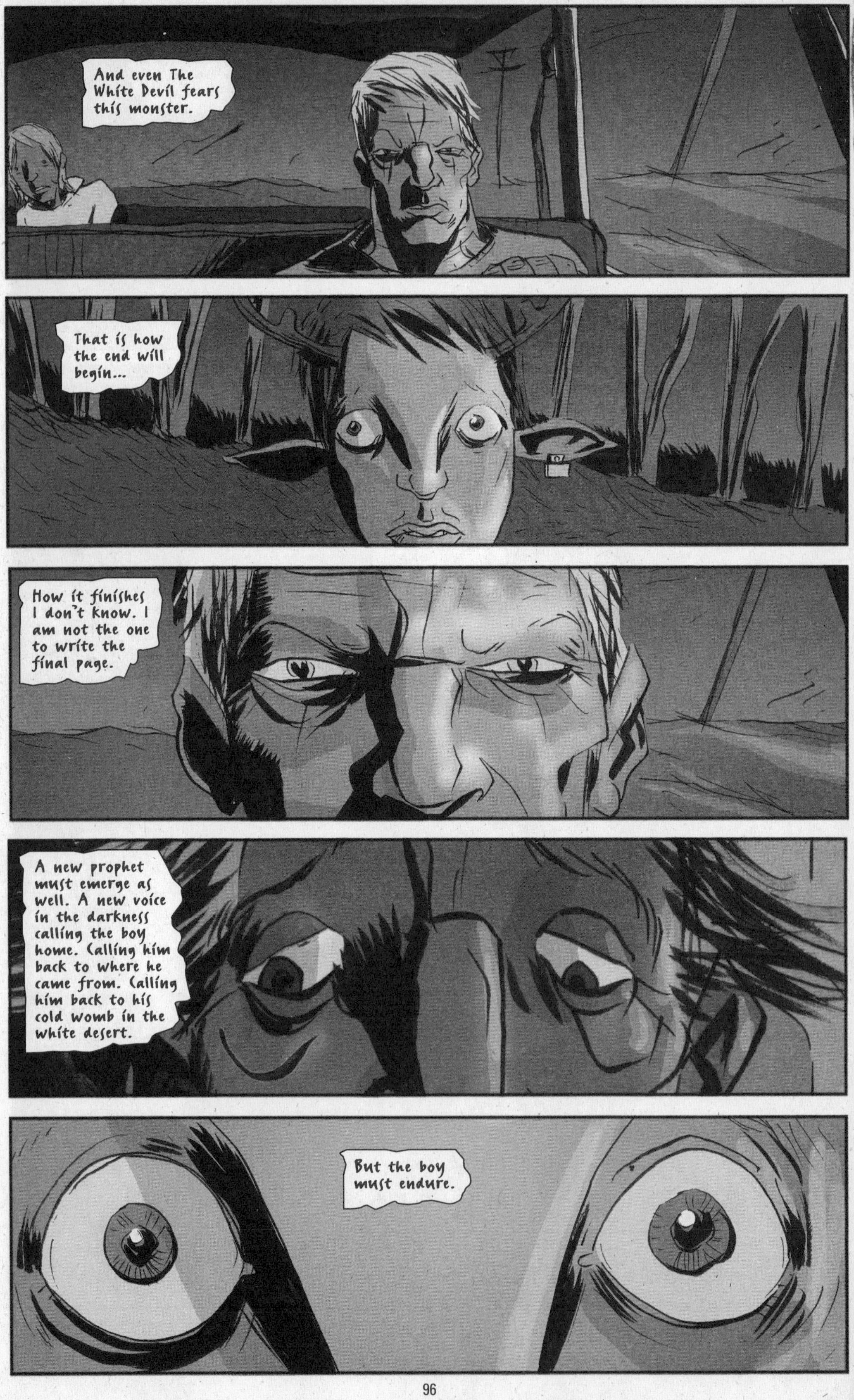
And even The White Devil fears this monster.
That is how the end will begin...
How it finishes I don't know. I am not the one to write the final page.
A new prophet must emerge as well. A new voice in the darkness calling the boy home. Calling him back to where he came from. Calling him back to his cold womb in the white desert.
But the boy must endure.

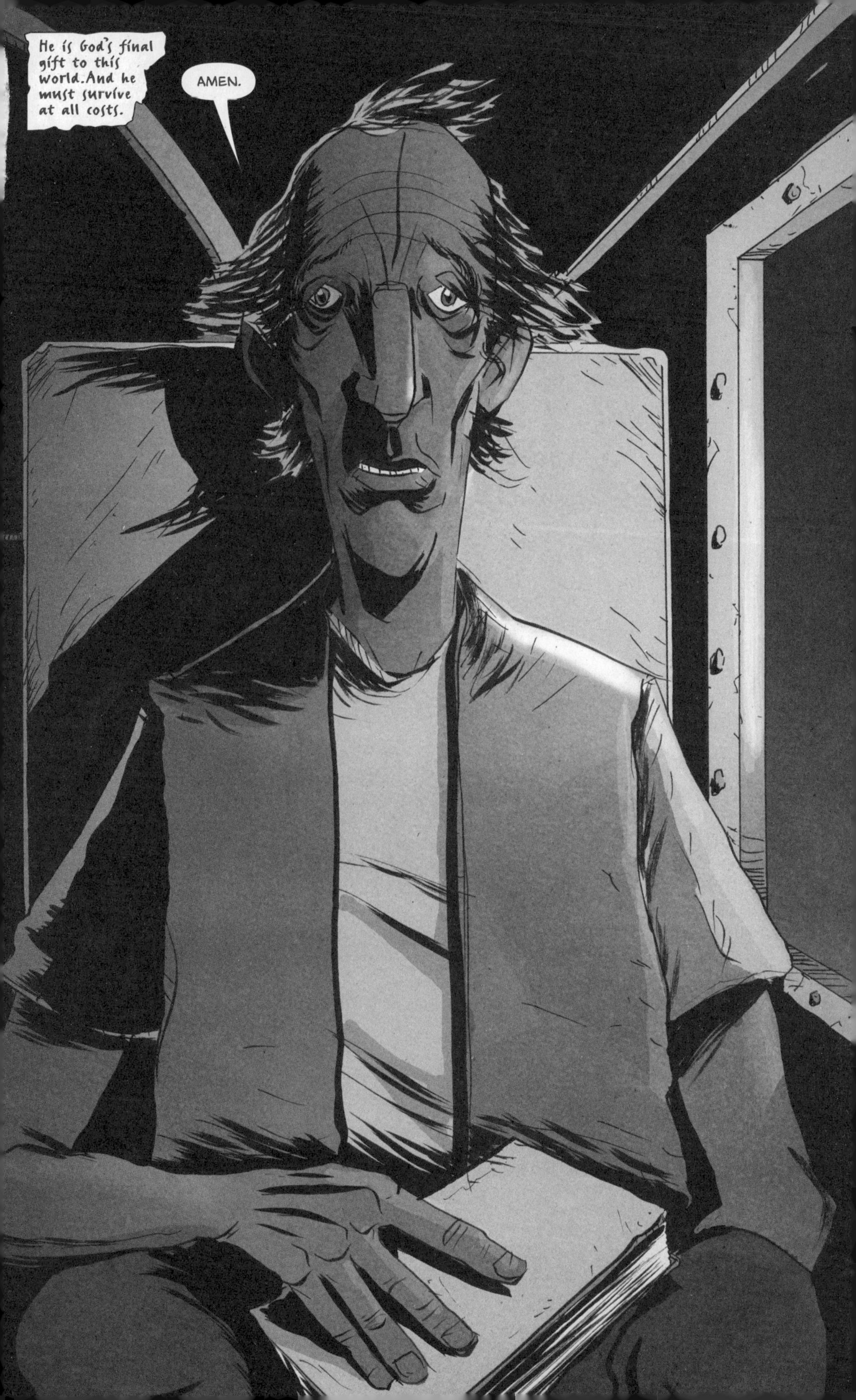
He is God's final gift to this world. And he must survive at all costs.
AMEN.

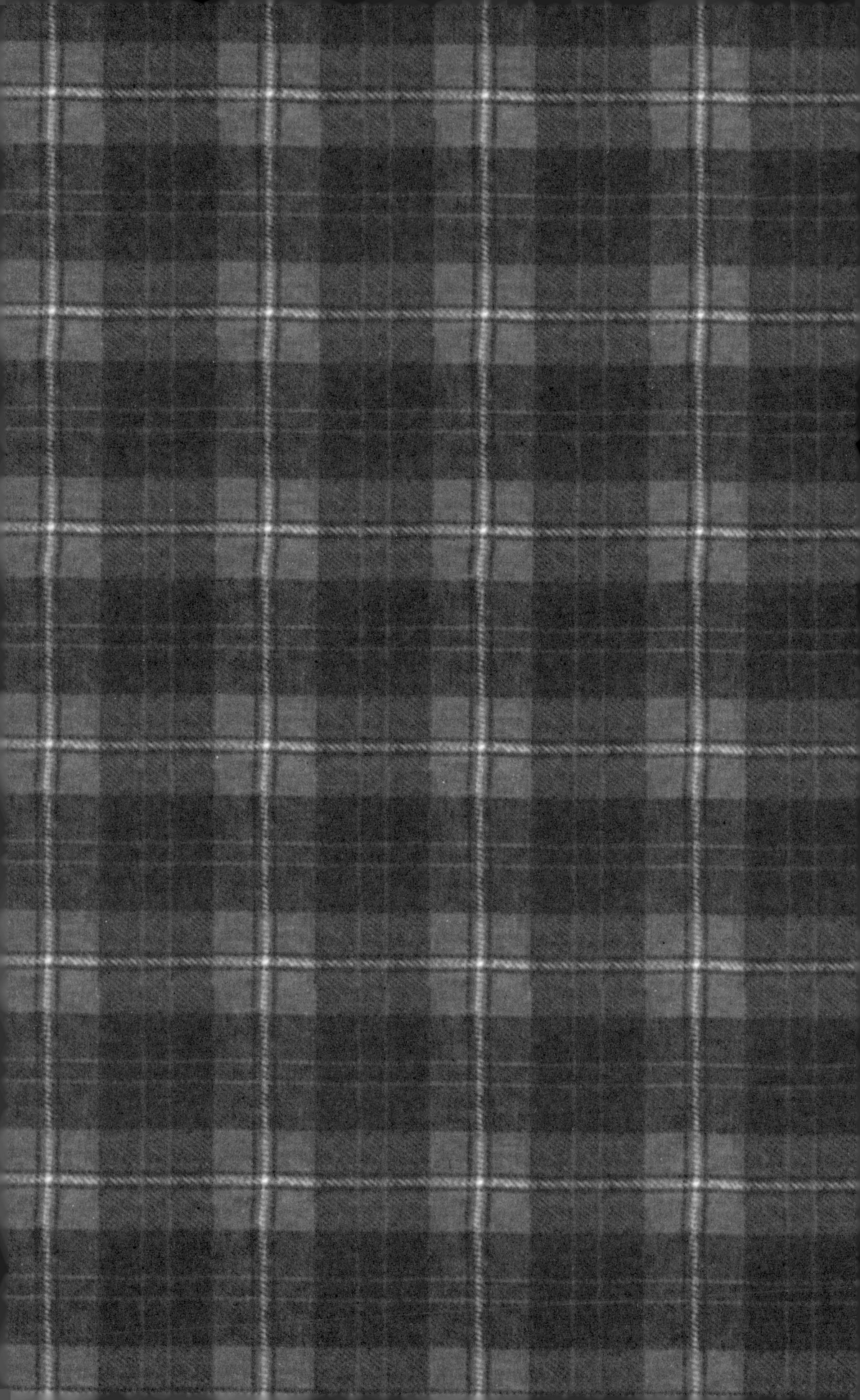

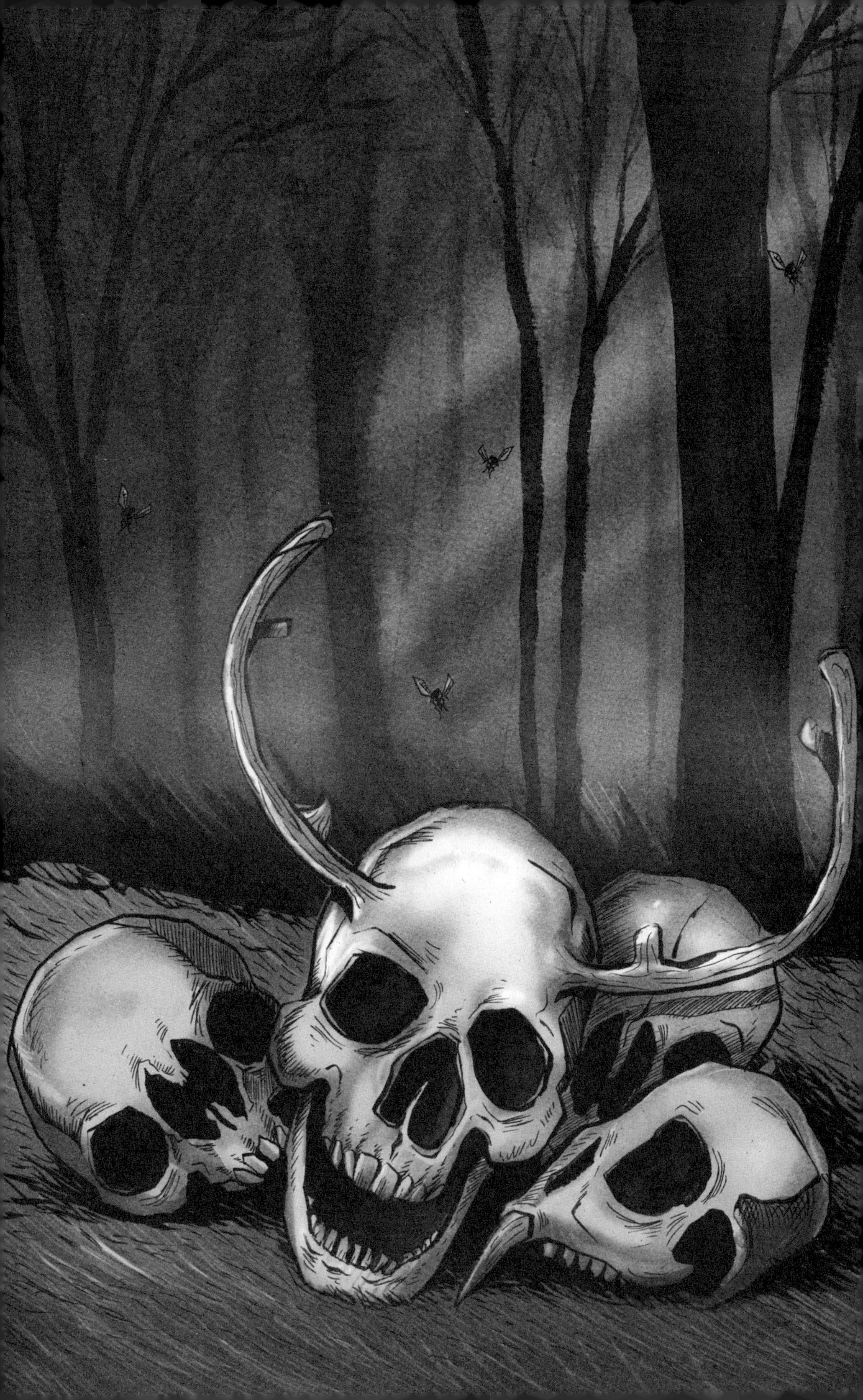

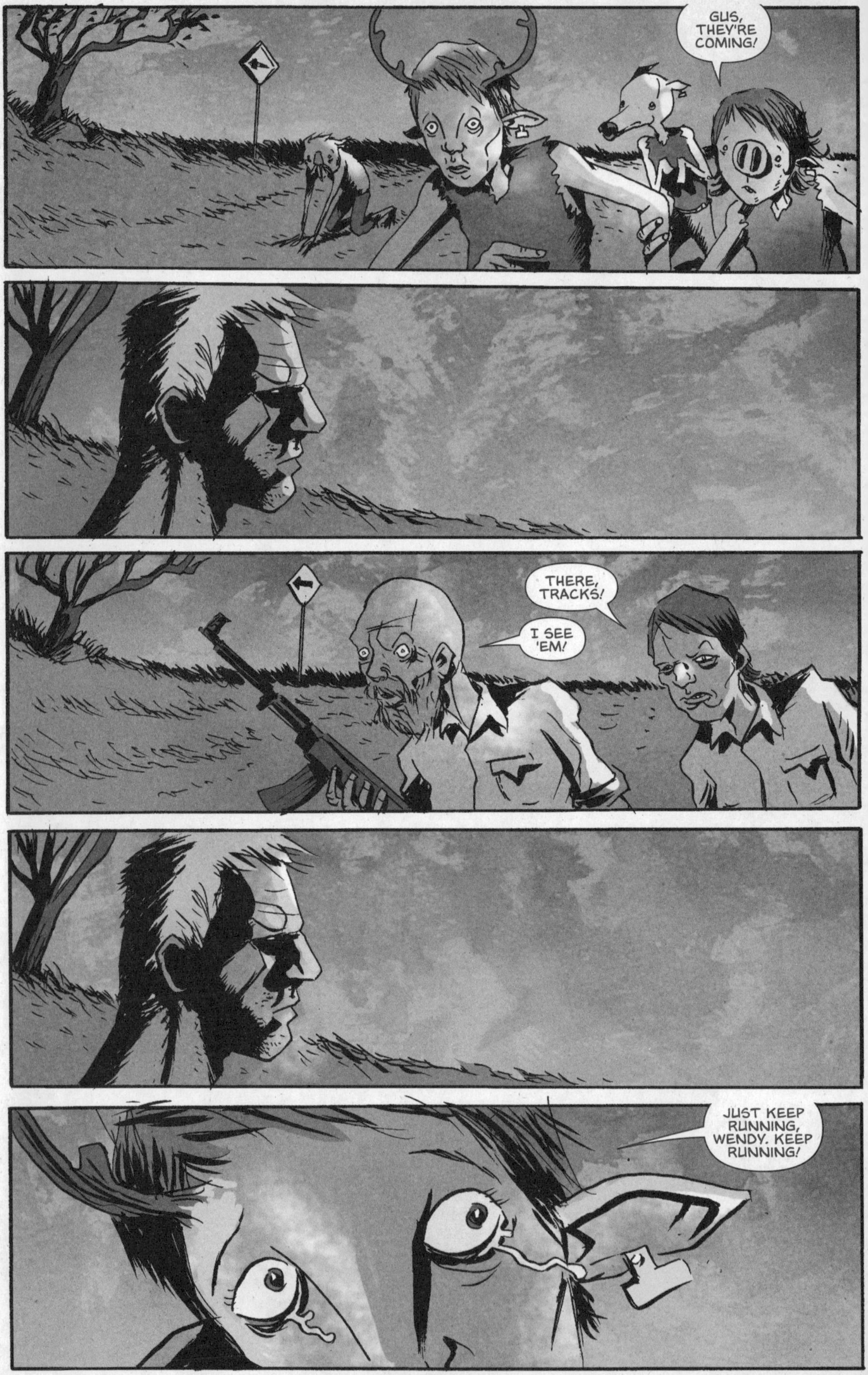
GUS, THEY'RE COMING!
THERE, TRACKS!
I SEE 'EM!
JUST KEEP RUNNING, WENDY. KEEP RUNNING!

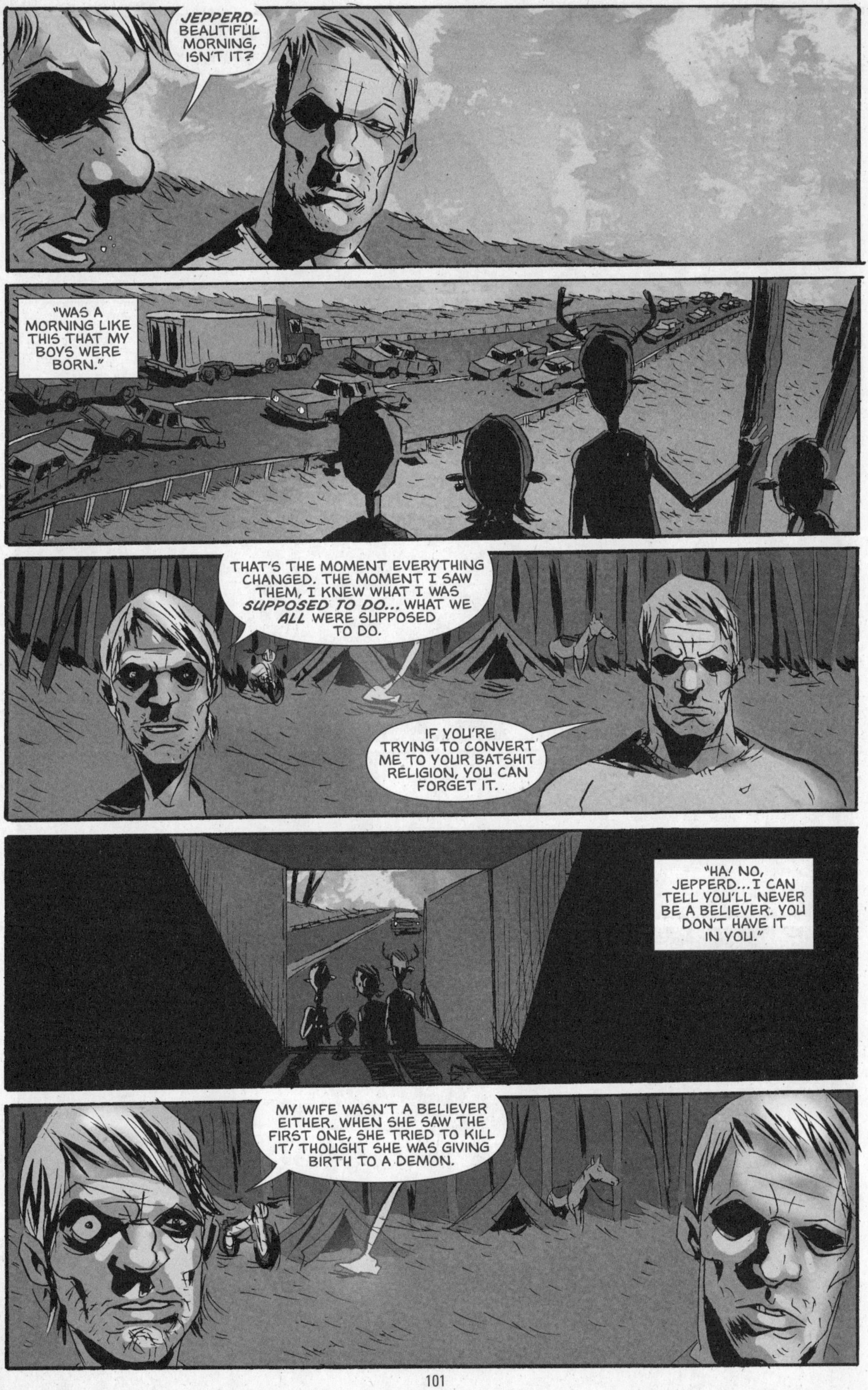
JEPPERD. BEAUTIFUL MORNING, ISN'T IT?
"WAS A MORNING LIKE THIS THAT MY BOYS WERE BORN."
THAT'S THE MOMENT EVERYTHING CHANGED. THE MOMENT I SAW THEM, I KNEW WHAT I WAS SUPPOSED TO DO... WHAT WE ALL WERE SUPPOSED TO DO.
IF YOU'RE TRYING TO CONVERT ME TO YOUR BATSHIT RELIGION, YOU CAN FORGET IT.
"HA! NO, JEPPERD... I CAN TELL YOU'LL NEVER BE A BELIEVER. YOU DON'T HAVE IT IN YOU."
MY WIFE WASN'T A BELIEVER EITHER. WHEN SHE SAW THE FIRST ONE, SHE TRIED TO KILL IT! THOUGHT SHE WAS GIVING BIRTH TO A DEMON.

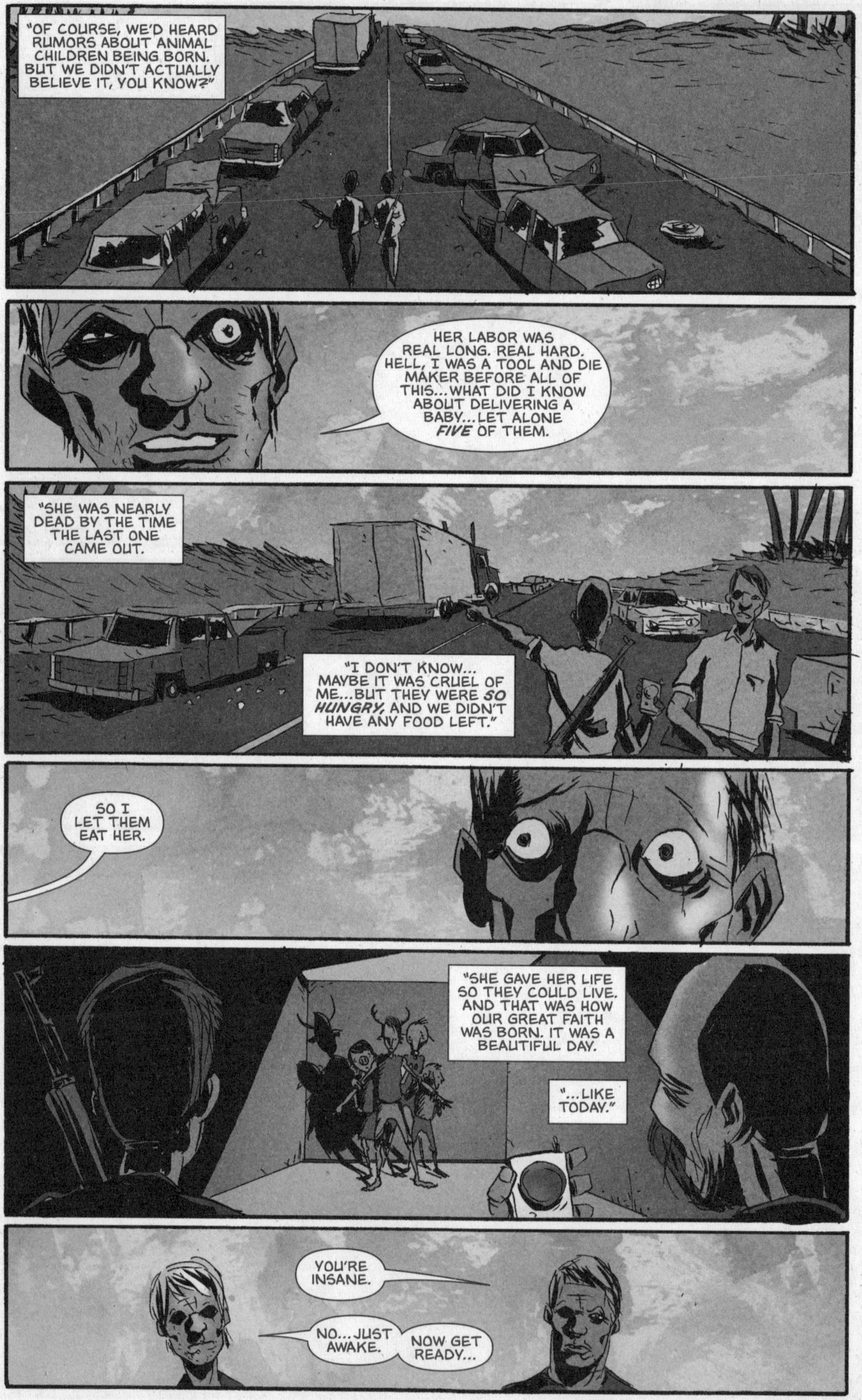
"OF COURSE, WE'D HEARD RUMORS ABOUT ANIMAL CHILDREN BEING BORN. BUT WE DIDN'T ACTUALLY BELIEVE IT, YOU KNOW?"
HER LABOR WAS REAL LONG. REAL HARD. HELL, I WAS A TOOL AND DIE MAKER BEFORE ALL OF THIS...WHAT DID I KNOW ABOUT DELIVERING A BABY...LET ALONE *FIVE* OF THEM.
"SHE WAS NEARLY DEAD BY THE TIME THE LAST ONE CAME OUT.
"I DON'T KNOW... MAYBE IT WAS CRUEL OF ME...BUT THEY WERE *SO HUNGRY,* AND WE DIDN'T HAVE ANY FOOD LEFT."
SO I LET THEM EAT HER.
"SHE GAVE HER LIFE SO THEY COULD LIVE. AND THAT WAS HOW OUR GREAT FAITH WAS BORN. IT WAS A BEAUTIFUL DAY.
"...LIKE TODAY."
YOU'RE INSANE.
NO...JUST AWAKE.
NOW GET READY...

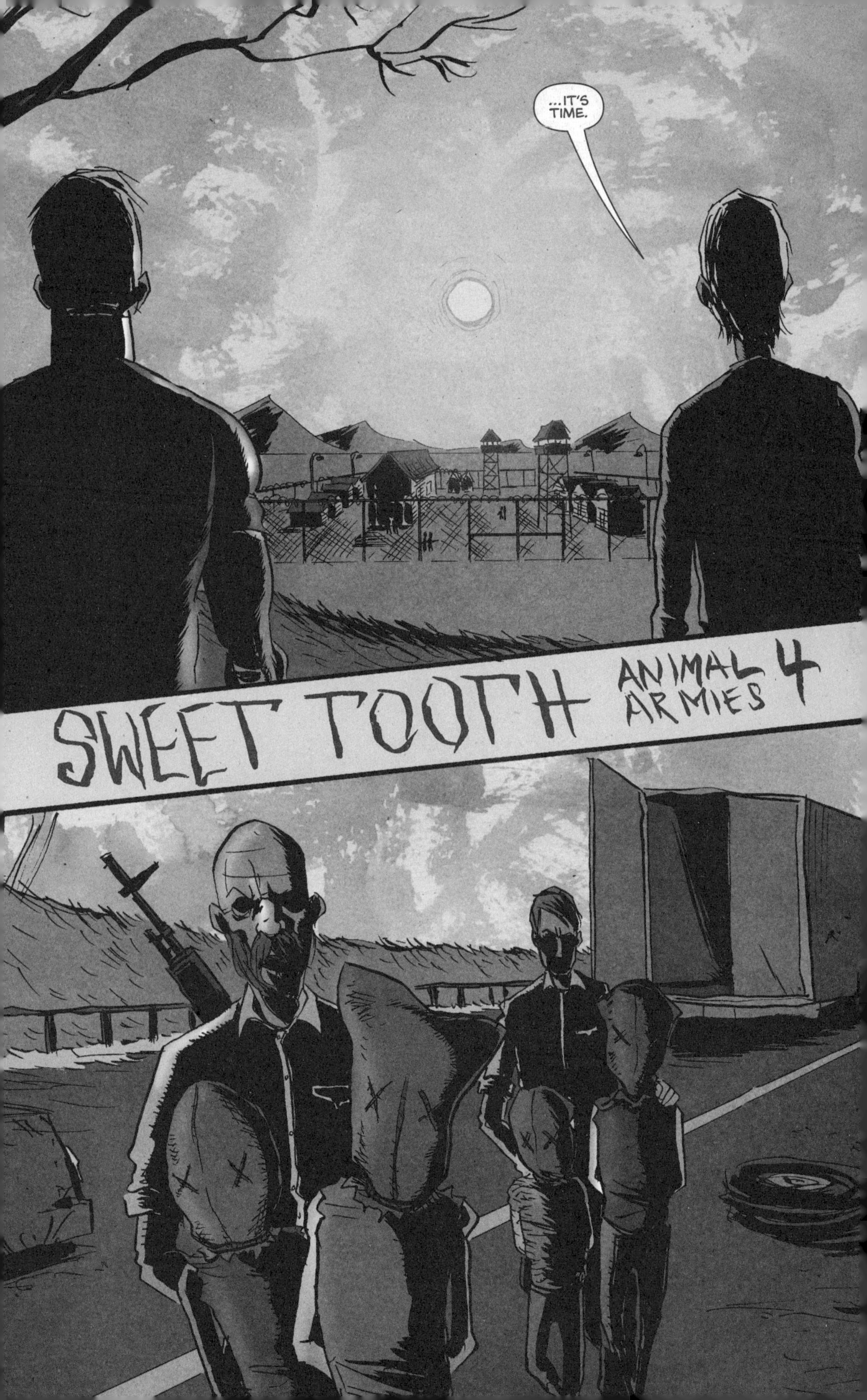
...IT'S TIME.
SWEET TOOTH
ANIMAL ARMIES 4

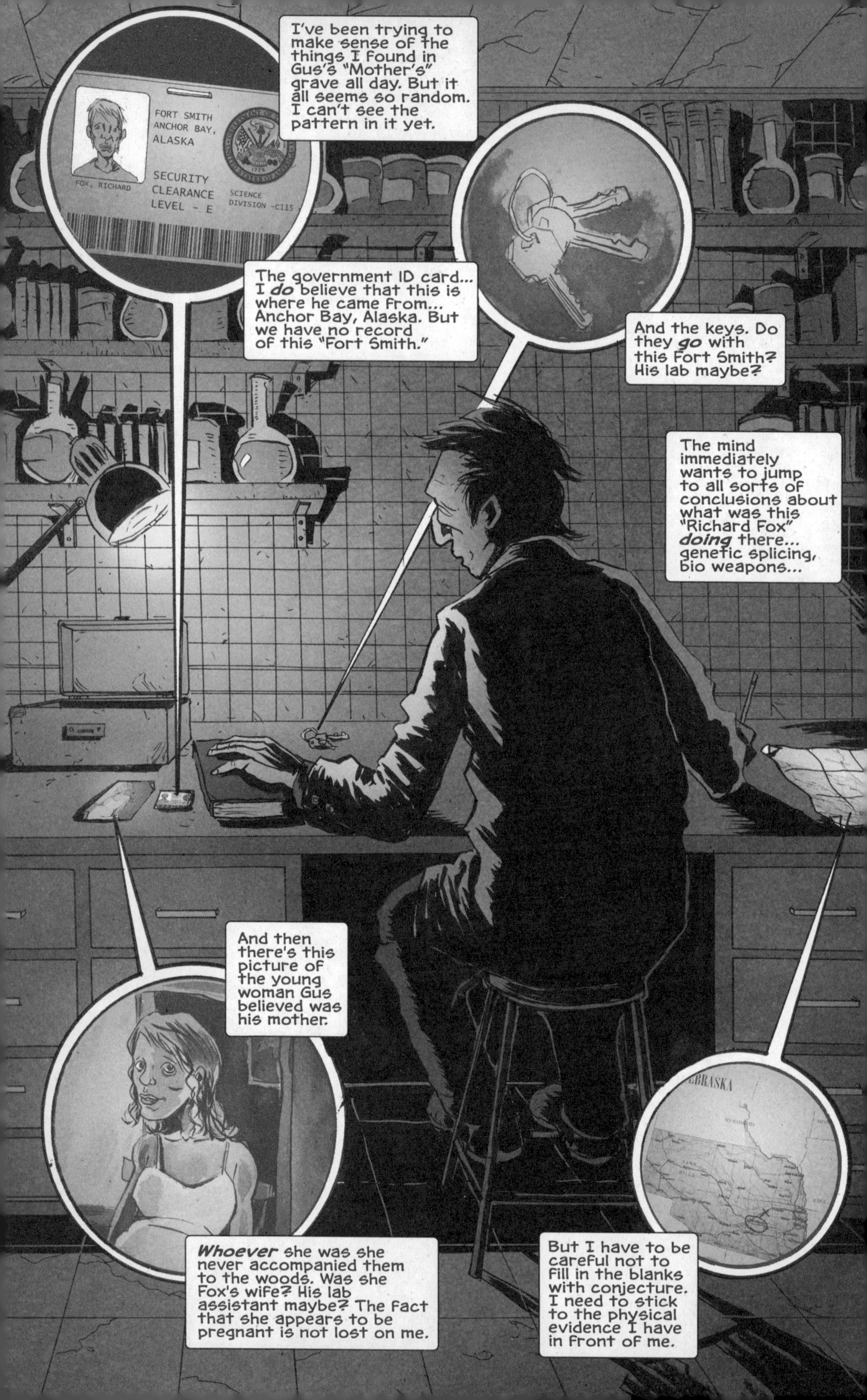

I've been trying to make sense of the things I found in Gus's "Mother's" grave all day. But it all seems so random. I can't see the pattern in it yet.
FORT SMITH ANCHOR BAY, ALASKA
SECURITY CLEARANCE LEVEL - E
SCIENCE DIVISION -C115
FOX, RICHARD
The government ID card... I *do* believe that this is where he came from... Anchor Bay, Alaska. But we have no record of this "Fort Smith."
And the keys. Do they *go* with this Fort Smith? His lab maybe?
The mind immediately wants to jump to all sorts of conclusions about what was this "Richard Fox" *doing* there... genetic splicing, bio weapons...
And then there's this picture of the young woman Gus believed was his mother.
Whoever she was she never accompanied them to the woods. Was she Fox's wife? His lab assistant maybe? The fact that she appears to be pregnant is not lost on me.
But I have to be careful not to fill in the blanks with conjecture. I need to stick to the physical evidence I have in front of me.

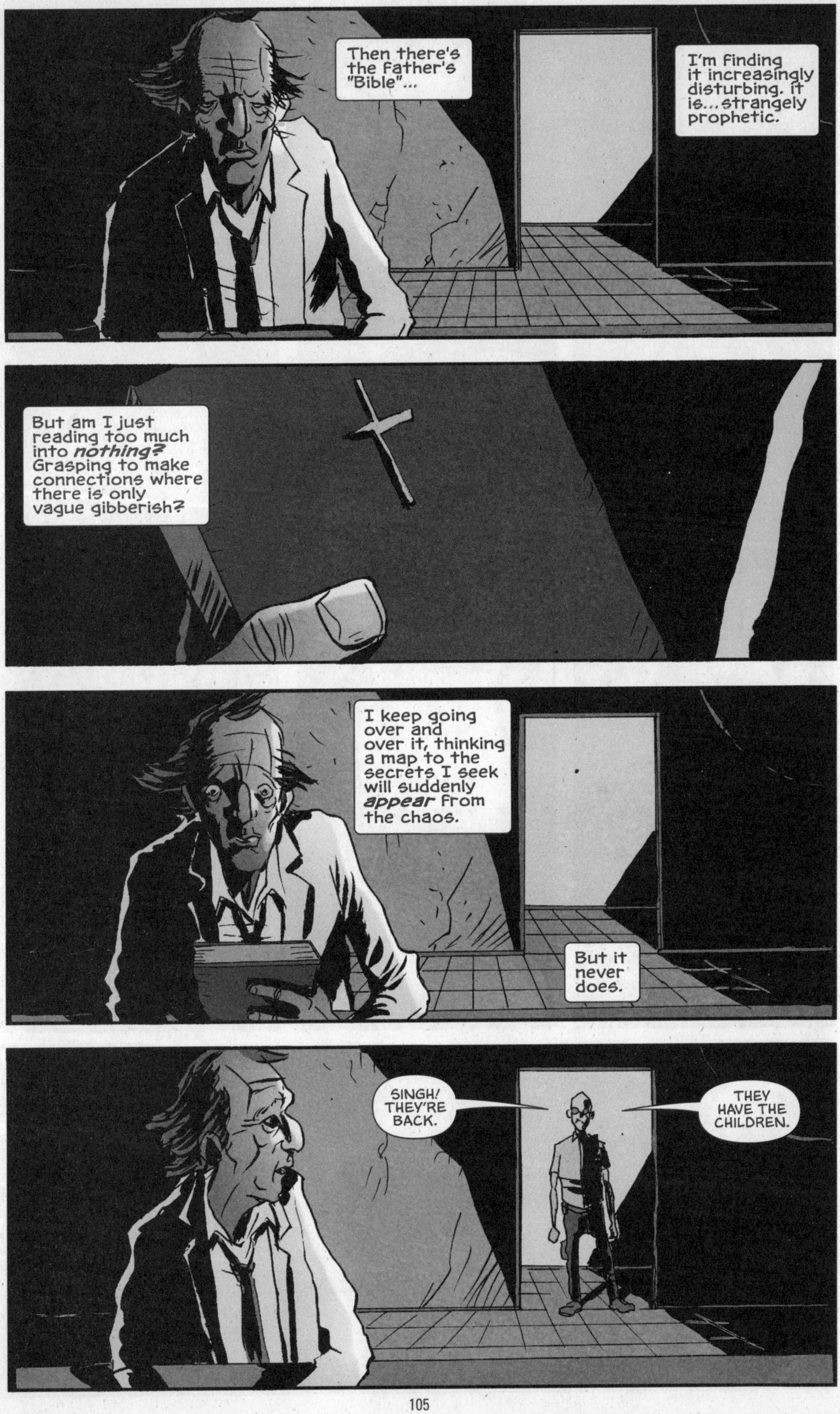
Then there's the Father's "Bible"...
I'm finding it increasingly disturbing. it is...strangely prophetic.
But am I just reading too much into *nothing?* Grasping to make connections where there is only vague gibberish?
I keep going over and over it, thinking a map to the secrets I seek will suddenly *appear* from the chaos.
But it never does.
SINGH! THEY'RE BACK.
THEY HAVE THE CHILDREN.

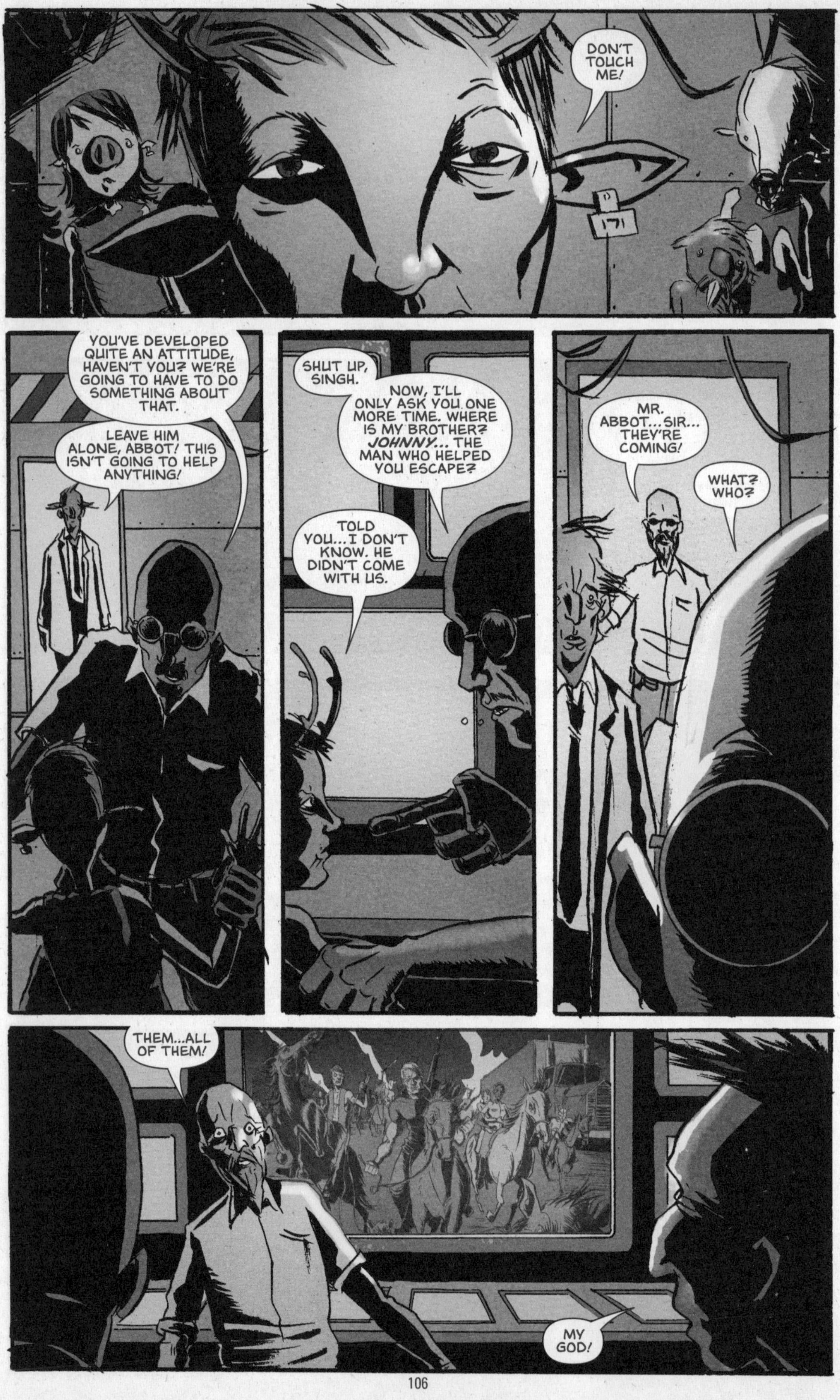
DON'T TOUCH ME!
YOU'VE DEVELOPED QUITE AN ATTITUDE, HAVEN'T YOU? WE'RE GOING TO HAVE TO DO SOMETHING ABOUT THAT.
LEAVE HIM ALONE, ABBOT! THIS ISN'T GOING TO HELP ANYTHING!
SHUT UP, SINGH.
NOW, I'LL ONLY ASK YOU ONE MORE TIME. WHERE IS MY BROTHER? *JOHNNY*... THE MAN WHO HELPED YOU ESCAPE?
TOLD YOU...I DON'T KNOW. HE DIDN'T COME WITH US.
MR. ABBOT...SIR... THEY'RE COMING!
WHAT? WHO?
THEM...ALL OF THEM!
MY GOD!

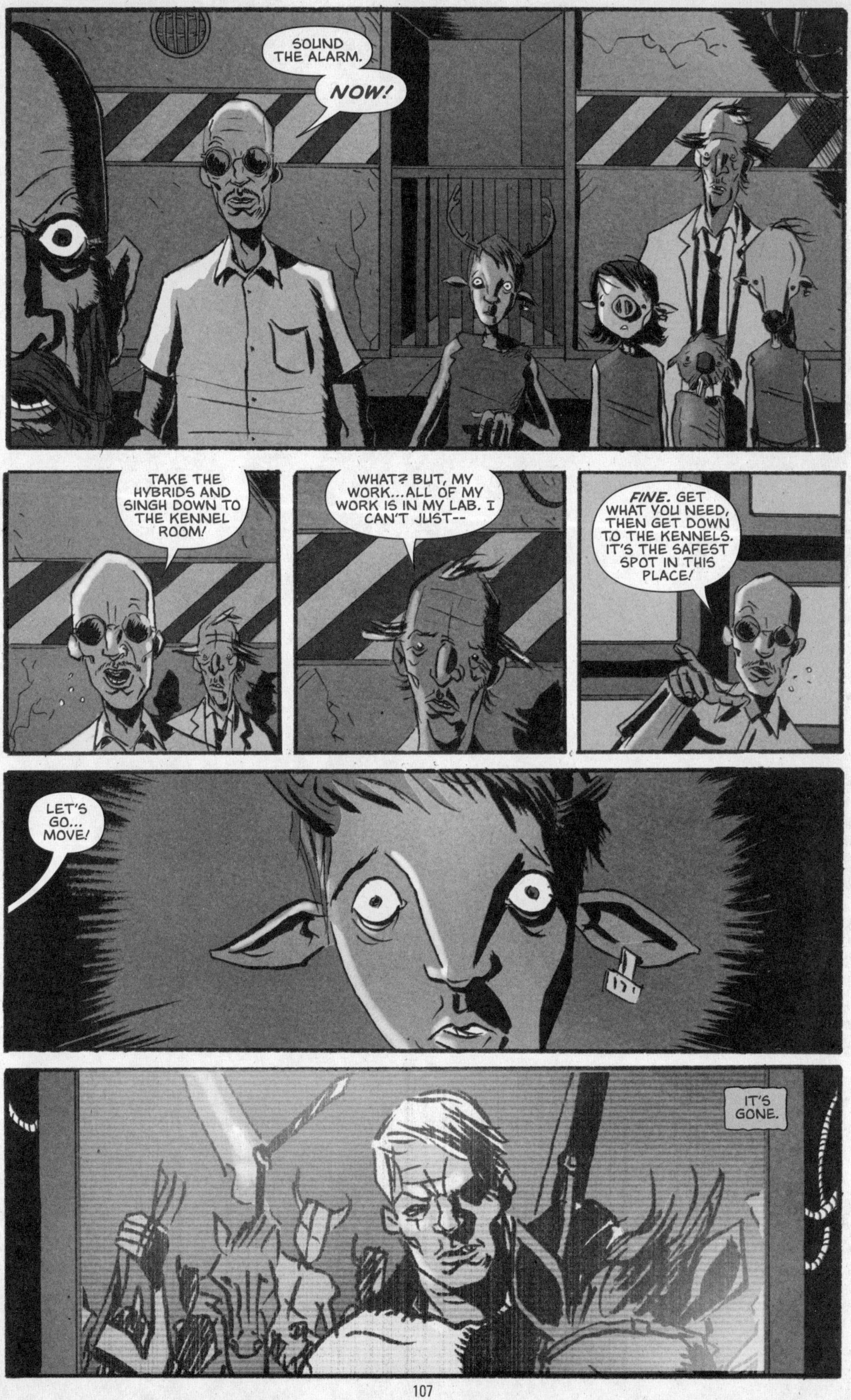
SOUND THE ALARM.
NOW!
TAKE THE HYBRIDS AND SINGH DOWN TO THE KENNEL ROOM!
WHAT? BUT, MY WORK... ALL OF MY WORK IS IN MY LAB. I CAN'T JUST--
FINE. GET WHAT YOU NEED, THEN GET DOWN TO THE KENNELS. IT'S THE SAFEST SPOT IN THIS PLACE!
LET'S GO... MOVE!
IT'S GONE.

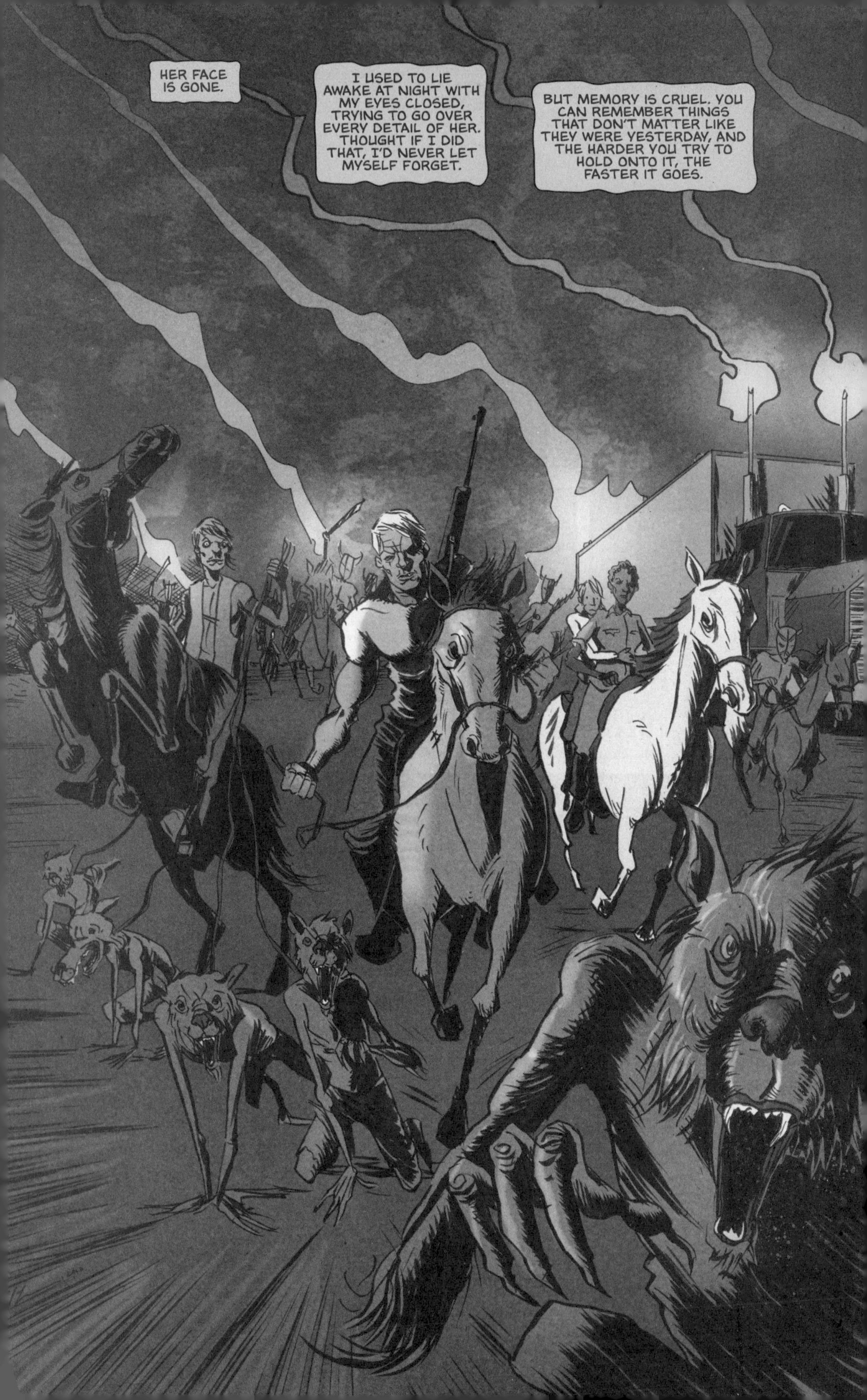
HER FACE IS GONE.
I USED TO LIE AWAKE AT NIGHT WITH MY EYES CLOSED, TRYING TO GO OVER EVERY DETAIL OF HER. THOUGHT IF I DID THAT, I'D NEVER LET MYSELF FORGET.
BUT MEMORY IS CRUEL. YOU CAN REMEMBER THINGS THAT DON'T MATTER LIKE THEY WERE YESTERDAY, AND THE HARDER YOU TRY TO HOLD ONTO IT, THE FASTER IT GOES.

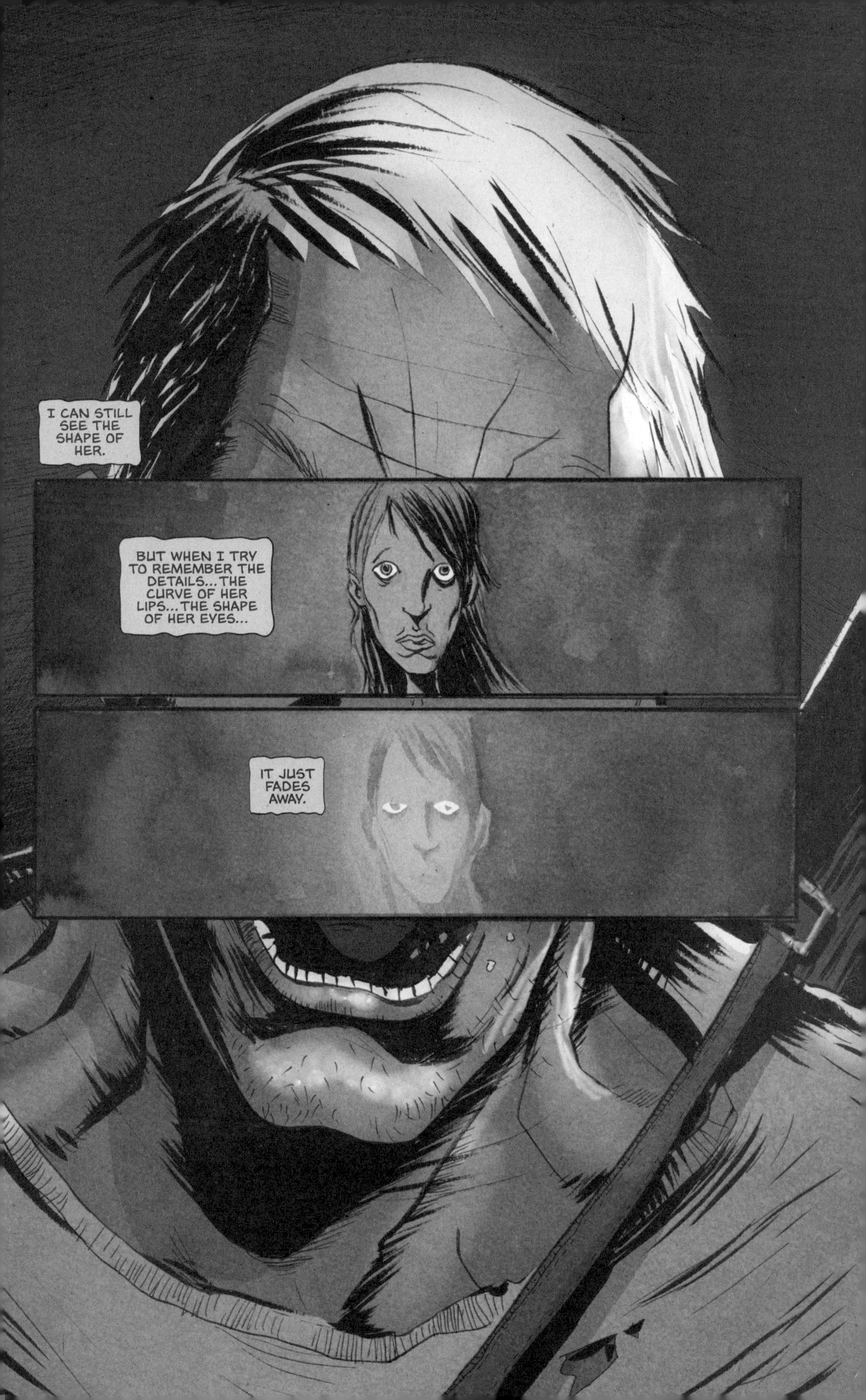
I CAN STILL SEE THE SHAPE OF HER.
BUT WHEN I TRY TO REMEMBER THE DETAILS...THE CURVE OF HER LIPS...THE SHAPE OF HER EYES...
IT JUST FADES AWAY.

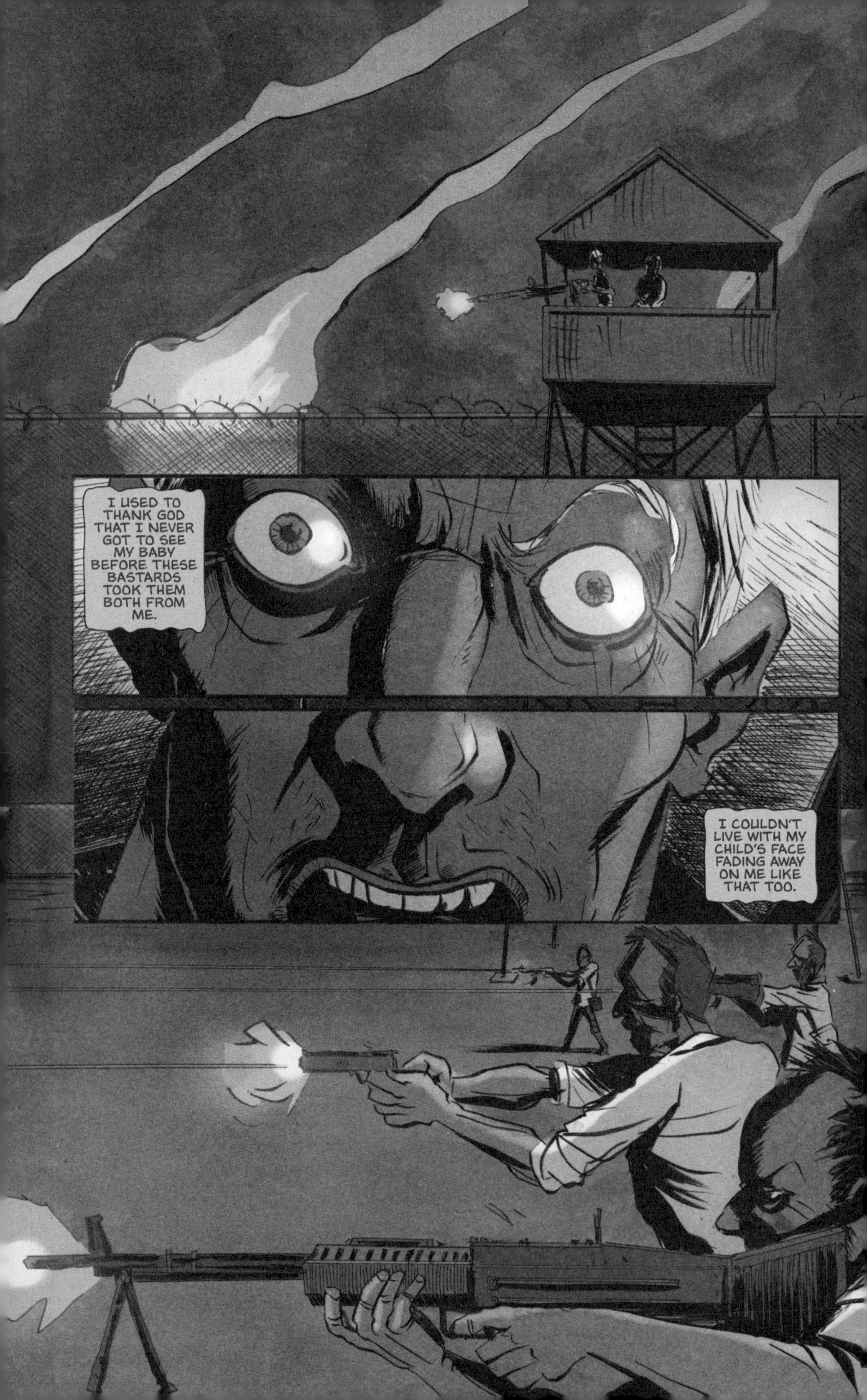
I USED TO THANK GOD THAT I NEVER GOT TO SEE MY BABY BEFORE THESE BASTARDS TOOK THEM BOTH FROM ME.
I COULDN'T LIVE WITH MY CHILD'S FACE FADING AWAY ON ME LIKE THAT TOO.

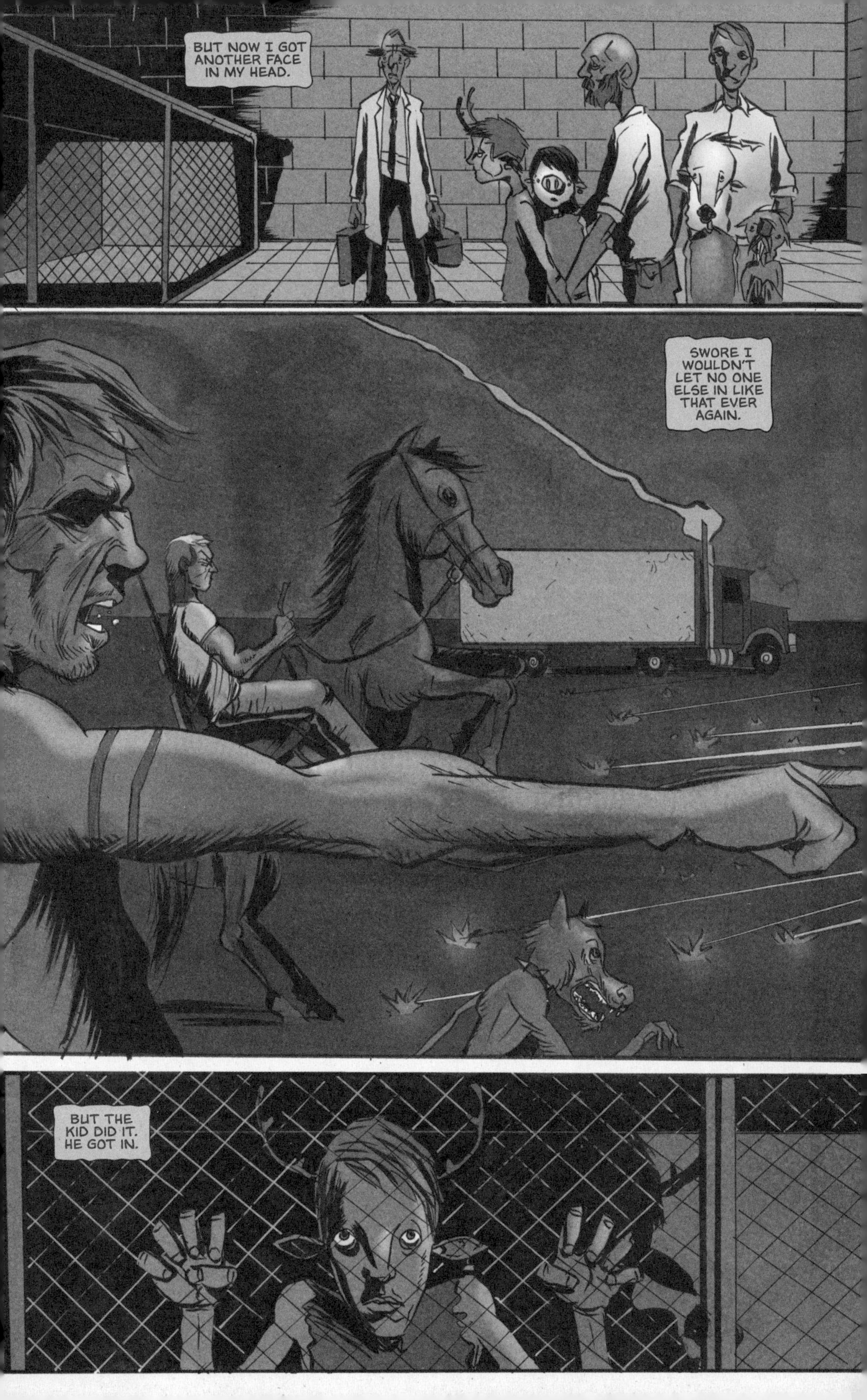
BUT NOW I GOT ANOTHER FACE IN MY HEAD.
SWORE I WOULDN'T LET NO ONE ELSE IN LIKE THAT EVER AGAIN.
BUT THE KID DID IT. HE GOT IN.

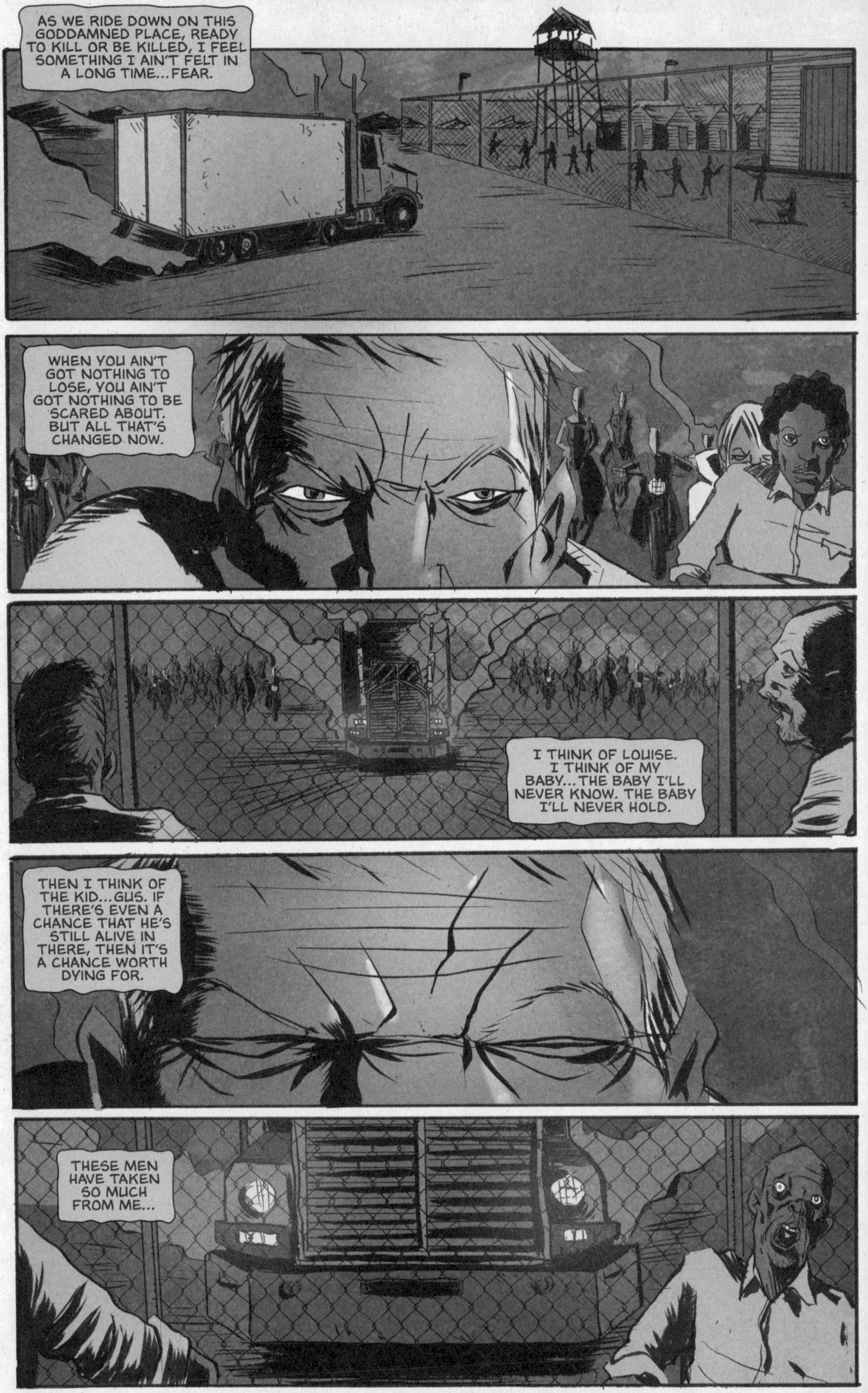
AS WE RIDE DOWN ON THIS GODDAMNED PLACE, READY TO KILL OR BE KILLED, I FEEL SOMETHING I AIN'T FELT IN A LONG TIME...FEAR.
WHEN YOU AIN'T GOT NOTHING TO LOSE, YOU AIN'T GOT NOTHING TO BE SCARED ABOUT. BUT ALL THAT'S CHANGED NOW.
I THINK OF LOUISE. I THINK OF MY BABY...THE BABY I'LL NEVER KNOW. THE BABY I'LL NEVER HOLD.
THEN I THINK OF THE KID...GUS. IF THERE'S EVEN A CHANCE THAT HE'S STILL ALIVE IN THERE, THEN IT'S A CHANCE WORTH DYING FOR.
THESE MEN HAVE TAKEN SO MUCH FROM ME...

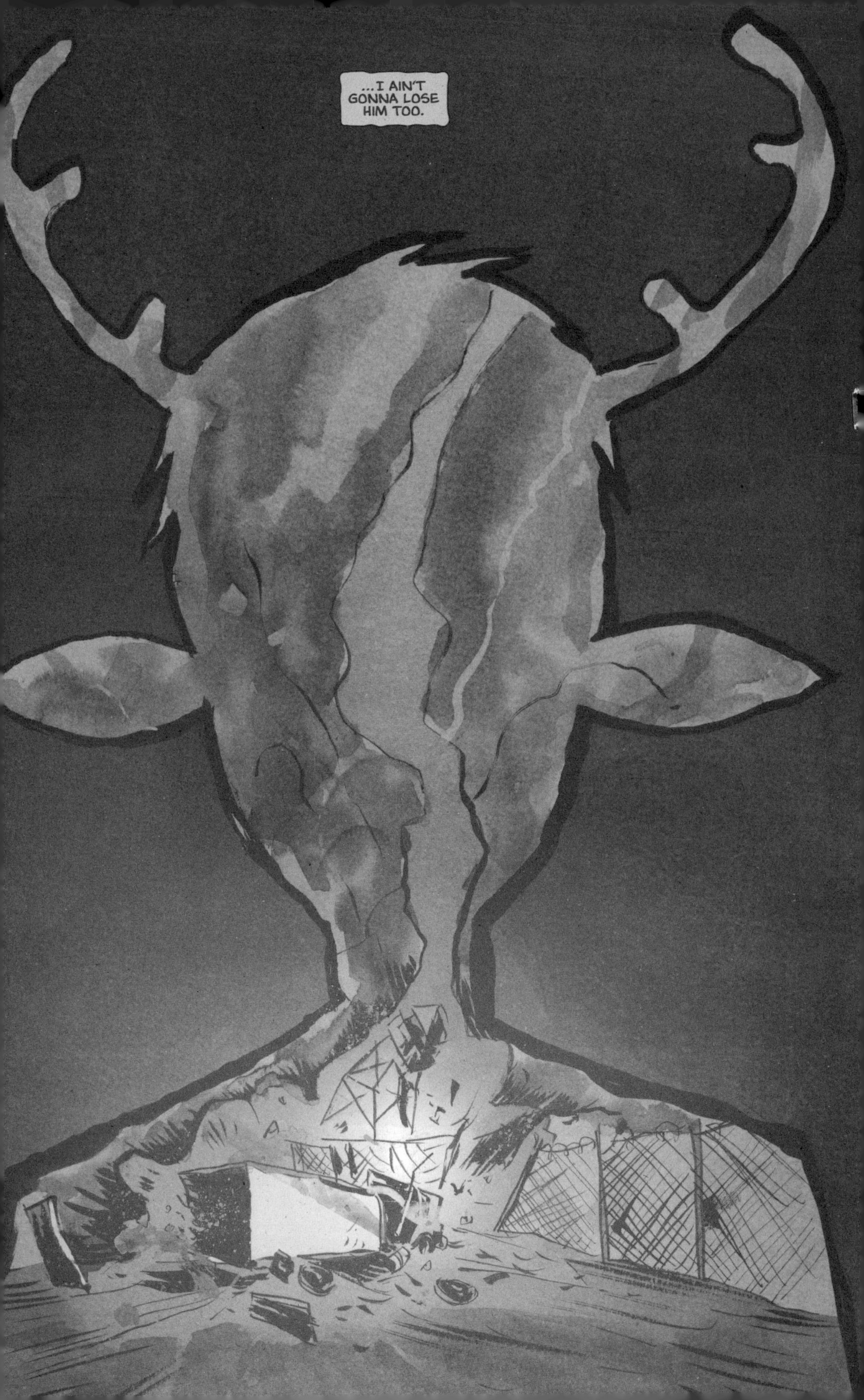
...I AIN'T GONNA LOSE HIM TOO.

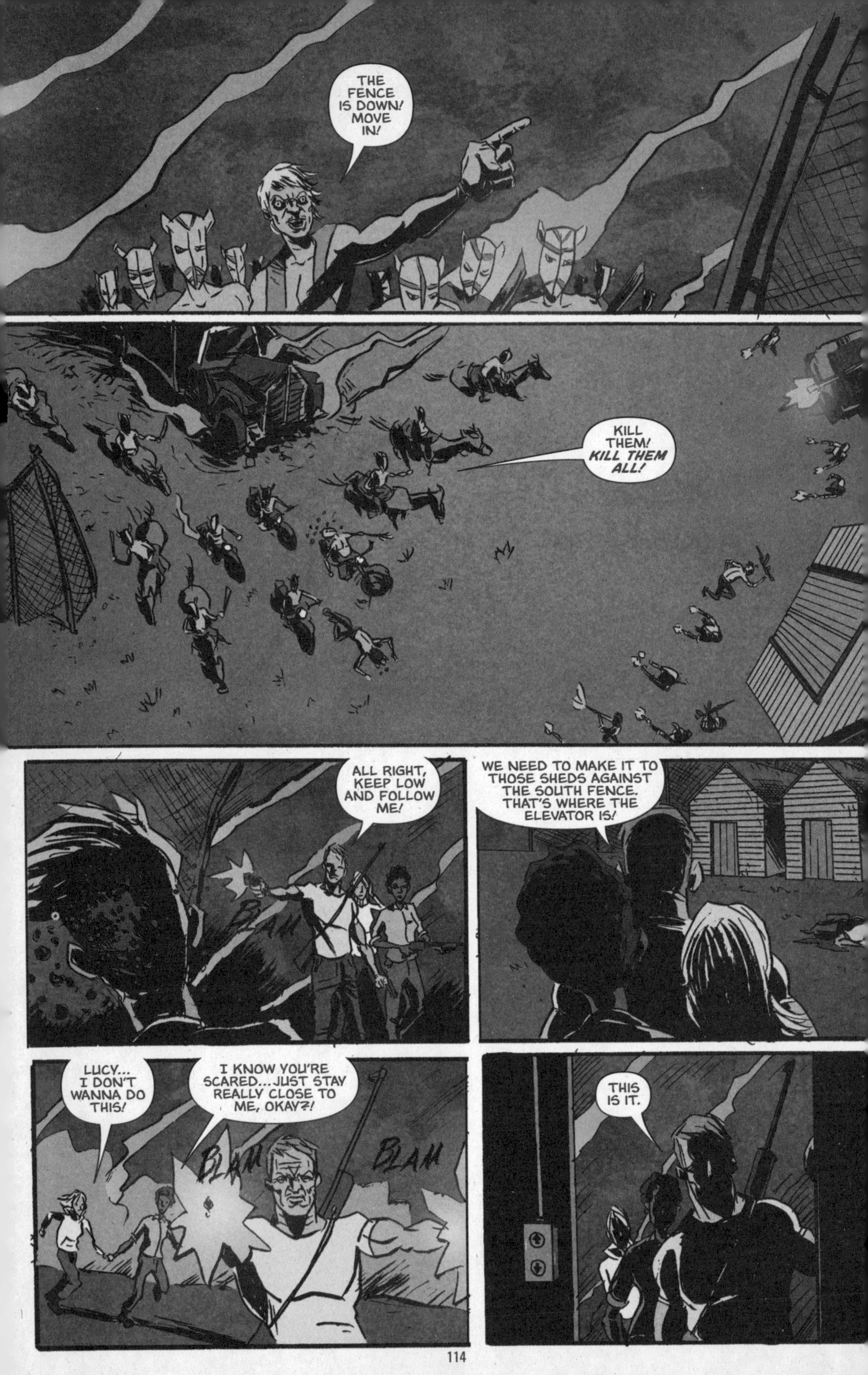
THE FENCE IS DOWN! MOVE IN!
KILL THEM! KILL THEM ALL!
ALL RIGHT, KEEP LOW AND FOLLOW ME!
BLAM
WE NEED TO MAKE IT TO THOSE SHEDS AGAINST THE SOUTH FENCE. THAT'S WHERE THE ELEVATOR IS!
LUCY... I DON'T WANNA DO THIS!
I KNOW YOU'RE SCARED... JUST STAY REALLY CLOSE TO ME, OKAY?!
BLAM
BLAM
THIS IS IT.

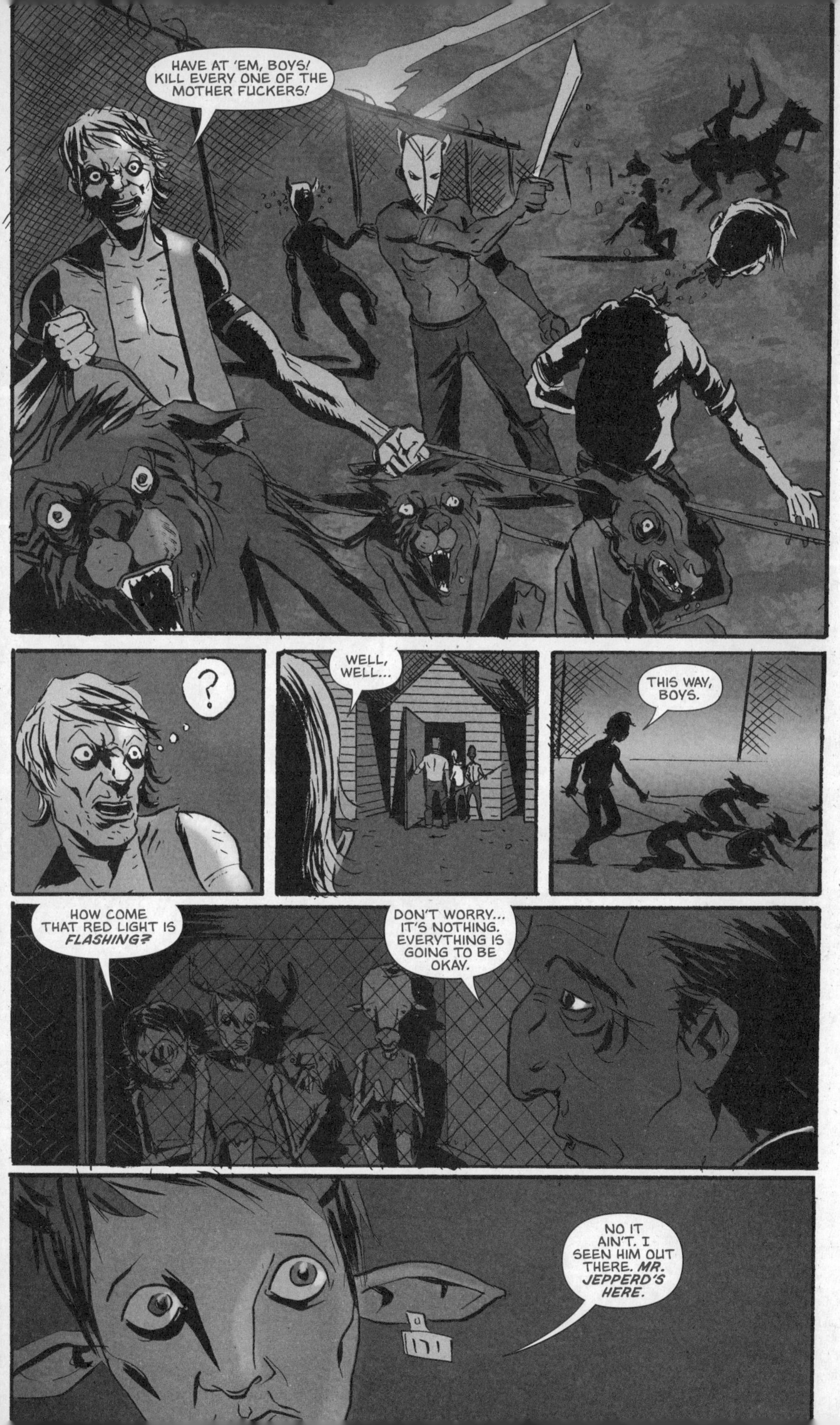
HAVE AT 'EM, BOYS! KILL EVERY ONE OF THE MOTHER FUCKERS!
?
WELL, WELL...
THIS WAY, BOYS.
HOW COME THAT RED LIGHT IS *FLASHING?*
DON'T WORRY... IT'S NOTHING. EVERYTHING IS GOING TO BE OKAY.
NO IT AIN'T. I SEEN HIM OUT THERE. *MR. JEPPERD'S HERE.*
171

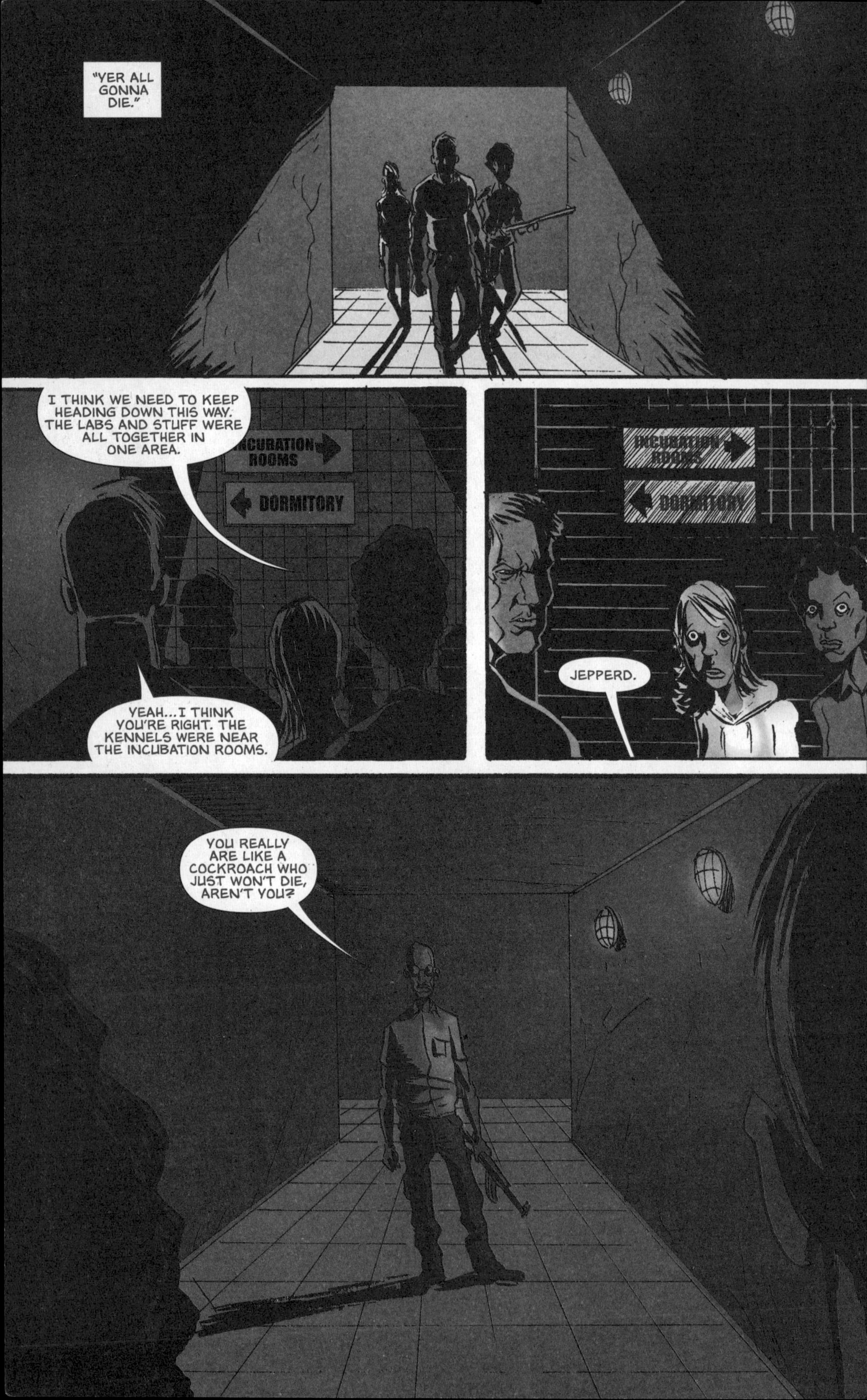
"YER ALL GONNA DIE."
I THINK WE NEED TO KEEP HEADING DOWN THIS WAY. THE LABS AND STUFF WERE ALL TOGETHER IN ONE AREA.
INCUBATION ROOMS
DORMITORY
YEAH...I THINK YOU'RE RIGHT. THE KENNELS WERE NEAR THE INCUBATION ROOMS.
INCUBATION ROOMS
DORMITORY
JEPPERD.
YOU REALLY ARE LIKE A COCKROACH WHO JUST WON'T DIE, AREN'T YOU?

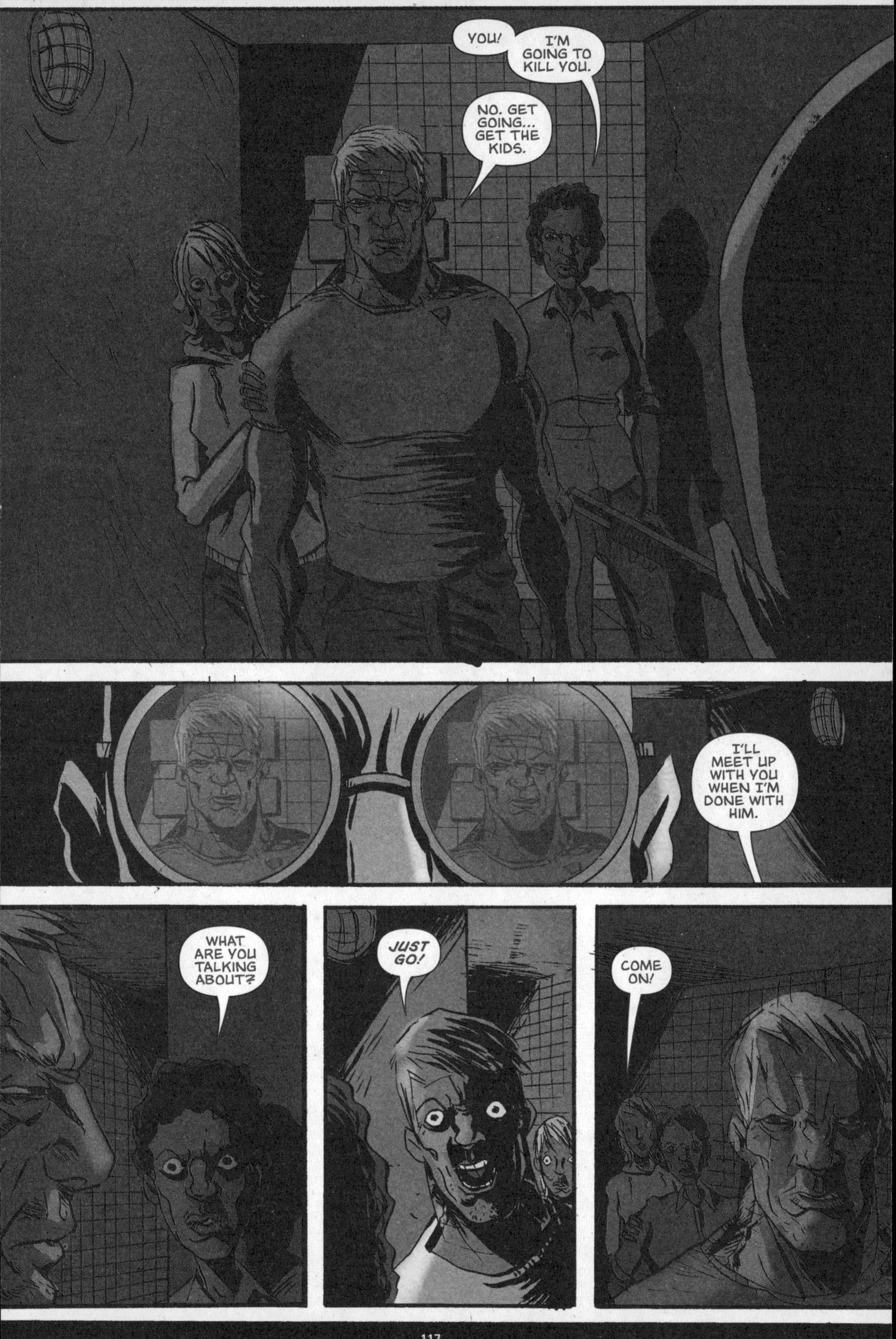
YOU!
I'M GOING TO KILL YOU.
NO. GET GOING... GET THE KIDS.
I'LL MEET UP WITH YOU WHEN I'M DONE WITH HIM.
WHAT ARE YOU TALKING ABOUT?
JUST GO!
COME ON!

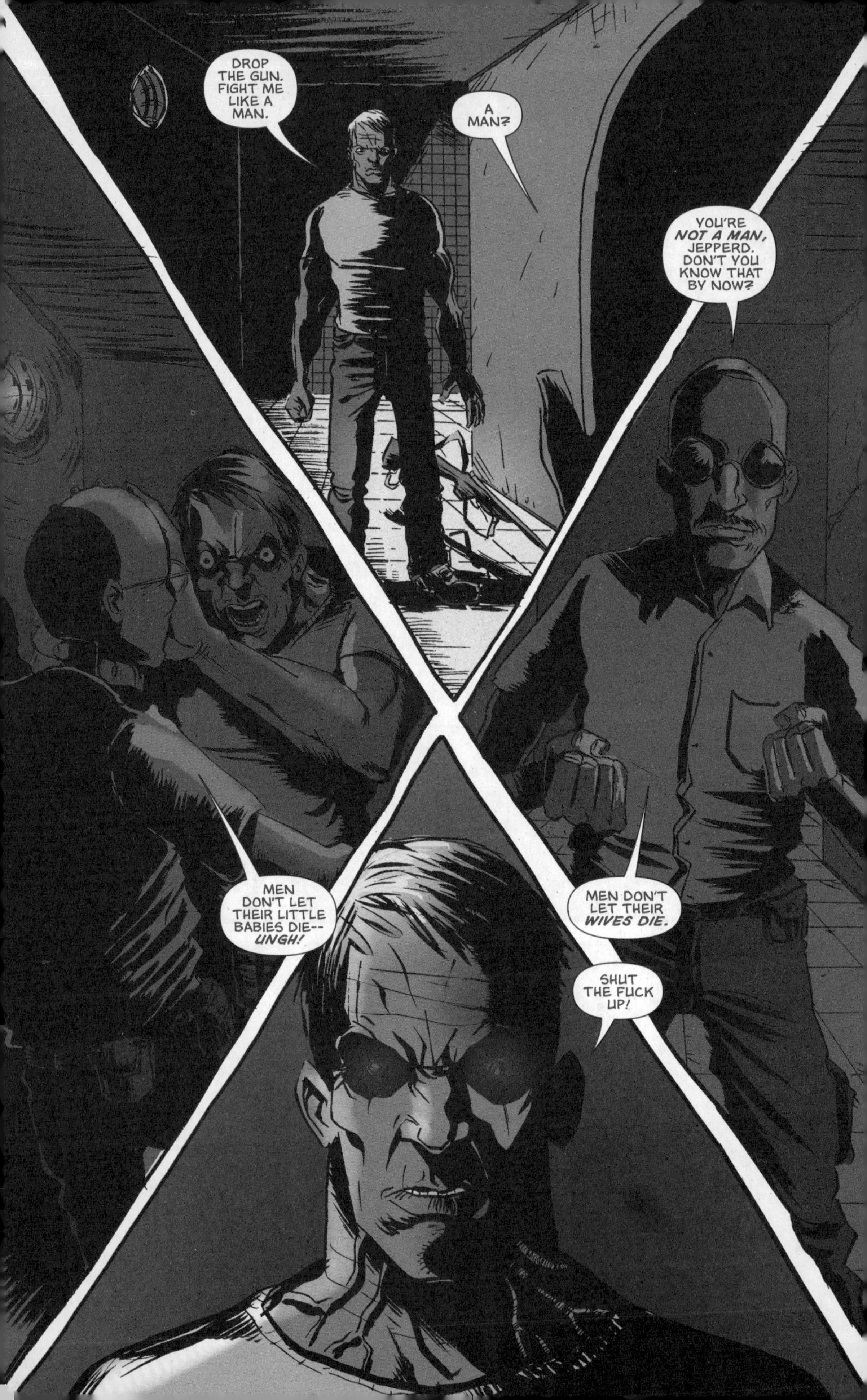
DROP THE GUN. FIGHT ME LIKE A MAN.
A MAN?
YOU'RE NOT A MAN, JEPPERD. DON'T YOU KNOW THAT BY NOW?
MEN DON'T LET THEIR LITTLE BABIES DIE-- UNGH!
MEN DON'T LET THEIR WIVES DIE.
SHUT THE FUCK UP!

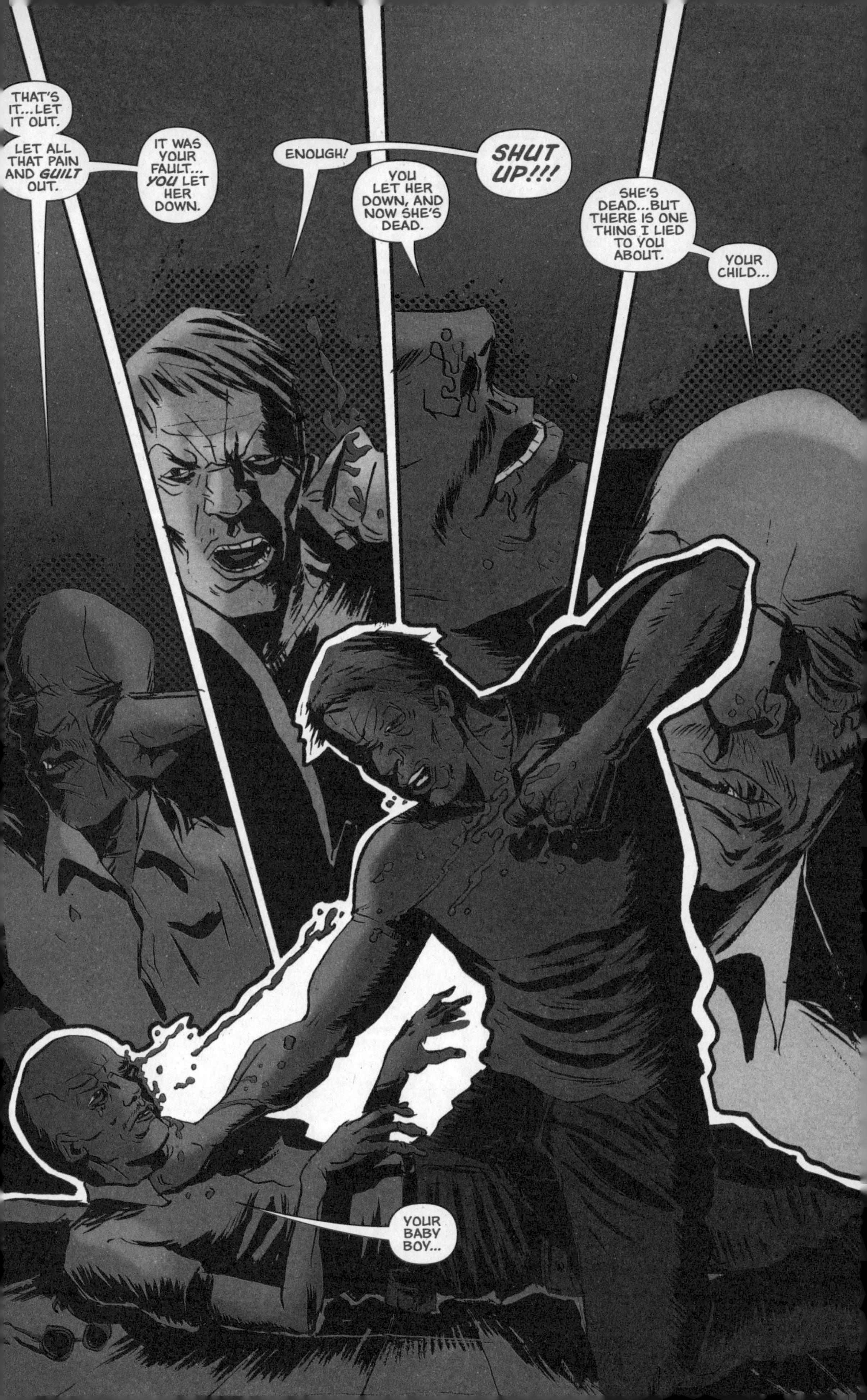
THAT'S IT...LET IT OUT.
LET ALL THAT PAIN AND *GUILT* OUT.
IT WAS YOUR FAULT... *YOU* LET HER DOWN.
ENOUGH!
YOU LET HER DOWN, AND NOW SHE'S DEAD.
SHUT UP!!!
SHE'S DEAD...BUT THERE IS ONE THING I LIED TO YOU ABOUT.
YOUR CHILD...
YOUR BABY BOY...

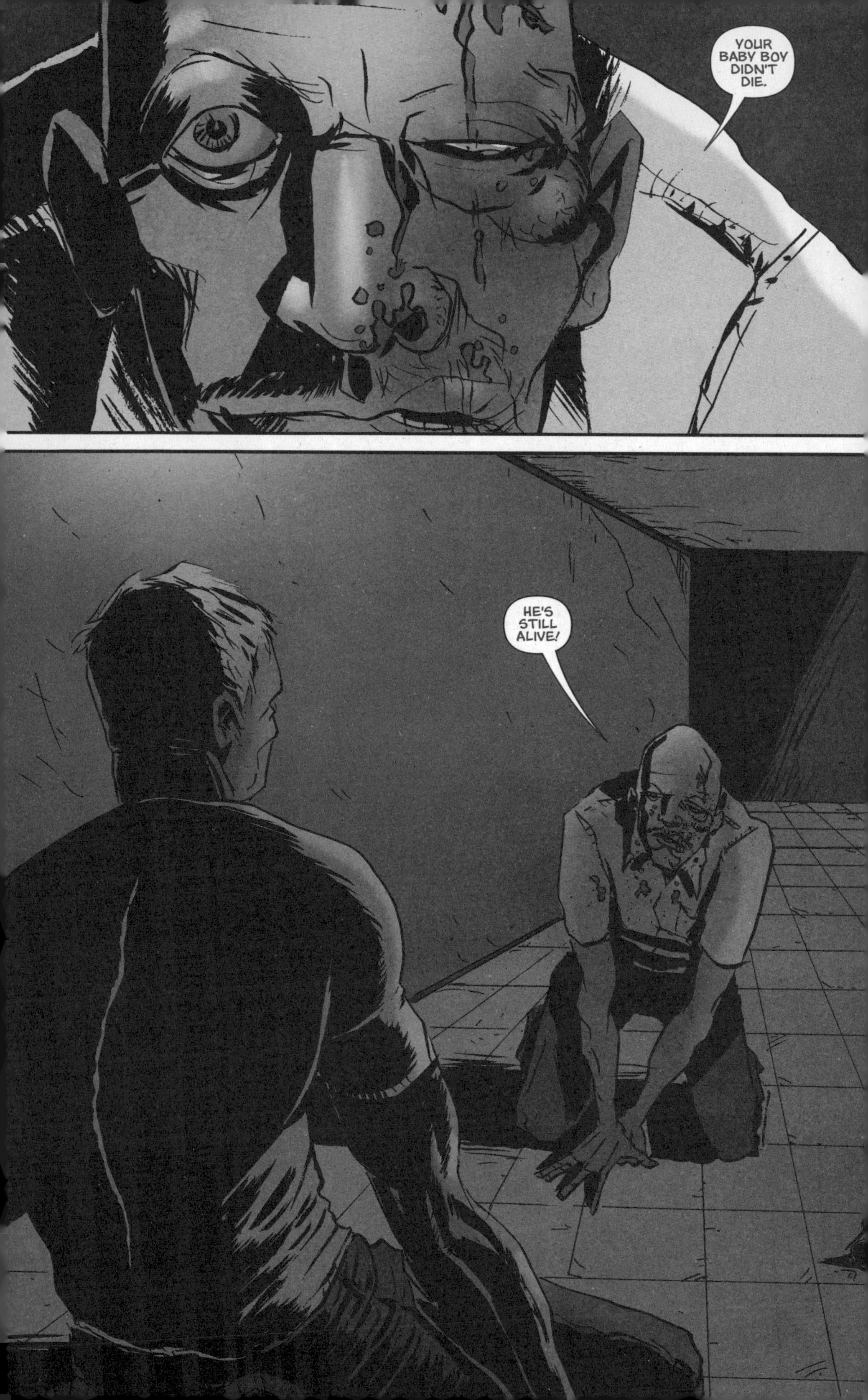
YOUR BABY BOY DIDN'T DIE.
HE'S STILL ALIVE!

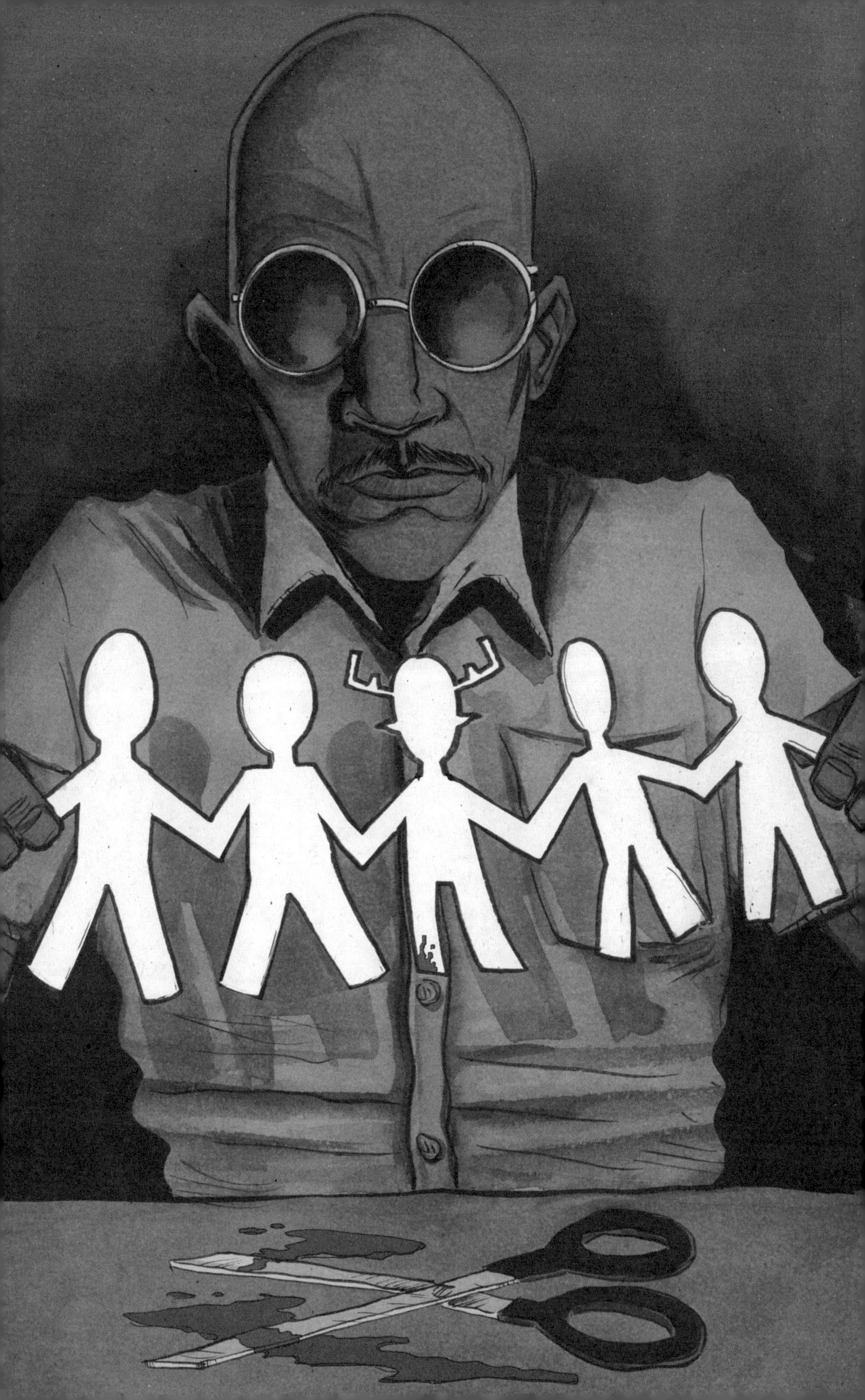

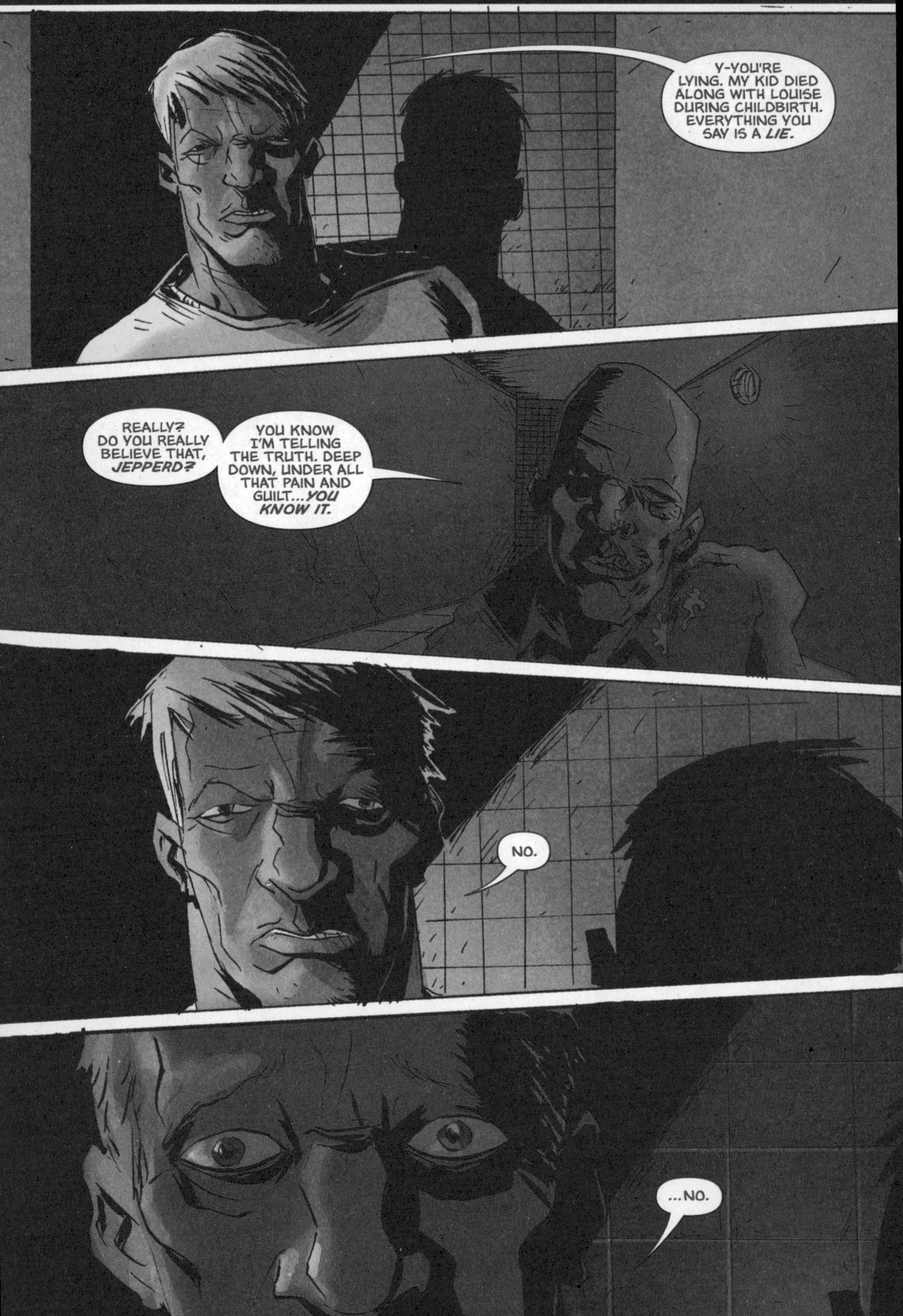
Y-YOU'RE LYING. MY KID DIED ALONG WITH LOUISE DURING CHILDBIRTH. EVERYTHING YOU SAY IS A *LIE*.
REALLY? DO YOU REALLY BELIEVE THAT, *JEPPERD?*
YOU KNOW I'M TELLING THE TRUTH. DEEP DOWN, UNDER ALL THAT PAIN AND GUILT... *YOU KNOW IT.*
NO.
...NO.

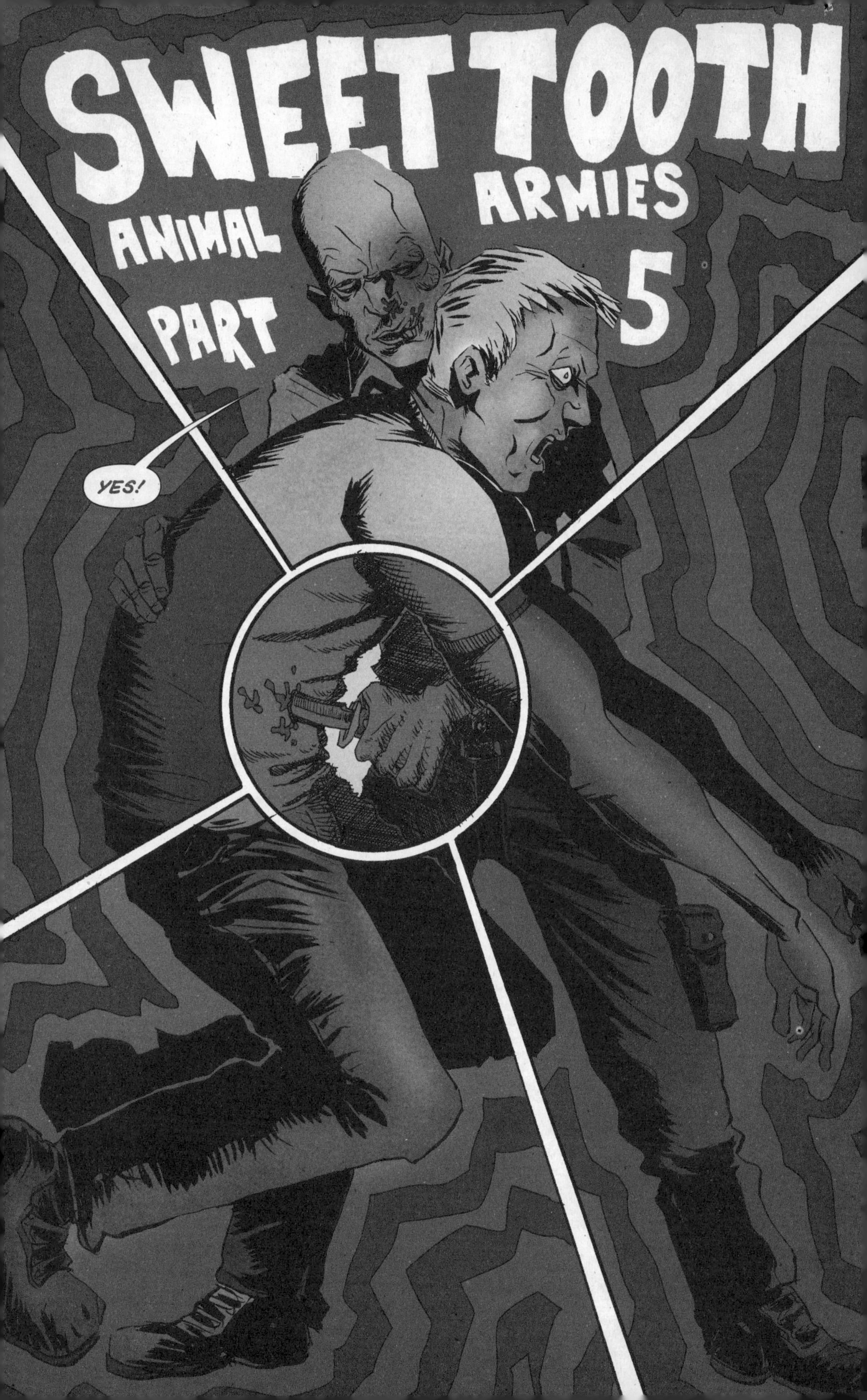
SWEET TOOTH
ANIMAL ARMIES
PART 5
YES!

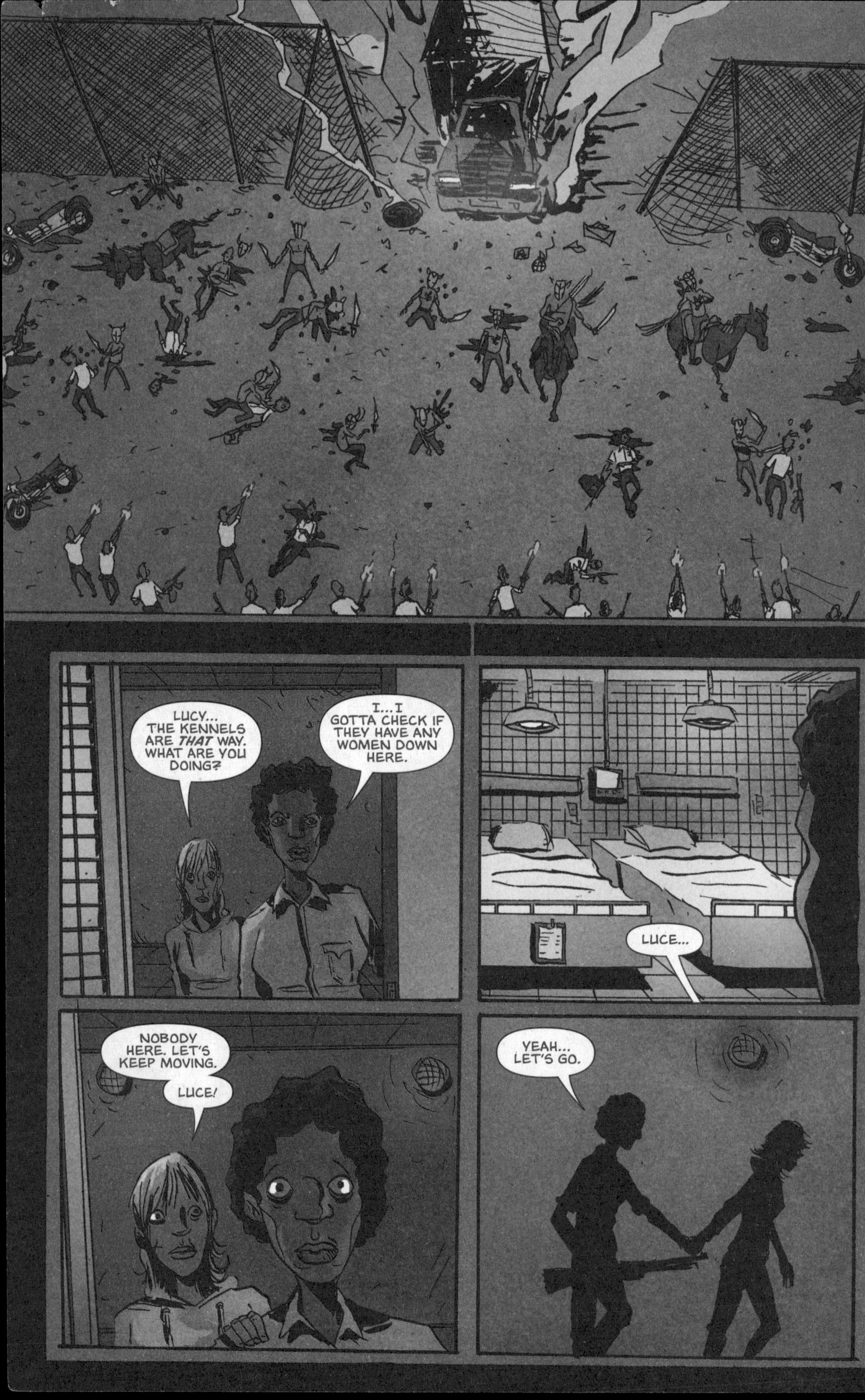
LUCY... THE KENNELS ARE *THAT* WAY. WHAT ARE YOU DOING?
I...I GOTTA CHECK IF THEY HAVE ANY WOMEN DOWN HERE.
LUCE...
NOBODY HERE. LET'S KEEP MOVING.
LUCE!
YEAH... LET'S GO.

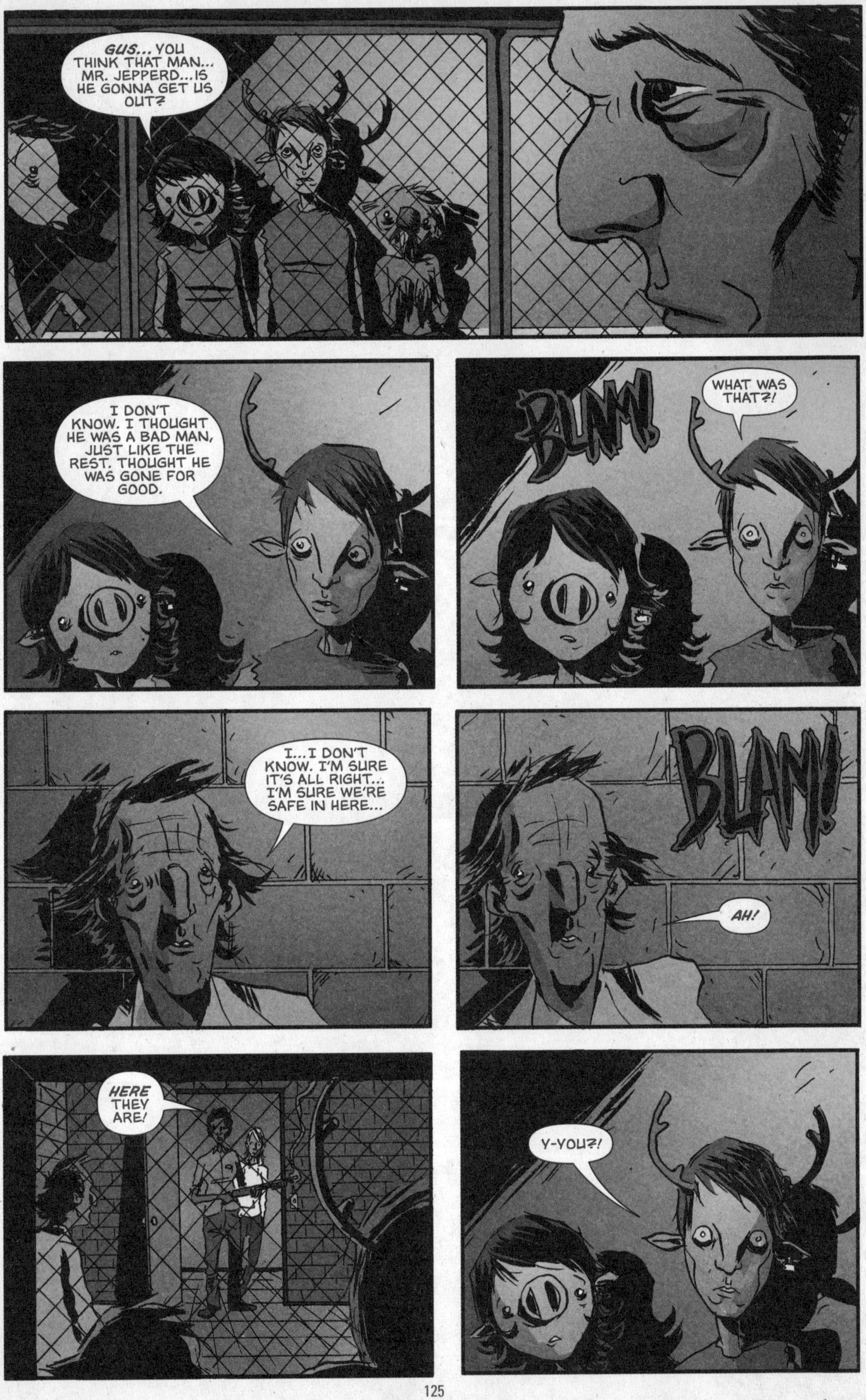
GUS... YOU THINK THAT MAN... MR. JEPPERD...IS HE GONNA GET US OUT?
I DON'T KNOW. I THOUGHT HE WAS A BAD MAN, JUST LIKE THE REST. THOUGHT HE WAS GONE FOR GOOD.
BLAM!
WHAT WAS THAT?!
I...I DON'T KNOW. I'M SURE IT'S ALL RIGHT... I'M SURE WE'RE SAFE IN HERE...
BLAM!
AH!
HERE THEY ARE!
Y-YOU?!

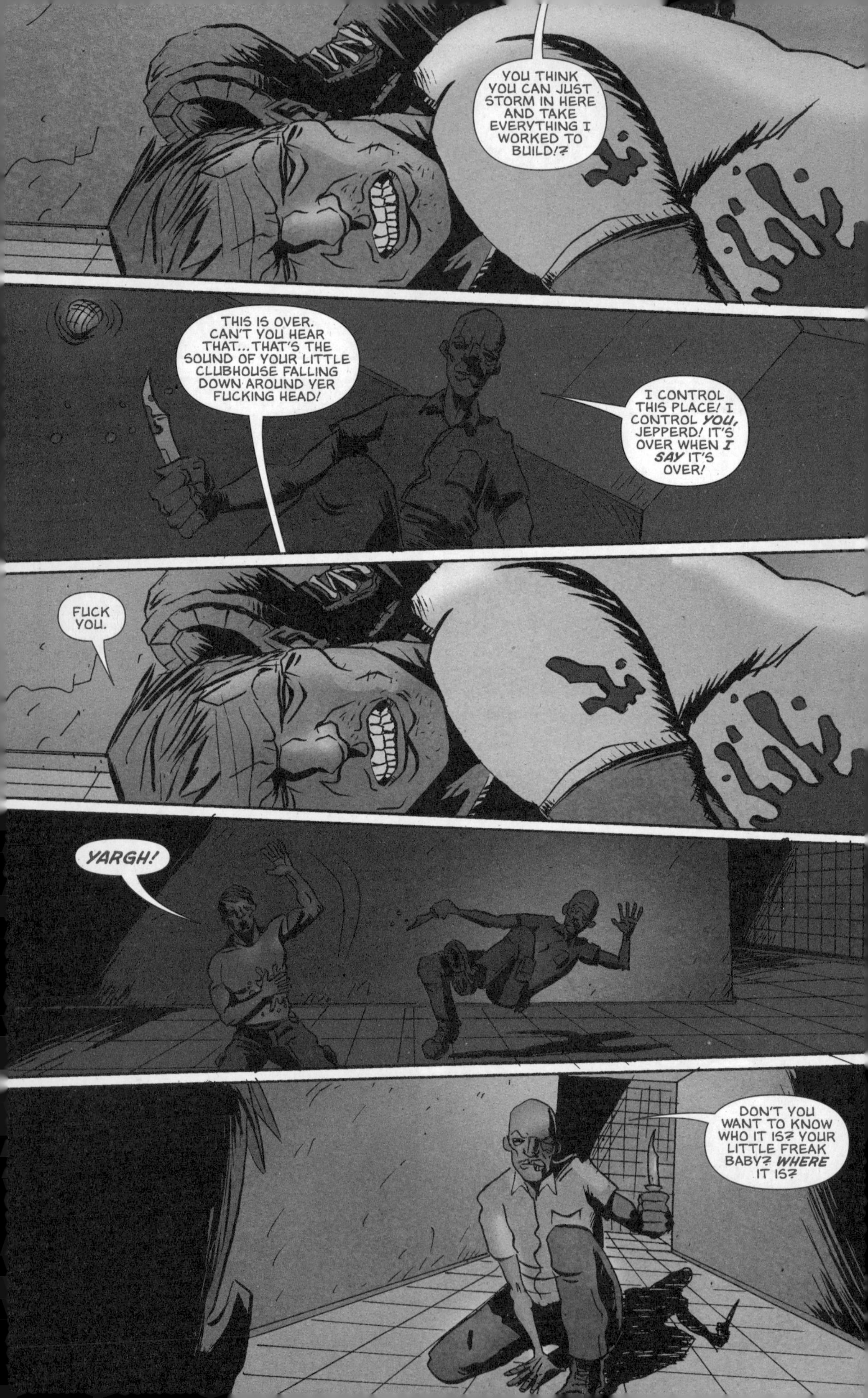
YOU THINK YOU CAN JUST STORM IN HERE AND TAKE EVERYTHING I WORKED TO BUILD!?
THIS IS OVER. CAN'T YOU HEAR THAT...THAT'S THE SOUND OF YOUR LITTLE CLUBHOUSE FALLING DOWN AROUND YER FUCKING HEAD!
I CONTROL THIS PLACE! I CONTROL YOU, JEPPERD! IT'S OVER WHEN I SAY IT'S OVER!
FUCK YOU.
YARGH!
DON'T YOU WANT TO KNOW WHO IT IS? YOUR LITTLE FREAK BABY? WHERE IT IS?

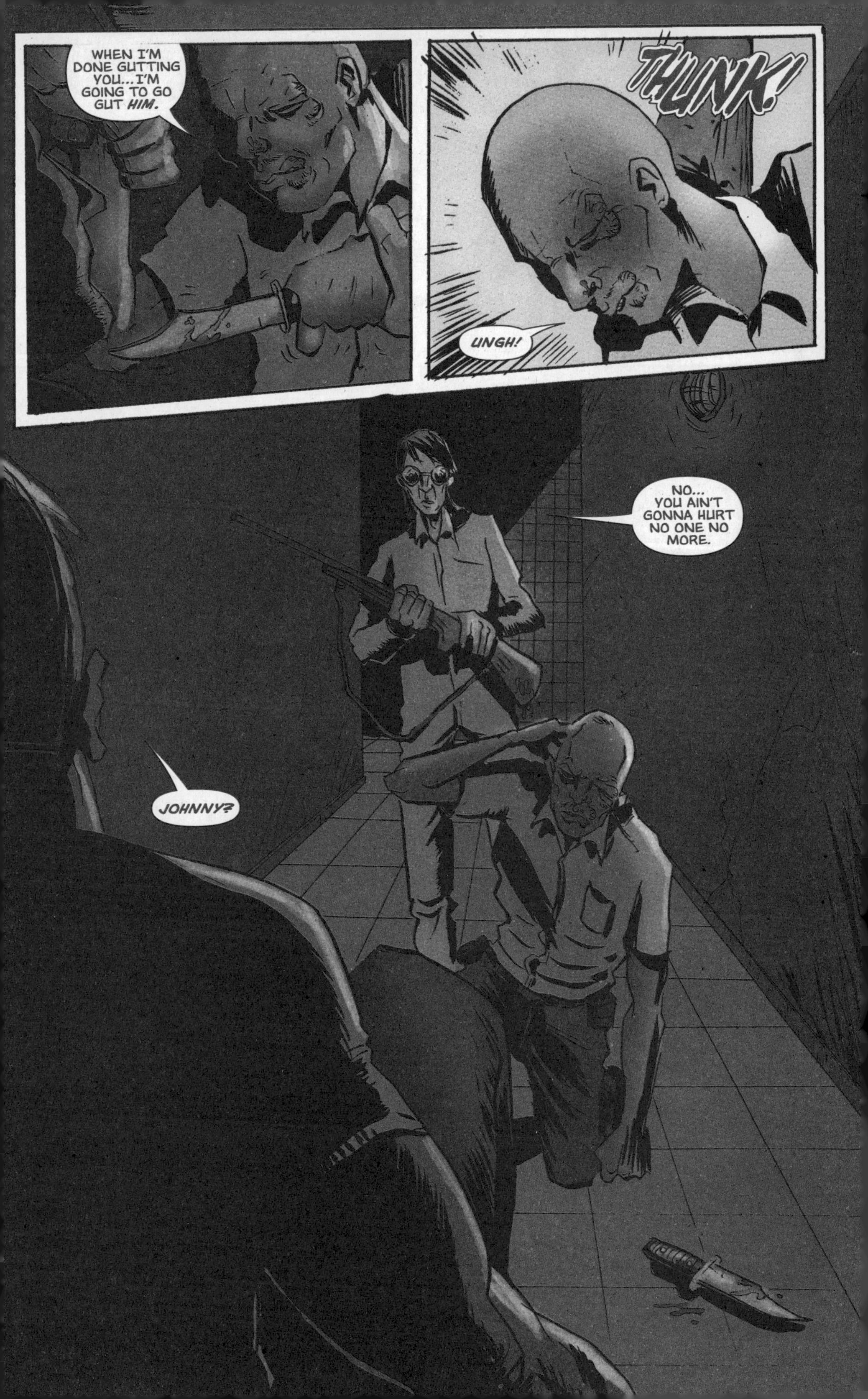
WHEN I'M DONE GUTTING YOU...I'M GOING TO GO GUT *HIM*.
THUNK!
UNGH!
NO... YOU AIN'T GONNA HURT NO ONE NO MORE.
JOHNNY?

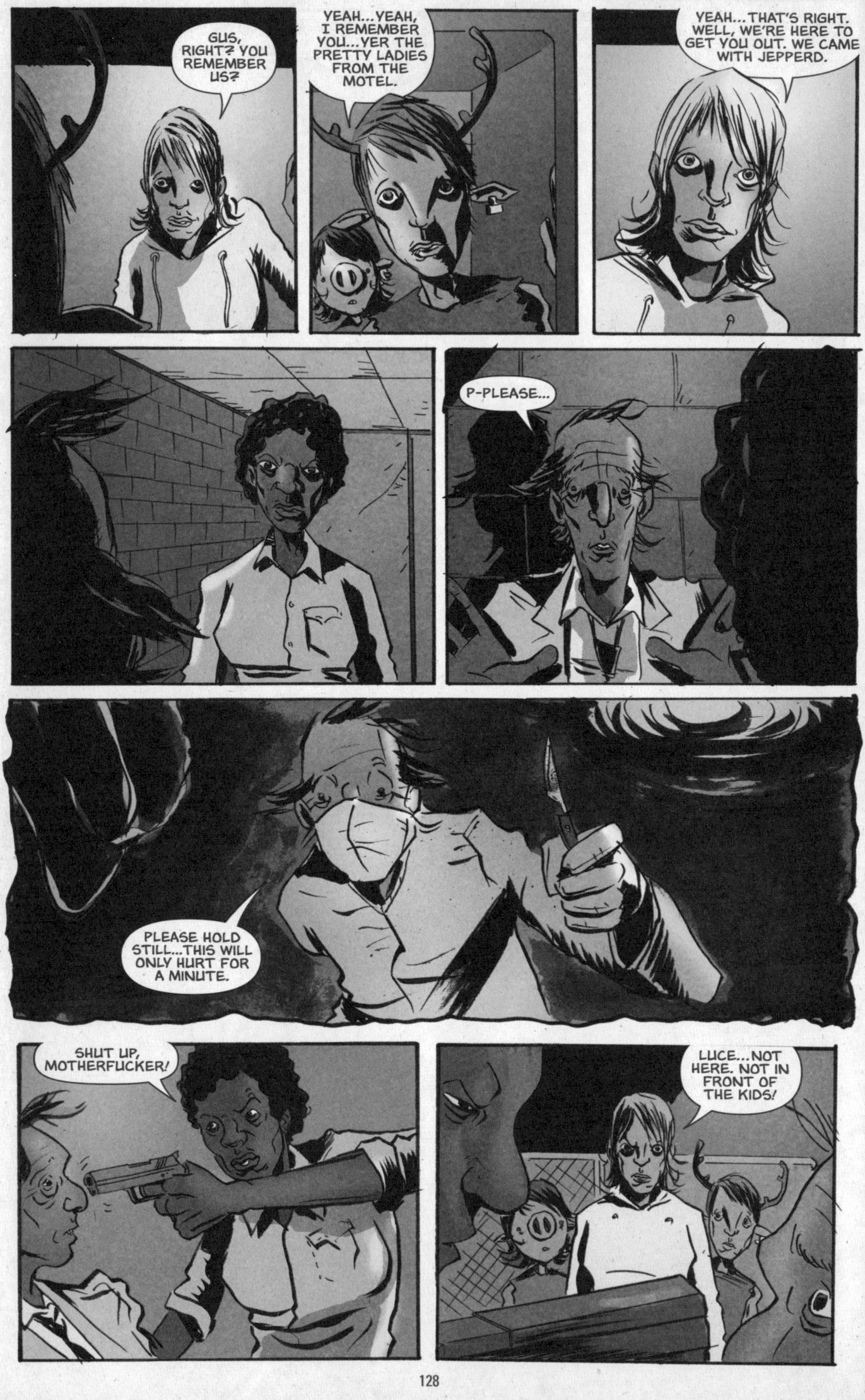
GUS, RIGHT? YOU REMEMBER US?
YEAH... YEAH, I REMEMBER YOU... YER THE PRETTY LADIES FROM THE MOTEL.
YEAH... THAT'S RIGHT. WELL, WE'RE HERE TO GET YOU OUT. WE CAME WITH JEPPERD.
P-PLEASE...
PLEASE HOLD STILL... THIS WILL ONLY HURT FOR A MINUTE.
SHUT UP, MOTHERFUCKER!
LUCE... NOT HERE. NOT IN FRONT OF THE KIDS!

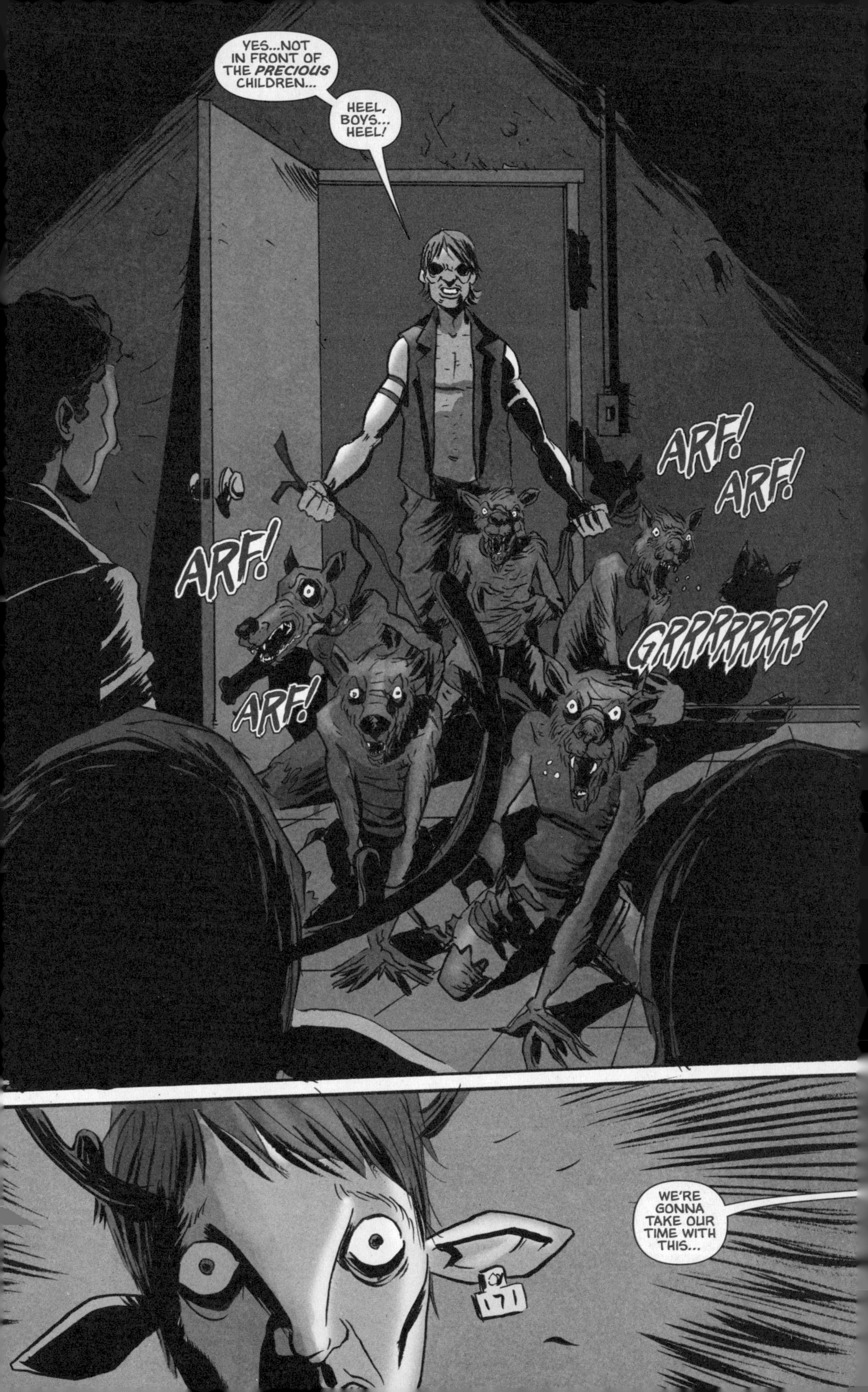
YES...NOT IN FRONT OF THE *PRECIOUS* CHILDREN...
HEEL, BOYS... HEEL!
ARF!
ARF!
ARF!
ARF!
GRRRRRRRR!
171
WE'RE GONNA TAKE OUR TIME WITH THIS...

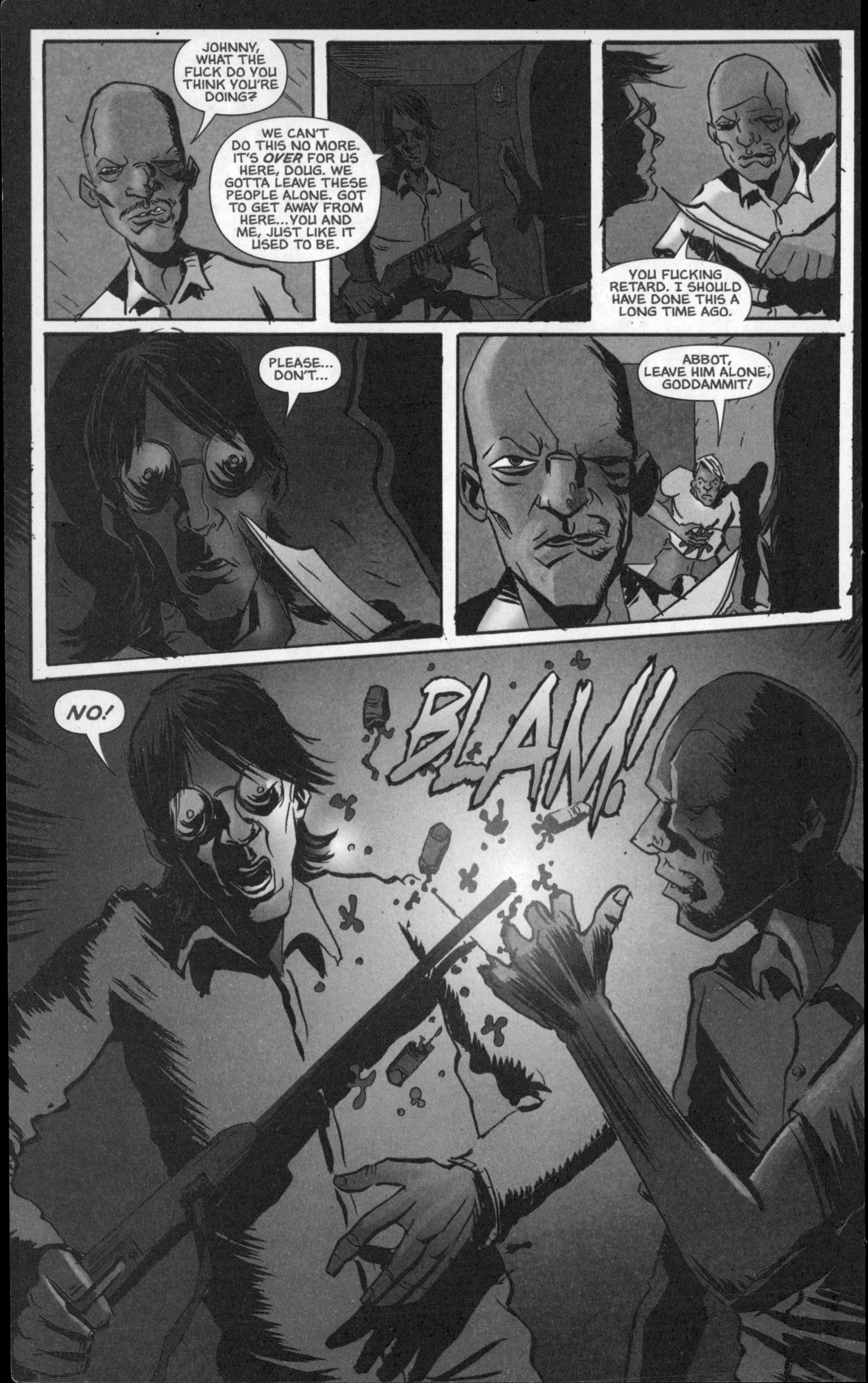

JOHNNY, WHAT THE FUCK DO YOU THINK YOU'RE DOING?
WE CAN'T DO THIS NO MORE. IT'S *OVER* FOR US HERE, DOUG. WE GOTTA LEAVE THESE PEOPLE ALONE. GOT TO GET AWAY FROM HERE...YOU AND ME, JUST LIKE IT USED TO BE.
YOU FUCKING RETARD. I SHOULD HAVE DONE THIS A LONG TIME AGO.
PLEASE... DON'T...
ABBOT, LEAVE HIM ALONE, GODDAMMIT!
NO!
BLAM!

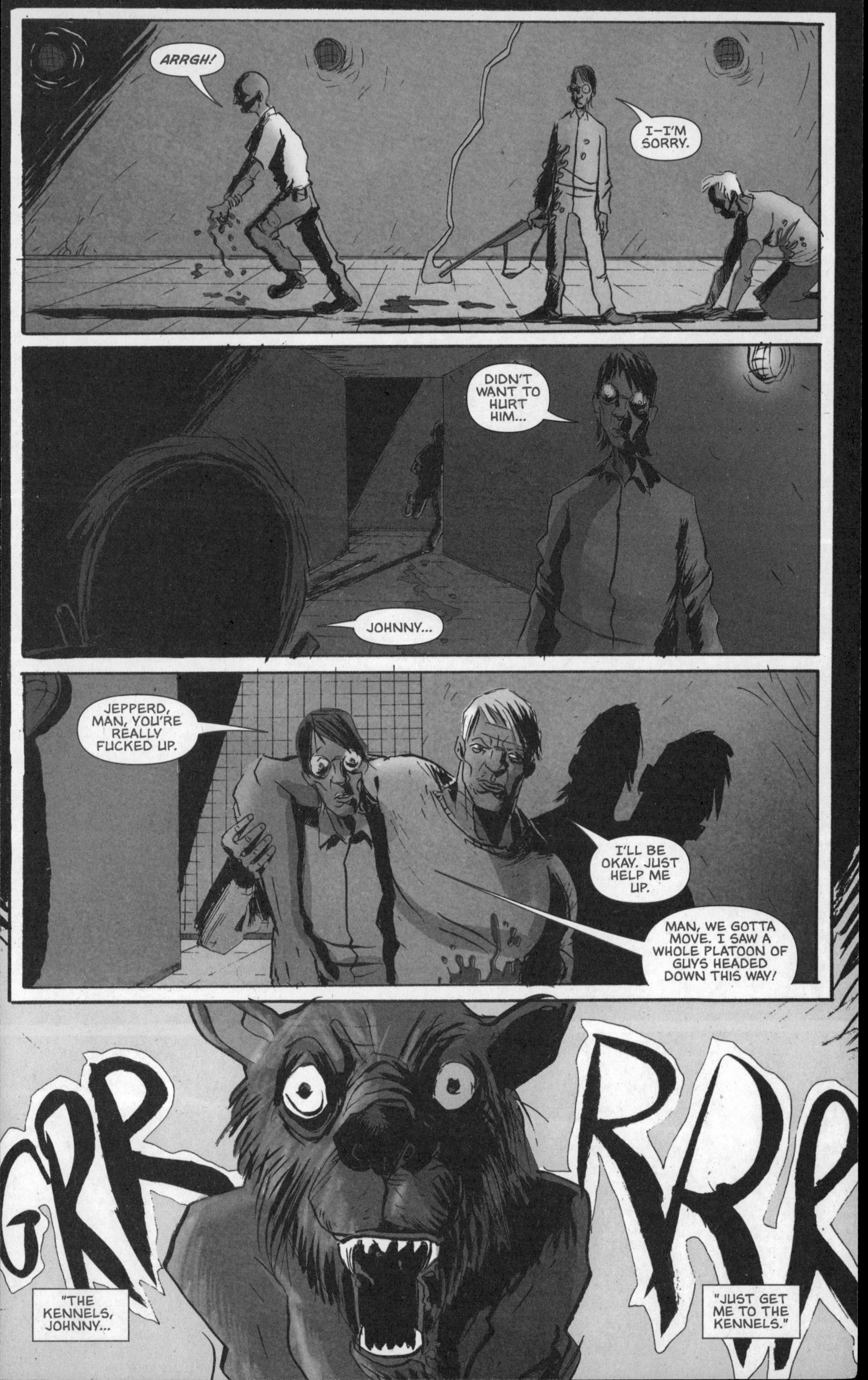
ARRGH!
I--I'M SORRY.
DIDN'T WANT TO HURT HIM...
JOHNNY...
JEPPERD, MAN, YOU'RE REALLY FUCKED UP.
I'LL BE OKAY. JUST HELP ME UP.
MAN, WE GOTTA MOVE. I SAW A WHOLE PLATOON OF GUYS HEADED DOWN THIS WAY!
GRRRRR
"THE KENNELS, JOHNNY...
"JUST GET ME TO THE KENNELS."

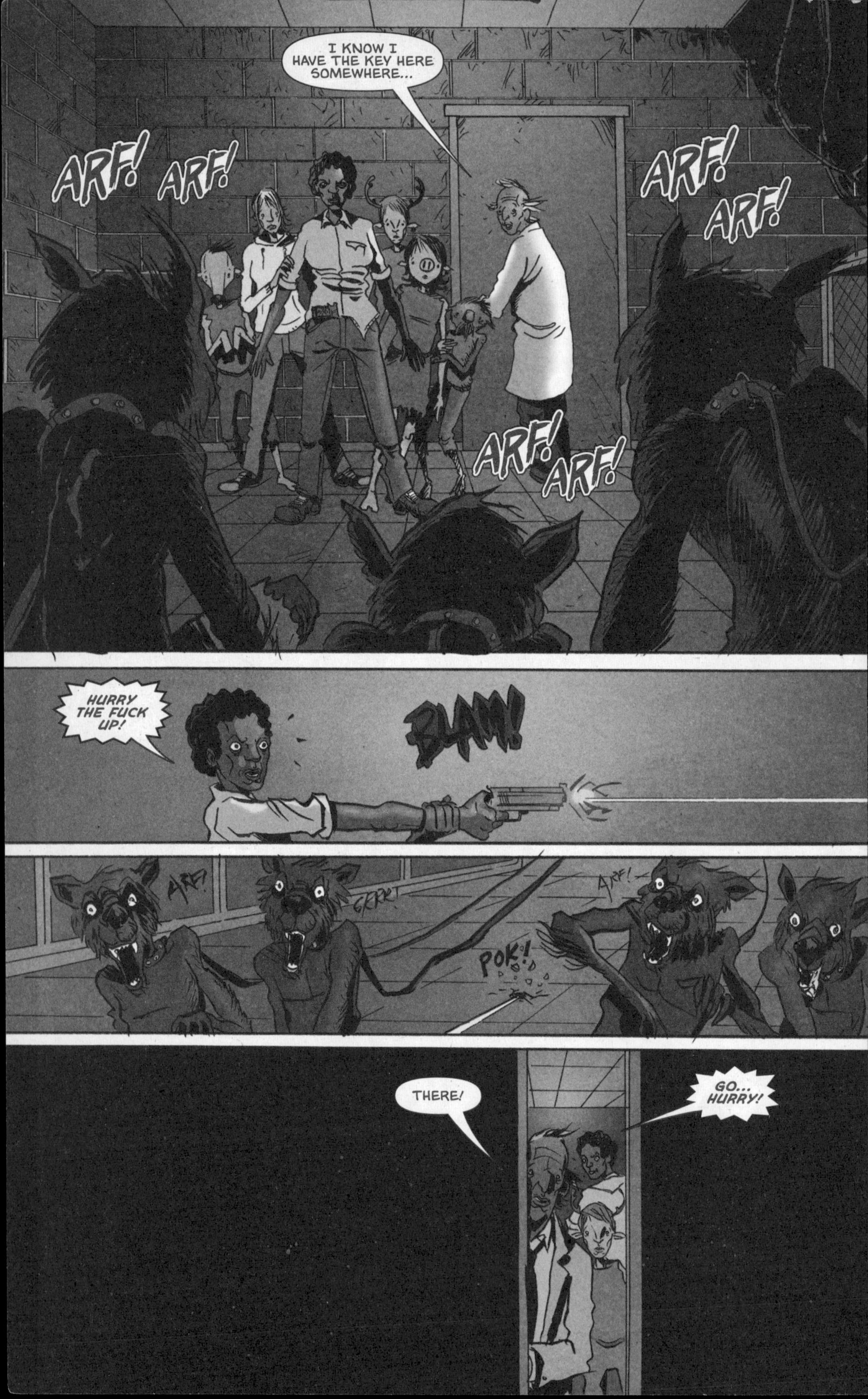
I KNOW I HAVE THE KEY HERE SOMEWHERE...
ARF! ARF!
ARF! ARF!
ARF! ARF!
HURRY THE FUCK UP!
BLAM!
ARF!
ARF!
POK!
THERE!
GO... HURRY!

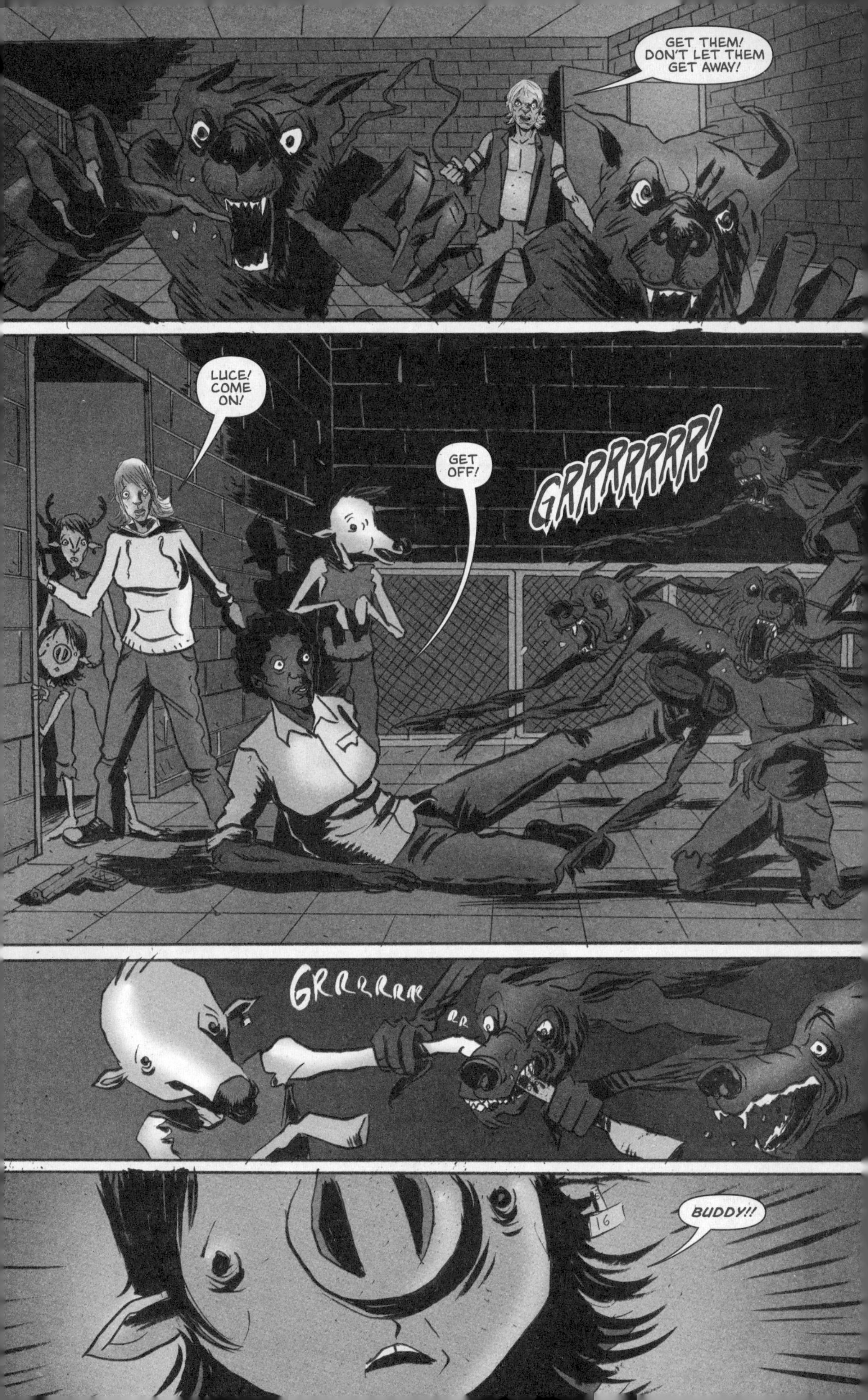
GET THEM! DON'T LET THEM GET AWAY!
LUCE! COME ON!
GET OFF!
GRRRRRRR!
GRRRRRRRR
BUDDY!!

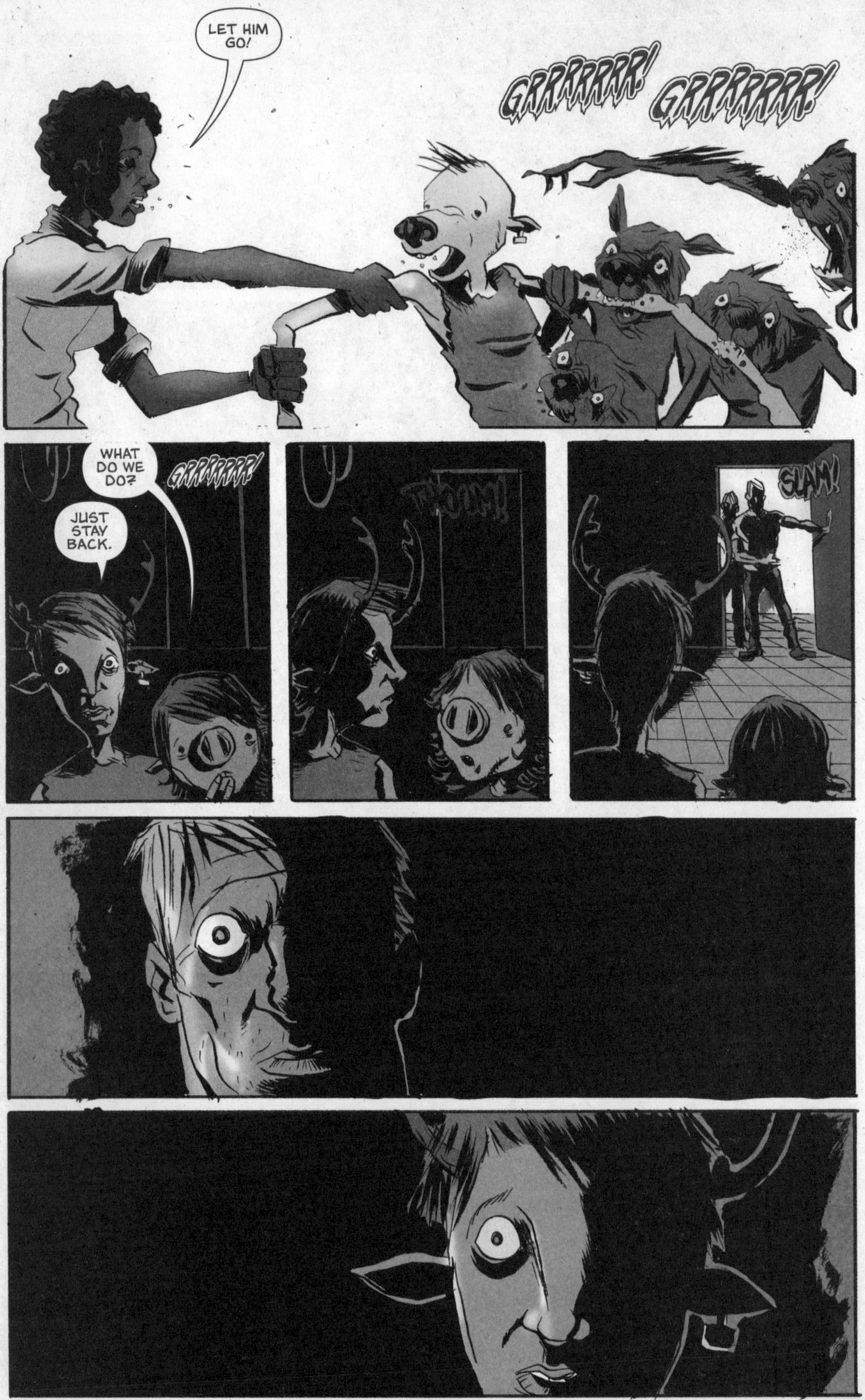
LET HIM GO!
GRRRRRRR!
GRRRRRRR!
WHAT DO WE DO?
GRRRRRRR!
JUST STAY BACK.
THOOM!
SLAM!

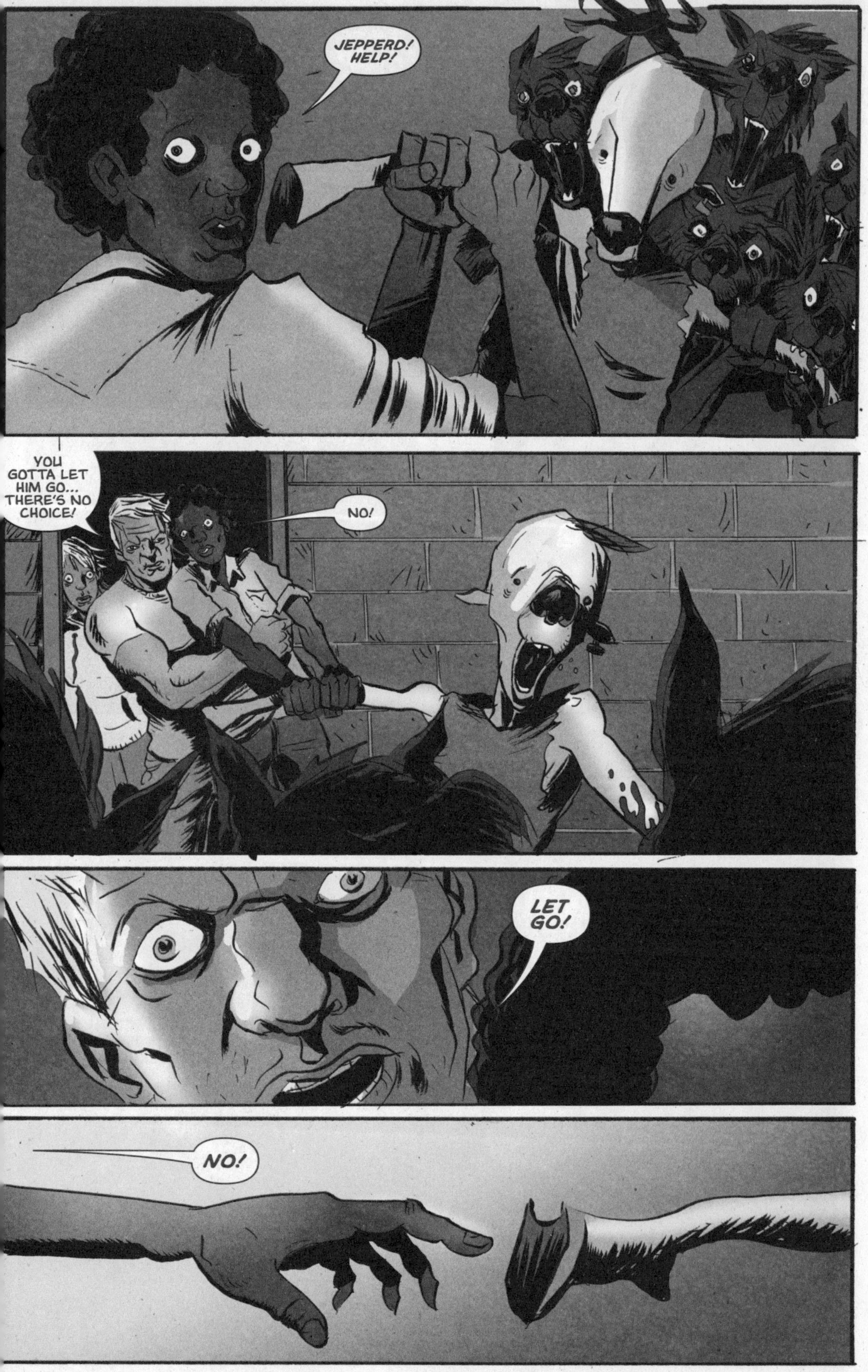
JEPPERD! HELP!
YOU GOTTA LET HIM GO... THERE'S NO CHOICE!
NO!
LET GO!
NO!

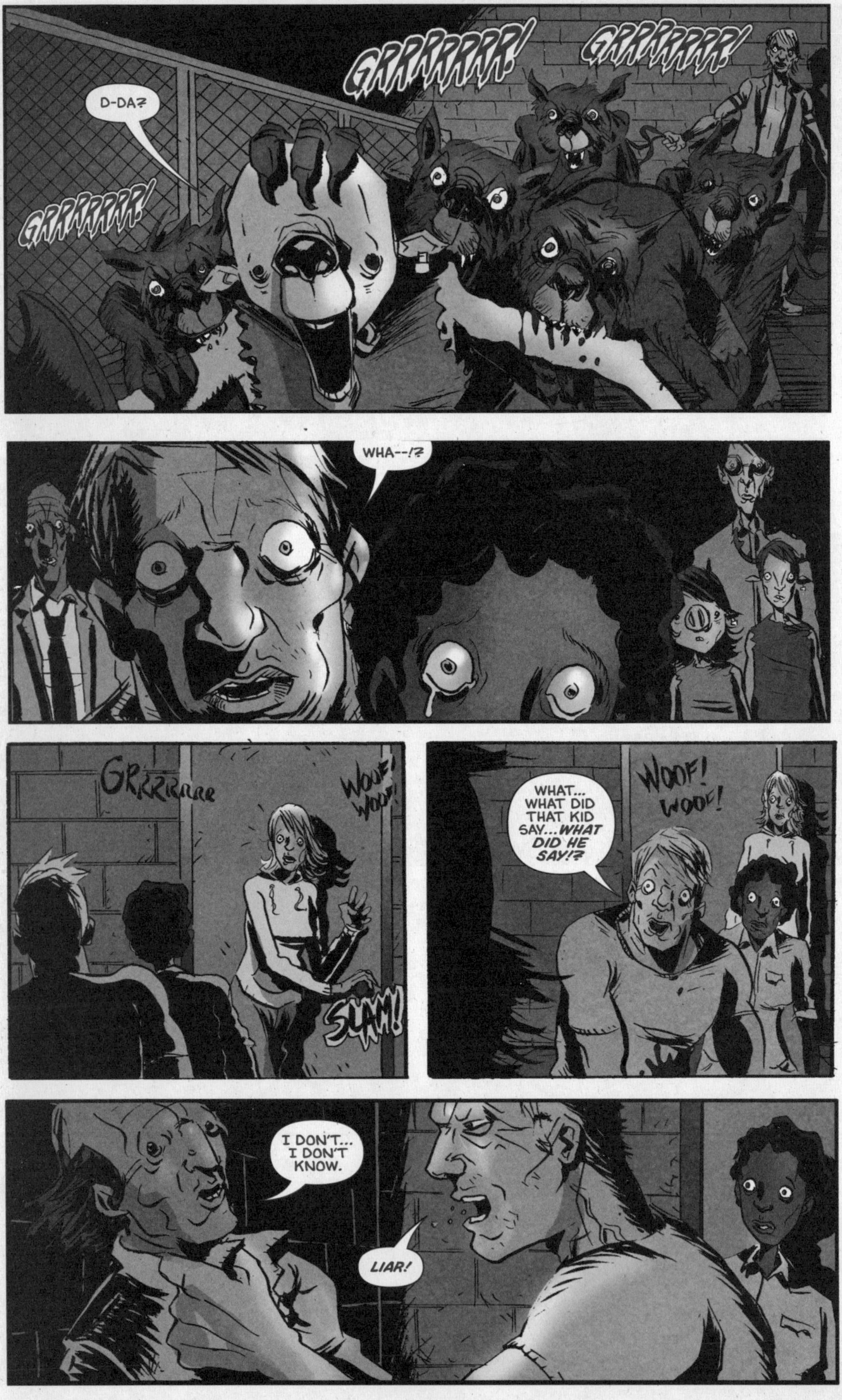
GRRRRRRR!
GRRRRRRR!
D-DA?
GRRRRRRR!
WHA--!?
GRRRRRRR
WOOF! WOOF!
SLAM!
WHAT... WHAT DID THAT KID SAY...WHAT DID HE SAY!?
WOOF! WOOF!
I DON'T... I DON'T KNOW.
LIAR!

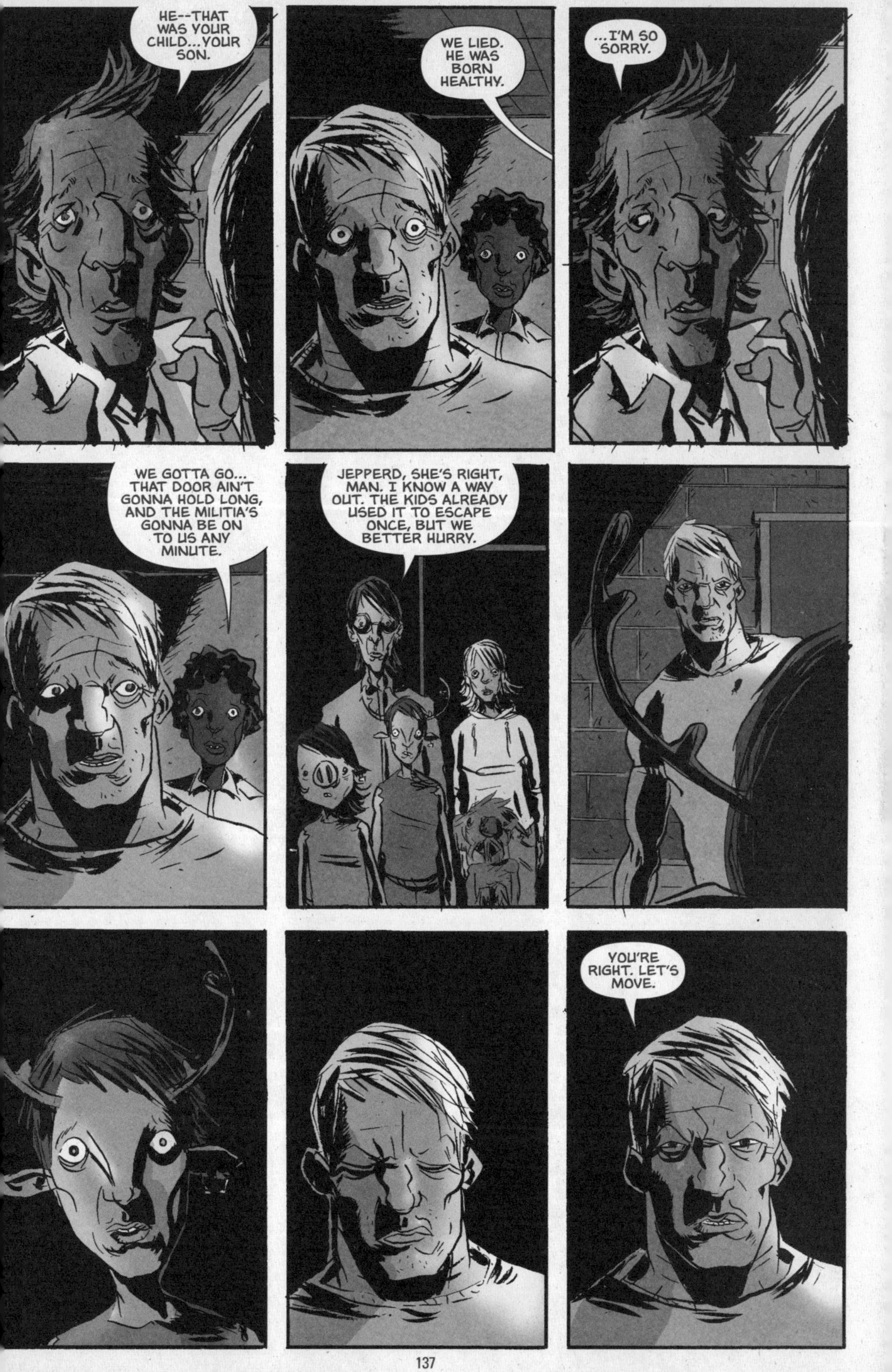
HE--THAT WAS YOUR CHILD...YOUR SON.
WE LIED. HE WAS BORN HEALTHY.
...I'M SO SORRY.
WE GOTTA GO... THAT DOOR AIN'T GONNA HOLD LONG, AND THE MILITIA'S GONNA BE ON TO US ANY MINUTE.
JEPPERD, SHE'S RIGHT, MAN. I KNOW A WAY OUT. THE KIDS ALREADY USED IT TO ESCAPE ONCE, BUT WE BETTER HURRY.
YOU'RE RIGHT. LET'S MOVE.

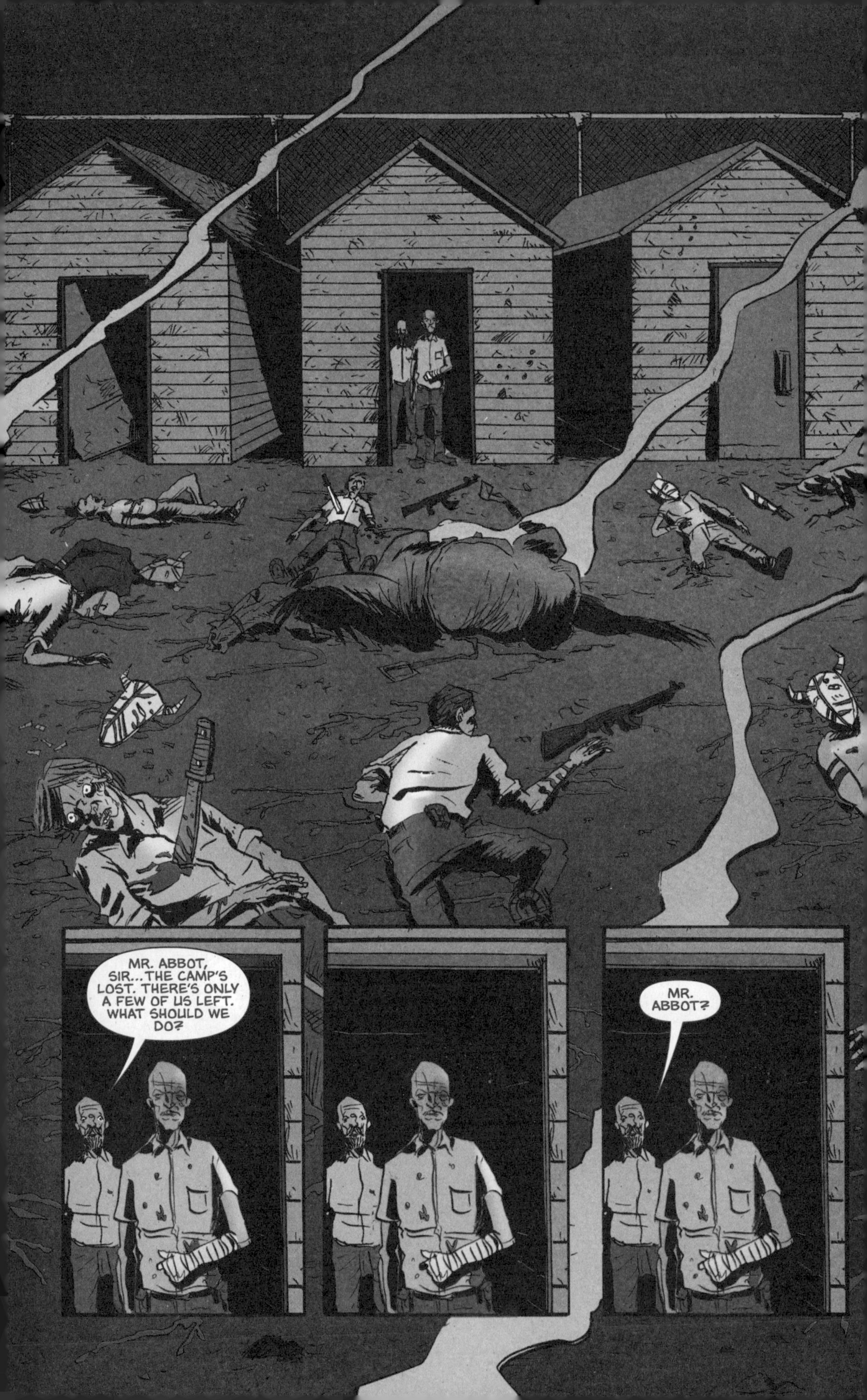
MR. ABBOT, SIR... THE CAMP'S LOST. THERE'S ONLY A FEW OF US LEFT. WHAT SHOULD WE DO?
MR. ABBOT?

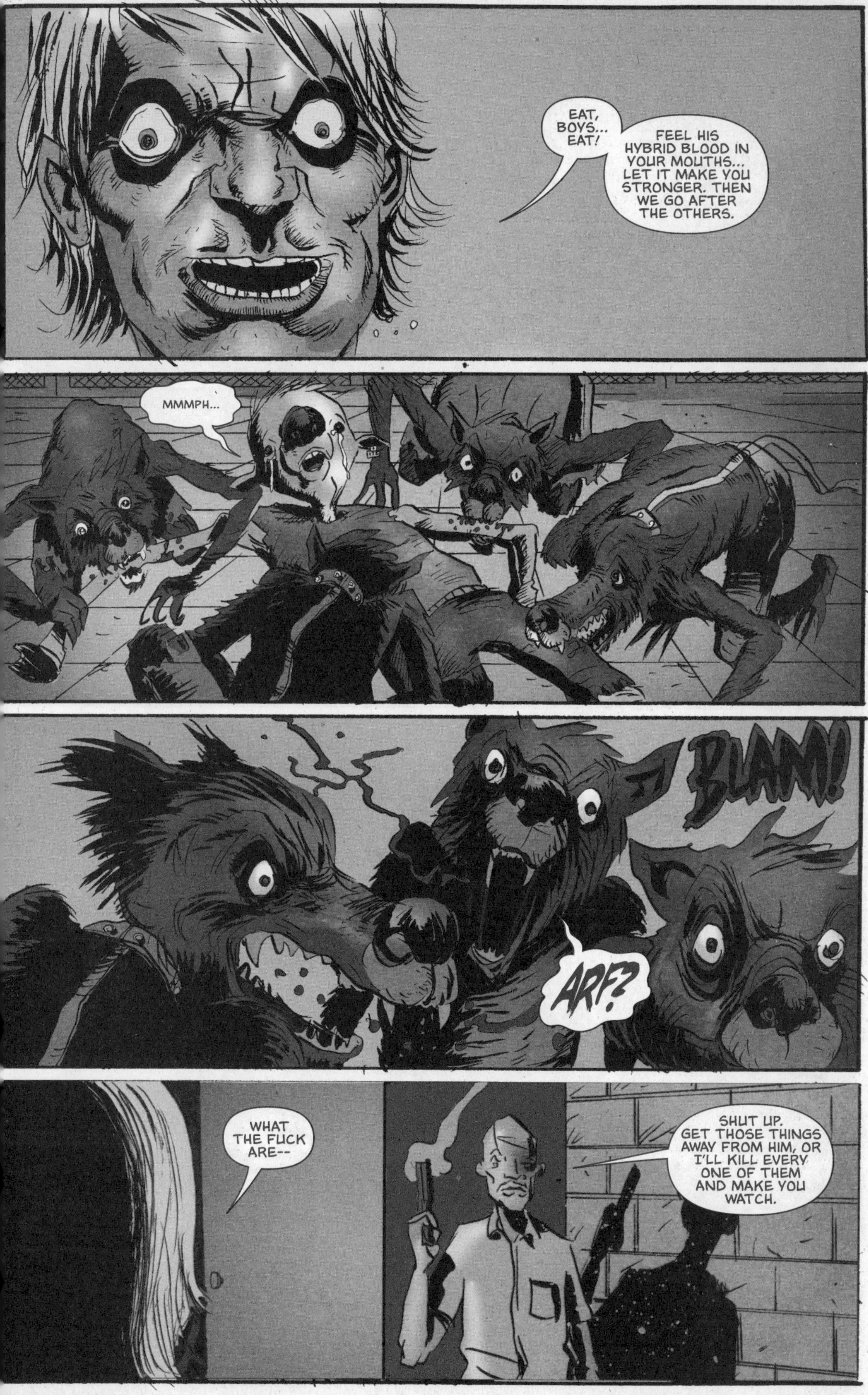
EAT, BOYS... EAT!
FEEL HIS HYBRID BLOOD IN YOUR MOUTHS... LET IT MAKE YOU STRONGER. THEN WE GO AFTER THE OTHERS.
MMMPH...
BLAM!
ARF?
WHAT THE FUCK ARE--
SHUT UP. GET THOSE THINGS AWAY FROM HIM, OR I'LL KILL EVERY ONE OF THEM AND MAKE YOU WATCH.

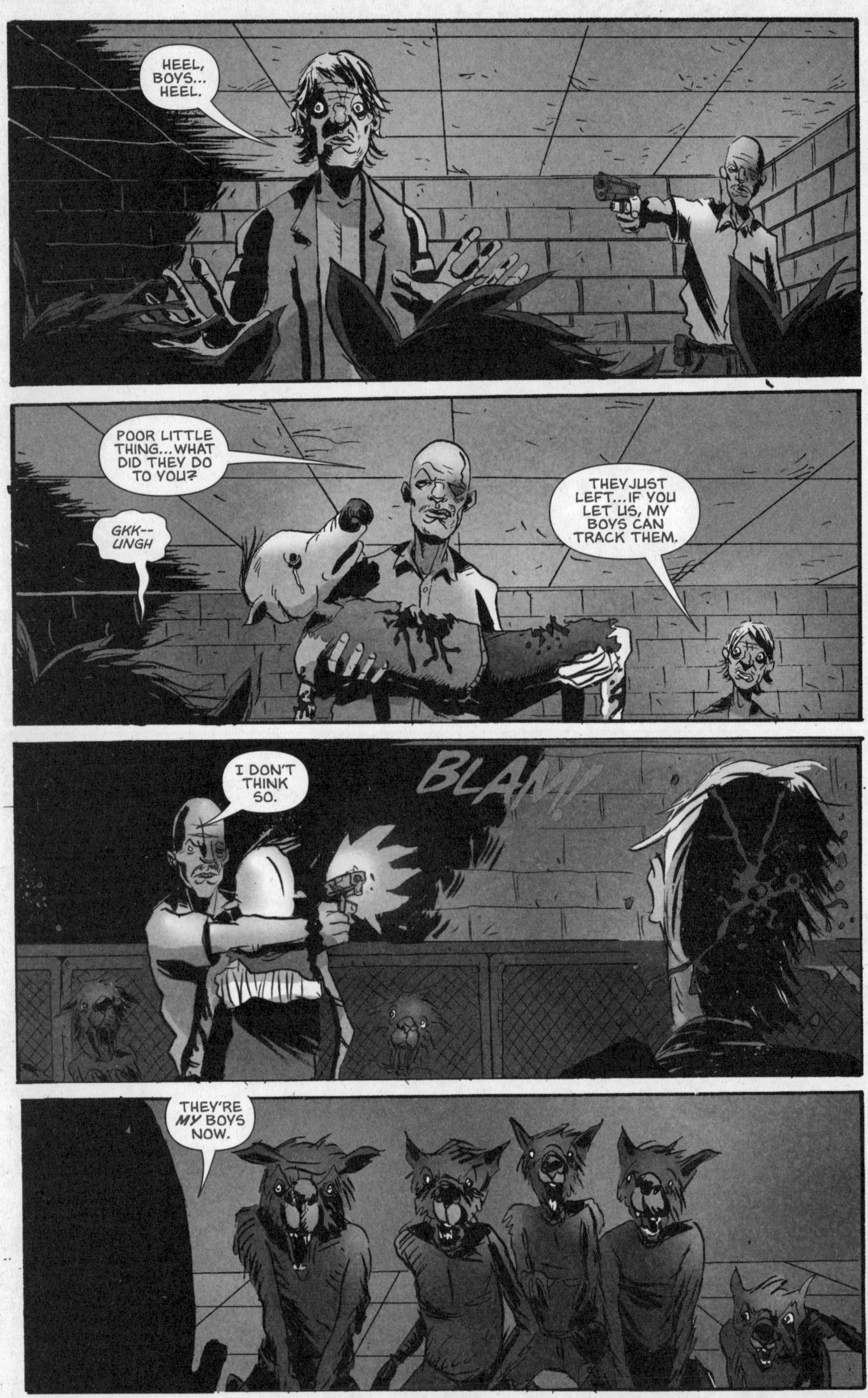
HEEL, BOYS... HEEL.
POOR LITTLE THING...WHAT DID THEY DO TO YOU?
GKK-- UNGH
THEYJUST LEFT...IF YOU LET US, MY BOYS CAN TRACK THEM.
I DON'T THINK SO.
BLAM!
THEY'RE *MY* BOYS NOW.

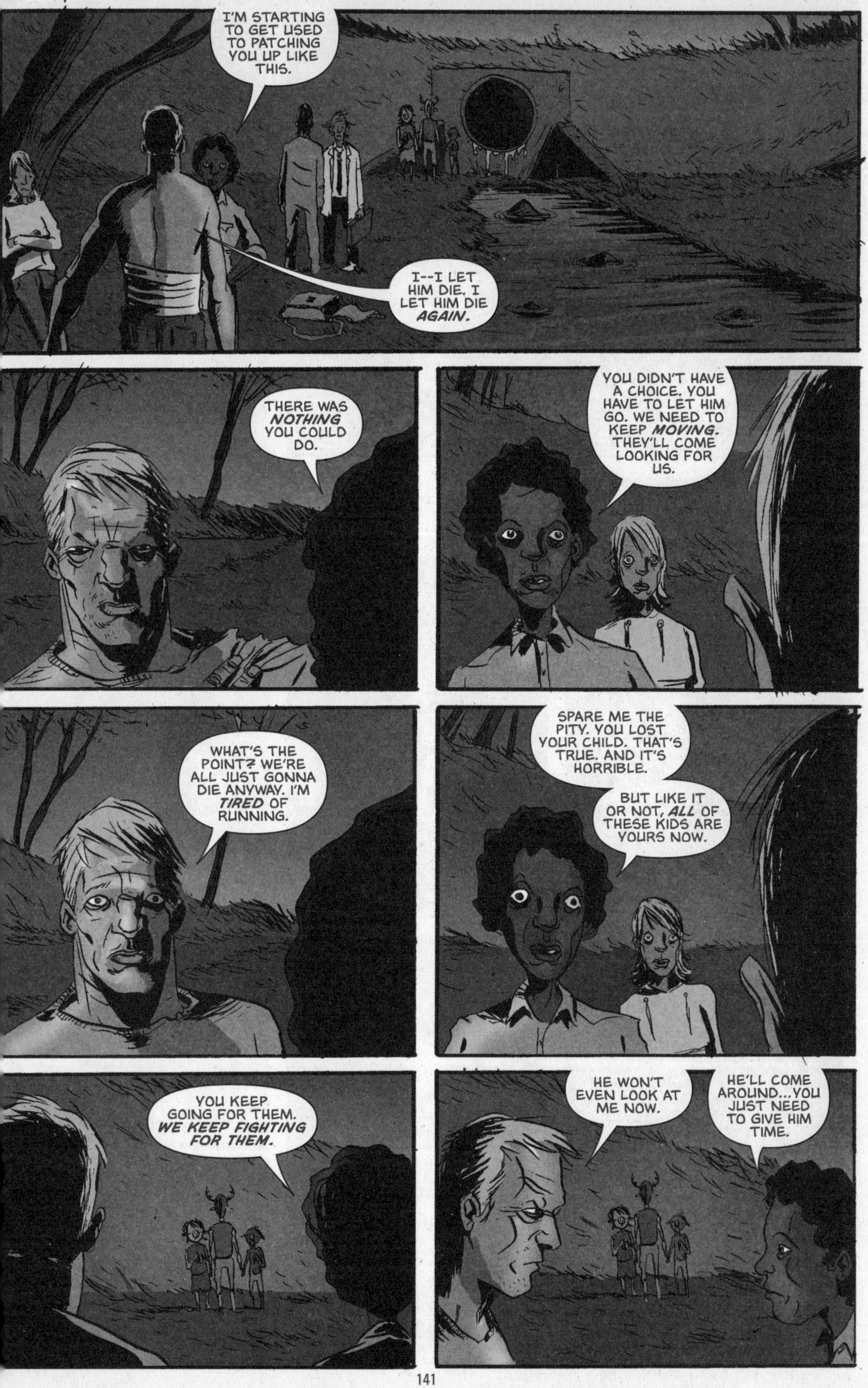
I'M STARTING TO GET USED TO PATCHING YOU UP LIKE THIS.
I--I LET HIM DIE. I LET HIM DIE AGAIN.
THERE WAS NOTHING YOU COULD DO.
YOU DIDN'T HAVE A CHOICE. YOU HAVE TO LET HIM GO. WE NEED TO KEEP MOVING. THEY'LL COME LOOKING FOR US.
WHAT'S THE POINT? WE'RE ALL JUST GONNA DIE ANYWAY. I'M TIRED OF RUNNING.
SPARE ME THE PITY. YOU LOST YOUR CHILD. THAT'S TRUE. AND IT'S HORRIBLE.
BUT LIKE IT OR NOT, ALL OF THESE KIDS ARE YOURS NOW.
YOU KEEP GOING FOR THEM. WE KEEP FIGHTING FOR THEM.
HE WON'T EVEN LOOK AT ME NOW.
HE'LL COME AROUND...YOU JUST NEED TO GIVE HIM TIME.

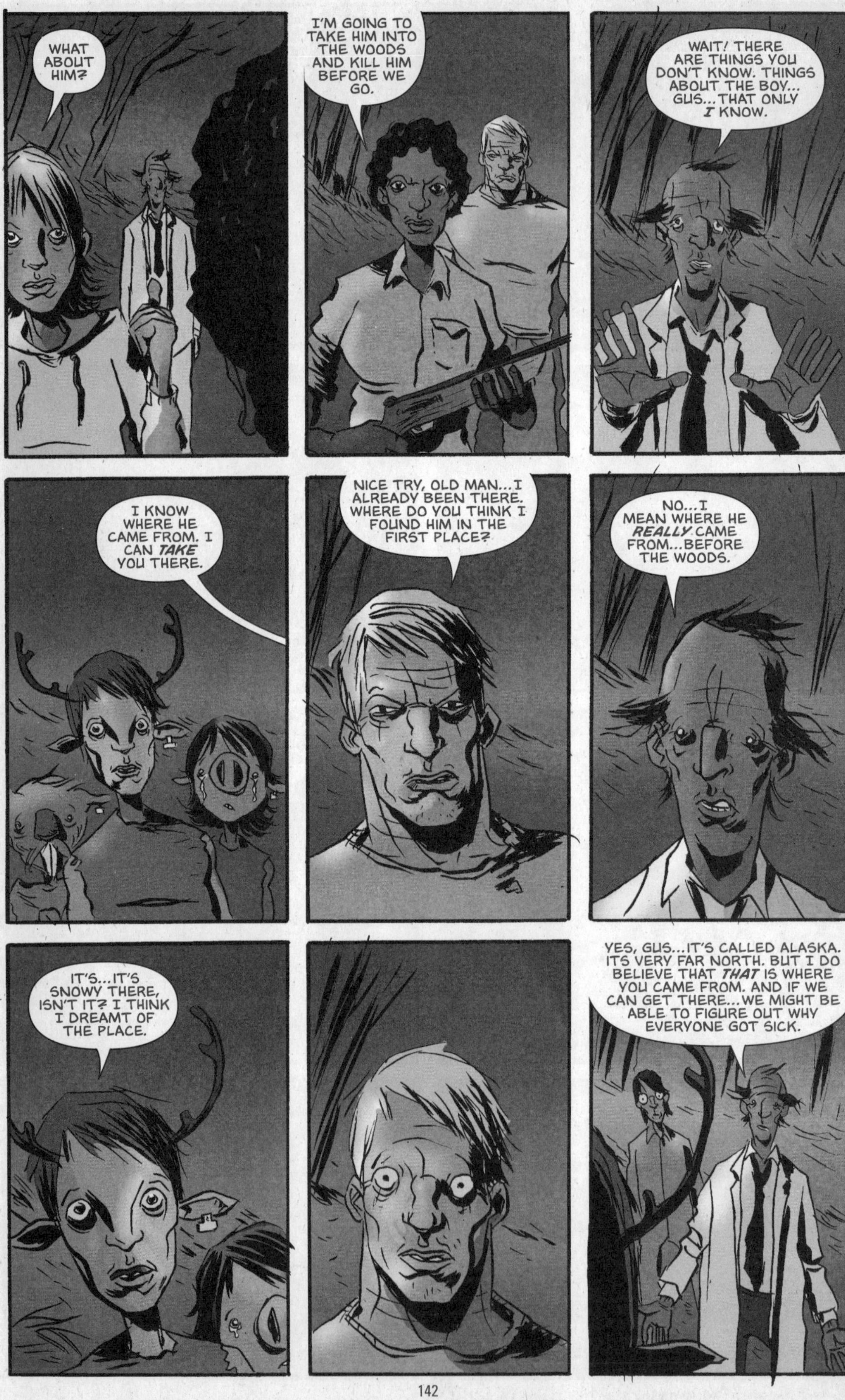
WHAT ABOUT HIM?
I'M GOING TO TAKE HIM INTO THE WOODS AND KILL HIM BEFORE WE GO.
WAIT! THERE ARE THINGS YOU DON'T KNOW. THINGS ABOUT THE BOY... GUS... THAT ONLY I KNOW.
I KNOW WHERE HE CAME FROM. I CAN TAKE YOU THERE.
NICE TRY, OLD MAN... I ALREADY BEEN THERE. WHERE DO YOU THINK I FOUND HIM IN THE FIRST PLACE?
NO... I MEAN WHERE HE REALLY CAME FROM... BEFORE THE WOODS.
IT'S... IT'S SNOWY THERE, ISN'T IT? I THINK I DREAMT OF THE PLACE.
YES, GUS... IT'S CALLED ALASKA. ITS VERY FAR NORTH. BUT I DO BELIEVE THAT THAT IS WHERE YOU CAME FROM. AND IF WE CAN GET THERE... WE MIGHT BE ABLE TO FIGURE OUT WHY EVERYONE GOT SICK.

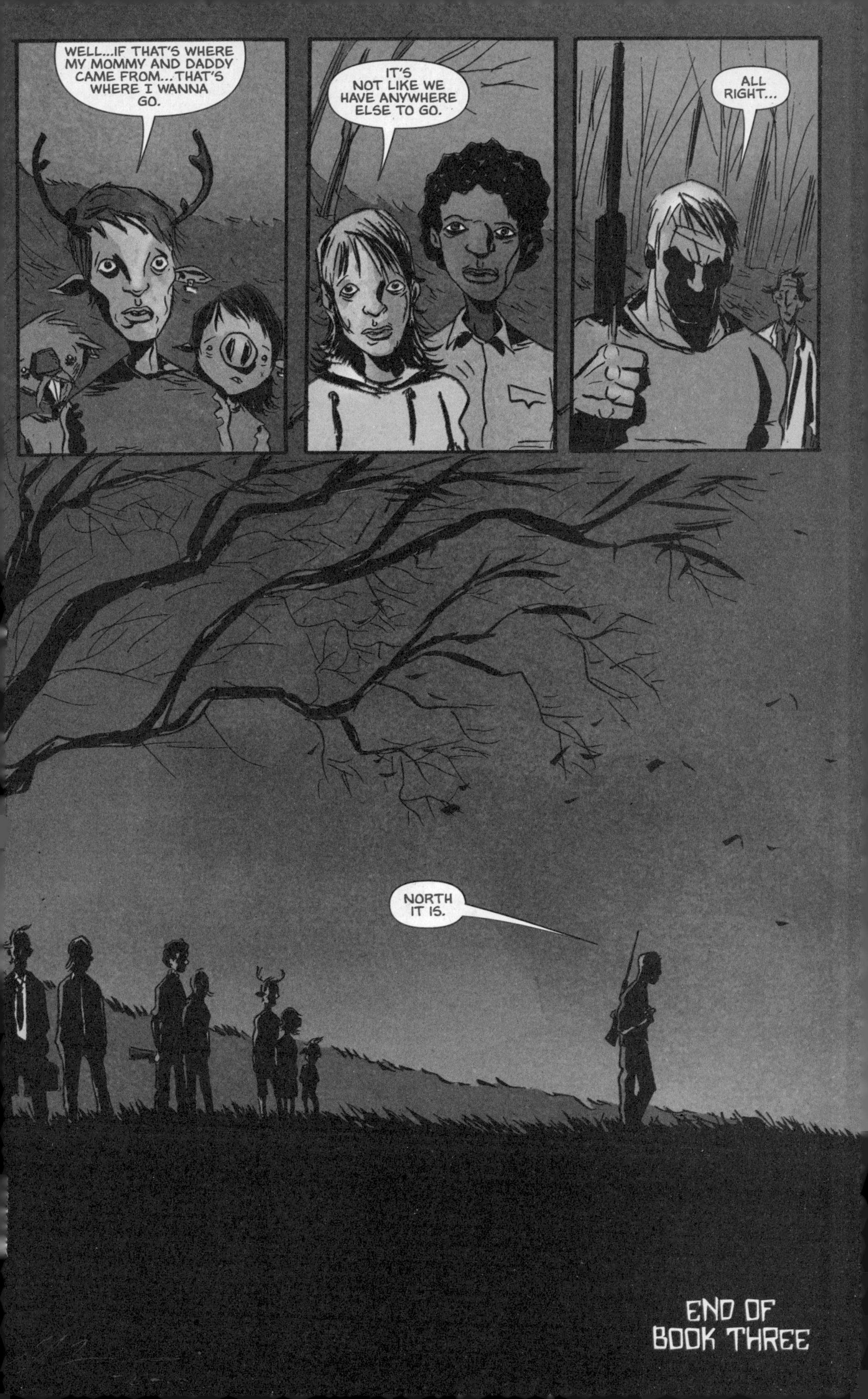
WELL...IF THAT'S WHERE MY MOMMY AND DADDY CAME FROM...THAT'S WHERE I WANNA GO.
IT'S NOT LIKE WE HAVE ANYWHERE ELSE TO GO.
ALL RIGHT...
NORTH IT IS.
END OF BOOK THREE

YOU'LL NEVER FORGET THE FIRST

AMERICAN VAMPIRE
VOL. I

DEMO
VOL. I

THE LOSERS
BOOK ONE

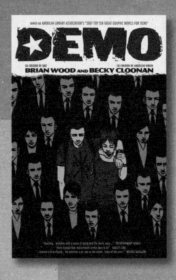

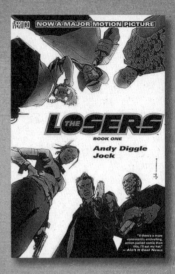

THE UNWRITTEN VOL. 1:
TOMMY TAYLOR AND
THE BOGUS IDENTITY

SWEET TOOTH VOL. I:
OUT OF THE DEEP WOODS

UNKNOWN SOLDIER VOL. I:
HAUNTED HOUSE

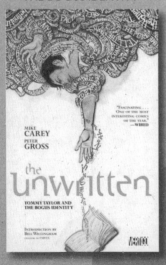